American
SPEAK
OUT

Intermediate
Student Book

with DVD/ROM and MP3 Audio CD

Antonia Clare • JJ Wilson

CONTENTS

DVD-ROM: ▶ DVD CLIPS AND SCRIPTS ▶ INTERVIEWS AND SCRIPTS

LISTENING/DVD	SPEAKING	WRITING
	talk about important dates in your life	write an email of introduction
listen to a set of instructions and do a test	talk about the differences beween men and women	
listen to three interviews	role-play an interview	
▶ **The Blind Painter:** watch a documentary about a blind artist	speak about yourself for 60 seconds	write a personal description
listen to a radio program about films	talk about life stories	
listen to news reports	talk about an important news event	write a news report
listen to a woman telling a story	tell a true story or a lie	
▶ **Hustle:** watch a drama about an art thief	tell a narrative	write a newspaper article
listen to people making plans	discuss your plans and arrangements	write a series of messages
	talk about predictions	
listen to a series of misunderstandings	explain misunderstandings	
▶ **YouTube:** watch a documentary about the rise of YouTube	discuss how to create a video channel	write a proposal
	discuss how important becoming a millionaire is for you	
listen to people describing dream jobs gone wrong	talk about past habits	write a cover letter
listen to people making decisions in a meeting	participate in a meeting	
▶ **Gavin and Stacey:** watch a comedy about a man's first day in a new job	describe a day in your life	write about your daily routine
	talk about inventions over the last 100 years	write an advantages/disadvantages essay
listen to people answering difficult questions	present and answer questions about your area of expertise	
listen to conversations about technical problems	explain/solve problems	
▶ **Top Gear:** watch a program about a race between a car and two people	present a new machine	write an advertisement

▶ CLASS AUDIO AND SCRIPTS

 CONTENTS

4

LISTENING/DVD	SPEAKING	WRITING
listen to a radio show about therapies	talk about emotions	
	discuss what you would do in different situations	write an email of advice
listen to conversations where people hear news	give/respond to news	
▶ **My Worst Week**: watch a program about a man's terrible day	talk about memorable moments	write a website entry

listen to a radio program about success	talk about success	
listen to a conversation about memory	talk about your abilities	write a summary
listen to a discussion about intelligence	give/clarify opinions	
▶ **Andy Murray**: watch a documentary about Andy Murray	describe an achievement	write an Internet post

	describe your neighborhood	
listen to descriptions of online communities	compare real-world and online activities	write a website review
listen to people describing guest/host experiences	discuss social situations	
▶ **Tribe: Anuta**: watch a documentary about a remote community	design a community	write a web advertisement

	talk about important events in history	write a short essay
listen to descriptions of past decades	talk about your own history	
listen to people taking a quiz about famous people in history	compile and take a quiz	
▶ **The Divine Michelangelo**: watch a documentary about the life and work of Michelangelo Buonarroti	describe a person who influenced you	write a wiki entry

	discuss ideas for reducing plastic waste	
listen to descriptions of the world's best food cities	recommend a city for food	write a restaurant review
listen to people giving advice/warnings	ask for/give travel advice	
▶ **Nature's Great Events: The Great Melt**: watch a documentary about the Arctic's melting ice caps	talk about an endangered place	write an email campaigning for action

COMMUNICATION BANK page 158   AUDIO SCRIPTS page 164

GRAMMAR

1 Read the text and find examples of ...

1 the past simple *he saw*
2 the past continuous
3 the present perfect
4 the past perfect
5 a modal verb
6 a superlative
7 a relative clause
8 a passive

> There have been some amazing coincidences throughout history, but this might be the best. In 1900, King Umberto of Italy was dining in a restaurant when he saw that the owner looked exactly like him. The man, who was also called Umberto, was born in Turin on the same day as the king and, like the king, married a woman called Margherita. Amazingly, their weddings had been on the same day. The king invited the restaurant owner to an gymnastics competition the next day. As the king sat down, he was told that the other Umberto had died in a mysterious shooting accident. Just as the king heard this news, an anarchist shot him dead.

PRONUNCIATION

2 A Find pairs of words that have the same vowel sound.

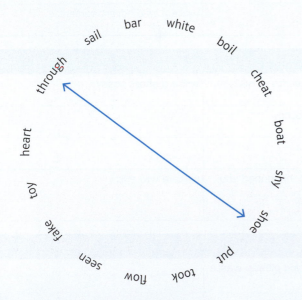

B Listen and check your answers.

C Work in pairs. Think of other words in English that use the same sounds.

VOCABULARY

3 A Complete the common phrases below using the correct verb from the box.

> ~~have~~   take   check   watch   chat   go
> meet   play (x2)   do

1	*have* a meeting	6	_____ some work
2	_____ your email	7	_____ on the Internet
3	_____ out with friends	8	_____ a break
4	_____ some sports	9	_____ a DVD
5	_____ a colleague	10	_____ some music

B Add phrases 1–10 above to the word webs below.

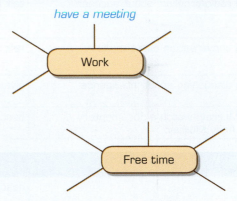

C Can you add any more phrases to the word webs? Which of these things do you do on a normal day?

COMMON ERRORS

4 A Correct the mistakes.

1 She likes listening music.
2 I am architect.
3 Are you feeling alright?
4 When I can visit your house?
5 Let's discuss about this tomorrow.
6 He don't come here often.
7 We come from germany.
8 Where you go yesterday?
9 I live in this town all my life.
10 My wife is a really good cooker.

B Which mistakes are connected with ...

a) verb–noun agreement   *6*
b) spelling
c) verb tense
d) punctuation/capitalization
e) prepositions
f) articles
g) vocabulary
h) word order
i) missing auxiliary verb
j) extra words

sports / capitalization   sport / capitalisation

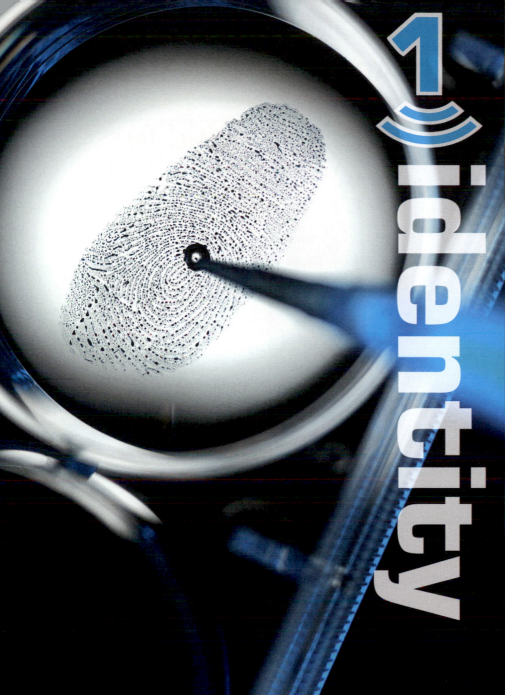

1)) identity

ME AND MY LANGUAGES p8

SAME OR DIFFERENT p11

TELL ME ABOUT YOURSELF p14

THE BLIND PAINTER p16

What does family mean to you?

INTERVIEWS

1.1)) ME AND MY LANGUAGES

G question forms
P intonation: *wh-* questions
V language

VOCABULARY

LANGUAGE

BILINGUALS: EXOTIC BIRDS OR EVERYDAY PEOPLE?

by Johan Acosta

1 A Read questions 1–10. What do the words in bold mean? Check with other students or your teacher. Then think about your answers to the questions.

1 Why are you **learning** English? For work, exams, travel, etc.?

2 Do you speak any languages apart from your **mother tongue** and English?

3 Who is the best **language learner** in your family?

4 Did you use any **learning strategies** when studying your second language? Which?

5 When was the first time you used a **foreign** language outside the classroom?

6 Do you have the chance to speak/write to **native speakers** regularly?

7 Is it important for you to learn **slang** or **jargon** in English, or do you only want to learn standard English?

8 Which is more important to you when you learn to speak a language: **fluency** or **accuracy**?

9 Which **skill** is the hardest for you: speaking, listening, reading, or writing? Which is the easiest?

10 Do you know anyone who is **bilingual**? What advantages might they have in life?

B Work in groups. Discuss your answers to questions 1–10.

2 Answer the questions.

1 Which words in bold in questions 1–10 have silent letters?

2 What are the silent letters in these words: **science, talk, listen, know, right, wrong, hours, guess?**

3 Which statement (a or b) do you think is true?

a Most words in English are spelled differently from how they are pronounced.

b Under twenty percent of words in English are spelled differently from how they are pronounced.

American Speak out TIP | Around fourteen percent of English words have irregular spelling; they are spelled differently from how they are pronounced. When you learn new words, try to hear them. Watch out for silent letters!

Grandpa shouts, "Dinner's ready" in Danish. My mother asks me in English to set the table. As I do so, I catch the theme tune of the Brazilian soap opera on TV in the living room, where my sister is relaxing. She speaks perfect Portuguese. My father asks her to record the program in his native Spanish, and we take our places at the table. And what's on the menu? Italian meatballs.

We know we aren't a normal family. At any moment, you might hear conversations in four different languages, and almost everyone understands almost everything. But what is normal these days? My mother is half-Danish, half-English, and my father, who is from Bolivia, speaks Spanish and Guaraní. Because of my mother's work (she's now retired), we lived in Brazil, Italy and Germany, so we picked up three more languages. Now as adults, my sister and I both speak six languages.

Being bilingual, or in our case multilingual, has so many advantages. All the recent research suggests we benefit in many ways: social, cultural, economic, academic and intellectual. The research has also destroyed some of those persistent myths.

READING

3 A Read the title of the text. What do you think it will discuss? Read to find out.

B Read the text again and answer the questions.

1 What six languages do you think the writer and his sister speak?

2 How do you think the writer learned each of his languages?

3 How many of the world's people are thought to be bilingual?

4 What are those who learn their second language as children better at compared to those who learn a second language as adults?

5 What health benefit of being bilingual is mentioned in the text?

spelled / set the table / program / learned — spelt / lay the table / programme / learnt

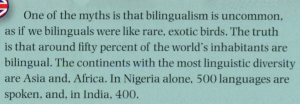

One of the myths is that bilingualism is uncommon, as if we bilinguals were like rare, exotic birds. The truth is that around fifty percent of the world's inhabitants are bilingual. The continents with the most linguistic diversity are Asia and, Africa. In Nigeria alone, 500 languages are spoken, and, in India, 400.

Some people believe that you have to learn both languages as a child to be truly bilingual. My sister and I are fortunate in this respect, but we know countless people who have mastered a second language as adults. They may not have such perfect pronunciation as those who acquire their second language as children, but they are still completely fluent and accurate.

Another myth about bilinguals concerns identity. Some people think we have split personalities. As kids, my sister and I were often asked, "But where are you really from? Don't you get confused?" Not at all. I am me, the product of many cultures. I can switch languages easily, according to where I am and whom I'm with, and this seems completely natural to me.

As for the benefits, bilinguals do better on certain tests, are better protected against mental illnesses such as Alzheimer's, gain insights into other cultures, have access to more of the world's information, and are in some contexts more employable. Being bilingual has made me who I am, and for that I'm grateful.

> **"** One of the myths is that bilingualism is uncommon, as if we bilinguals were like rare, exotic birds. **"**

C Underline words or phrases in the text that match meanings 1—6 below.

1 relating to the language you grew up speaking (paragraph 1)
2 learned by listening/watching other people (paragraph 2)
3 speaking many languages (paragraph 3)
4 false ideas that people continue to believe and repeat (paragraph 3)
5 learn without needing to try hard, e.g., a language (paragraph 5)
6 understand important truths about a subject (paragraph 7)

D Discuss the questions with other students.

1 Do you agree with the writer's list of the advantages of being bilingual?
2 Do you think there are any disadvantages to being bilingual?
3 Do you know any families that are bilingual or multilingual? Are they similar to the family in the text?

GRAMMAR
QUESTION FORMS

4 A Read questions 1—6 and answer questions a)—e).

1 Do you <u>speak</u> other languages?
2 Did you use any learning strategies?
3 Whom did you talk to?
4 What happened?
5 What did you talk about?
6 Who is the best language learner in your family?

a) Underline the main verb in each question. (The first has been done for you.)
b) Circle the auxiliary verbs. Which auxiliary refers to the past? Which refers to the present?
c) Which two questions are yes/no questions?
d) Which two questions end in a preposition: *of, by,* etc.?
e) Which two questions use *wh-* words to refer to the subject (the person who does the action or the action itself) and don't use an auxiliary verb?

▶ page 128 LANGUAGE**BANK**

B INTONATION: *wh-* questions Listen to the questions in Exercise 4A. Are the question words (*wh-* words) in 3—6 said in a higher or a lower voice?

C Listen and say the questions at the same time.

5 A Put the words in the correct order to make questions.

1 do / every / you / day / study?
2 your / any / did / languages / teach / parents / you / other?
3 is / learner / who / the / best / you / language / know?
4 was / teacher / your / English / first / who?
5 do / you / remember / what / English / words / to / do?
6 languages / you / what / do / to / like / listening?
7 do / what / watch / you / English / in / TV / programs?
8 foreign / did / speak / first / when / language / a / you?

B Choose three of the questions to ask other students.

SPEAKING

6 A Write four dates, four names and four places that are important to you.

Dates: *7 May 2008—My son was born.*

Names:

Places:

B In groups, take turns explaining what you wrote. As you listen, think of three questions to ask afterward.

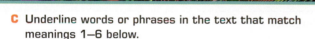
whom / afterward   who / afterwards

WRITING

EMAILS OF INTRODUCTION; LEARN TO WRITE FORMAL AND INFORMAL EMAILS

7 A When would you write a letter or email to introduce yourself?

B Read the emails. Why are the people writing? Which sentences tell us?

To   ramirezh@languagestar.nett

Subject   Spanish Conversation Class

Hi Hernán,

My name's Julia Brown. I heard from my friend Nicola Lazarus that you're running a Spanish conversation class. She said you'd be happy to accept a few more people. My mother tongue is English, but I picked up some Spanish years ago when I was traveling in Latin America. I really want to develop my fluency and accuracy, so I'd love to join the class. Hope to hear from you soon.

All the best,

Julia 😃

To   GND staff

Subject   Greetings

Dear Colleagues,

As you probably know, next month I will start work as the new director of the Language Teaching Education Program. For those of you who don't know me, I would like to take this opportunity to introduce myself. Since 2010, I have worked at the School of Education at Borodive University. I have been involved in a number of language teacher education projects across Europe, and I worked extensively on the Star Placement Initiative that placed six thousand native speakers in language classrooms in eight countries. I am married with two children, and my family is bilingual in English and Turkish.

I look forward to working with you.

Yours faithfully,

Talya Osman

---

8 Read the five steps for good email writing. Do you think the emails in Exercise 7B follow steps 1–3?

1 **A**im for your **a**udience: think about whom you are writing to. Is the email formal or informal?

2 **B**e **b**rief: try not to use too many words. Emails shouldn't go on for pages.

3 **C**ommunicate **c**learly: use simple, clear language and simple sentence structure.

4 **D**o two **d**rafts: write a first version and then rewrite.

5 **E**dit **e**verything: check grammar, vocabulary, spelling and punctuation before sending.

> In more formal emails, if you know the name of the addressee, you close with "Sincerely," (American English) or "Yours sincerely," (British English); otherwise, "Yours faithfully" is used.

9 A Look at the emails in Exercise 7B again. Which one is formal and which is informal? How do you know?

B Answer questions 1–4 with formal (F) or informal (I).

1 Which email uses full forms of verbs (*I will*, *I would*) instead of contractions (*you're*, *I'd*)?

2 Which email leaves out words (e.g., *Hope to* ... instead of *I hope to* ...)?

3 Which email sounds more like spoken English?

4 Which email uses longer, more complex sentences?

C Complete the notes with phrases from the email.

Greeting
(formal):   1 _____.
(informal):   Hi/Hello.

Introduction
(formal):   I would like to take this 2 _____.
(informal):   My name's ...

Final message
(formal):   I look forward to ...
(informal):   3 _____.

Goodbye
(formal):4 _____.
(informal):All the best.

10 Choose a situation below and write an email. Think about whom you are writing to, the reason for writing and the style: formal or informal.

Situation 1
You are going to join an English conversation class. Write an email introducing yourself to the teacher and the class. Mention your experience of learning and speaking English and say why you want to join the class.

Situation 2
Next week you start a new job in a multinational company. Your colleagues speak over twenty languages, and all of them read English. Write to introduce yourself. Mention your previous work experience and the languages you know and add something personal.

traveling   travelling

1.2)) SAME OR DIFFERENT?

G question forms
P intonation: *wh-* questions
V language

VOCABULARY
RELATIONSHIPS

1 A Work in pairs. Think of all the people you have talked to in the last 24 hours. What relationship do they have to you?

B Look at the words in the box and answer the questions.

> boss and employee   classmates
> partner   teammates   member
> godfather and godmother   mentor and mentee
> fiancée and fiancé

1 Which pair works together? *boss and employee*
2 Which pair promises to help guide a child through life?
3 Which pair is going to get married?
4 Which pair involves one person learning from the other?
5 Which word describes people who play on the same sports team?
6 Which word describes people who go to the same class?
7 Which word describes a person who is part of a club?
8 Which word is a general word for "someone whom you do something with"?

C Listen to six sentences. Check the words in the box in Exercise 1B that you hear.

D WORD STRESS Six of the words have two syllables. Find the words and underline the stressed syllable. Say the words aloud, putting the stress on the correct syllable.

▶ page 148 VOCABULARY**BANK**

> **American Speak out TIP** Remember: most two-syllable words in English have the stress on the first syllable. Hold a hand under your chin. Say the word slowly. The jaw (the bottom part of your chin) drops more on the stressed syllable.

2 Work in groups. Discuss the questions.

1 Can you think of one man and one woman who have played important roles in your life? Who were they? Why were the relationships important?
2 Do you think men and women are different in these roles? How?

LISTENING

3 A Read the text. Discuss. Do you think male and female brains are different? How? What are the stereotypes of men and women in your country?

Are men's and women's brains
wired differently?

Is it true that men are from Mars and women are from Venus? Some researchers think that male and female brains are wired differently, with male brains wired from back to front, and female brains wired from side to side. This might explain why men are good at performing a single task, like cycling or navigating, whereas women might be better at multi-tasking. Other researchers disagree, however. What do YOU think? Try the bike test to find out if your brain is male or female.

B Take a piece of paper. Listen to Parts 1 and 2 and follow the bike test instructions.

C Listen to the explanation in Part 3. Turn to page 158 and check your picture. How many parts did your bike have? Could it work? Does it have a person on it? Compare your picture with other students'.

D Discuss the questions.

1 Was the explanation correct for you?
2 Do you agree with the presenter's views about men and women?

> " Women think people are important. Men, on the other hand, are more interested in getting the machine right. "

mentee, student / on the same sports team
Check / that

pupil / in the same sports team
Tick / which

SPEAKING

4 A Read the information. Which comments do you agree/disagree with? Can you think of any opinions to add?

Are men & women really different?

We asked for comments, and this is what you said.

"Absolutely! Men can't watch sports on TV **and** talk to their girlfriends at the same time."

"WOMEN DON'T KNOW

HOW TO

READ MAPS."

"Women remember **every outfit they've worn** for the past twenty years. Men **can't remember** what they were wearing yesterday without looking on the floor."

"Men can buy a pair of shoes on the Internet in **90 seconds**. Women like to take three weeks."

"A baby is crying, a dog is barking, and a doorbell is ringing, but the man of the house is sleeping. **Men can sleep through anything**. Women can't."

"Men speak in sentences. Women speak in **paragraphs.**"

B Do the men and women in your life conform to the normal stereotypes? Why?/Why not?

GRAMMAR
REVIEW OF VERB TENSES

5 A Match the underlined verbs below with the tenses a)–d).

1 We <u>asked</u> for comments, and this is what you <u>said</u>.

2 Men can't remember what they <u>were wearing</u> yesterday.

3 Women <u>remember</u> every outfit they've worn for the past twenty years.

4 A baby <u>is crying</u>.

a) present simple

b) present continuous

c) past simple

d) past continuous

B Complete the rules with the correct tenses a)–d).

> **RULES**
>
> 1 We use _____ for actions, events or situations that are finished.
>
> 2 We use _____ for things that are going on at a particular moment in the present.
>
> 3 We use _____ for habits, routines and things that are always true.
>
> 4 We use _____ when someone was in the middle of an action at a particular moment in the past.

C Read about state verbs. Underline three examples in the text above.

> **RULES**
>
> Some verbs are not usually used in the continuous, e.g., *want, like, remember, understand, know*. These are called "state verbs."

▶ page 128 **LANGUAGEBANK**

6 A Read the text below and put the verbs in **parentheses** into the correct tense.

> My name is Matsuko Tamazuri. I am twenty-three, and I ¹_____ (be) a student. I study French and Spanish at college in Osaka, where I ²_____ (grow up), but, at the moment, I ³_____ (learn) English in New York. When I first ⁴_____ (get) here, everything ⁵_____ (seem) different: the food, the clothes and the weather. Now I ⁶_____ (enjoy) it, and it feels like home! I have a boyfriend called Josh. I ⁷_____ (meet) him three weeks ago when I ⁸_____ (look) for an Internet café! My hobbies ⁹_____ (be) surfing the net and singing. I ¹⁰_____ (sing) every day, usually in the bathroom!

B Work in pairs. Ask questions and write your partner's personal profile. Use the profile above to help.

parentheses / college   brackets / university

VOCABULARY *PLUS*
COLLOCATIONS

7 A Work in pairs and do the quiz.

B Turn to page 158 and read the text to check your answers.

8 A Look at the quiz again. Find and circle five expressions using *take*, *get*, *do* and *go*.

B Write the expressions in italics in the correct places in the word webs below.

1 *on a diet*, along with, for a drink/a walk/a meal, for broke

- **go** —
  - on a diet (start something)
  - _____ (commit)
  - _____ (do something)
  - _____ (to agree to/with)

2 *responsibility for, after someone, part in something, a taxi*

- **take** —
  - _____ (go in a vehicle)
  - _____ (join in)
  - _____ (phrasal verbs)
  - _____ (other expressions)

3 *married, a job/degree,*  along with someone, *here*

- **get** —
  - _____ (become)
  - _____ (obtain)
  - _____ (go somewhere)
  - _____ (phrasal verbs)

4 *homework, research, housework, someone a* favor

- **do** —
  - _____ (schoolwork at home)
  - _____ (responsibilities and tasks)
  - _____ (find information)
  - _____ (help someone)

▶ page 148 VOCABULARY**BANK**

SPEAKING

9 A Think about your classmates. Write down the name of someone who:

- never gets angry
- does research for his/her job
- took a test in the last six months
- went for a meal last weekend
- took up a new hobby recently
- always gets here early
- went for a walk today
- got a new job recently

B Work in groups. Ask the other students to check if they agree with your ideas.

What Women **Really** Think ...?

Stella magazine commissioned YouGov, a research agency, to interview over 1,000 women in the U.K. about everything from their eating habits to their relationships and family values to find out what they really think.

How do you think they responded?

1 **How many women in the U.K. would prefer to have a male boss?**
a) less than 30%   b) about 50%   c) over 70%

2 **How many women spend more than seven hours a week exercising?**
a) 4%   b) 15%   c) 30%

3 **What is the biggest challenge for women today?**
a) staying healthy   b) making enough money
c) balancing home and work life

4 **What do women think is the best age to get married?**
a) between 21 and 24   b) between 25 and 29
c) over 30

5 **What do 59% of women think fathers should take more responsibility for?**
a) their children   b) doing the housework
c) organizing vacations

6 **According to women, how much housework do they do?**
a) more than 50%   b) over 75%   c) nearly all of it

7 **How many women 45–54 years of age met their husbands through the Internet?**
a) 1%   b) 9%   c) 16%

8 **How many women have gone on a diet in the past?**
a) 20%   b) between 35% and 45%   c) over 50%

get along with someone
favor / organizing / vacation

get on with someone
favour / organising / holidays

1.3)) TELL ME ABOUT YOURSELF

G talking about yourself
P intonation: sounding polite
V interview advice

5 Tips to Help You Do Well in Interviews

How do you get into the college or get the job of your dreams? Even before the interview, you might need to catch someone's attention. The Dean of Admissions at Harvard University says he often receives flowers and chocolates from potential students. One student sent references every day for three months. Eventually, he even sent a letter from his dentist saying how nice his teeth were. He didn't get an interview.

For those of you who do make the interview stage, here are five top tips:

1 Be prepared. Do some research about the college or company so you know what questions to ask.

2 Dress appropriately. You don't have to dress fashionably, but you should look clean. And don't wear "bling" (large, showy jewelry).

3 Arrive on time. Fifteen minutes early is OK.

4 Shake hands firmly and make eye contact. First impressions are important.

5 Speak clearly and try to offer full answers rather than short responses. This shows your enthusiasm.

SPEAKING

1 A Look at the photos. What types of interviews could they be? Choose from the list below.

- job interview
- interview to get into college
- newspaper/magazine interview
- interview for a talk show/radio program
- placement interview for a language course

B Look at the list of interview types above. Answer questions 1–3.

1 Which types of interviews above have you experienced?

2 Which will you experience in the future?

3 Do you think it is possible to show "the real you" in a short interview? Why?/Why not?

VOCABULARY
INTERVIEW ADVICE

2 A Work in pairs. What should/shouldn't you do in an interview? Think of as many things as you can in two minutes.

You should try to ask questions.

B Look at topics 1–3 below and match them to the expressions in the box.

> dress fashionably *3*   speak clearly   answer briefly
> shake hands firmly   send references
> arrive on time   avoid eye contact   be prepared
> do some research   show enthusiasm

1 Should Do during an Interview

2 Shouldn't Do during an Interview

3 Might Do before an Interview

3 Read the text and answer the questions.

1 What type of things do some people do to get an interview at Harvard University?

2 According to the text, what should you do before and during an interview? Do you agree with the advice?

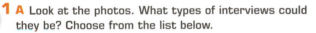

to get into college / fashionably, in the latest fashions / jewelry

for a place at university
smartly / jewellery

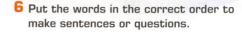

FUNCTION
TALKING ABOUT YOURSELF

4 A Listen to three extracts from interviews and answer the questions.

1 What types of interviews are they?
2 Which interviewee doesn't follow the five tips? How?

B Answer questions 1–6. Listen again to check.

Interview 1

1 What does the student want to practice?
2 What types of classes are in the afternoons?

Interview 2

3 What did the girl organize at summer camp?
4 What "can be difficult" according to the interviewer?

Interview 3

5 What does the man want to know?
6 Why are online courses more difficult than face-to-face courses?

5 A Read the extracts from the interviews. Underline the expressions that introduce a question.

Extract 1

T: OK … Is there anything else?
S: Could I ask a question?

Extract 2

I: There are a couple of things I'd like to ask about. Your résumé says you have some experience of looking after children?
A: Yes, I was a counselor at a summer camp last year.
I: Can I ask you about that? What types of things did you do?

Extract 3

I: I think that's about it. Do you have any questions?
S: Um, yes, actually I do have a question.

B Read the extracts below and underline the expressions that are used to introduce an opinion.

Extract 1

S: I've … spent time in the United States, but that was a few years ago. So, for me, the most important thing is to just refresh …

Extract 2

I: OK. And you enjoyed it?
A: Yes.
I: What aspect, what part did you enjoy, would you say?
A: I suppose I'd have to say I liked the games best …
I: … We often find that different ages together can be difficult.
A: It depends. In my opinion, you can usually get the older children to help the younger ones.

Extract 3

S: So I wouldn't need to attend classes?
I: Not for the online courses. But … well, one thing I'd like to say is that the online courses are, in many ways, more difficult than face-to-face courses.

▶ page 128 **LANGUAGEBANK**

6 Put the words in the correct order to make sentences or questions.

1 question / I / a / have
2 I / a / could / question / ask / ?
3 like / couple / of / are / about / I'd / things / to / a / ask / there
4 ask / you / I / can / that / about / ?
5 true / this / opinion / my / isn't / in
6 to / I'd / I / agree / have / say
7 thing / that / like / I'd / one / say / is / to / is / course / the / difficult
8 is / thing / important / most / for / the / me / to / study

LEARN TO
USE TWO-WORD RESPONSES

7 A Match expressions 1–5 with expressions a)–e).

1 Of course.   a) Please continue.
2 That's right.   b) You're correct.
3 I see.   c) You're welcome.
4 No problem.   d) Yes, definitely.
5 Go ahead.   e) I understand.

B Which expressions in Exercise 7A are more formal? Read audio script 1.5 on page 164 to see how the expressions are used.

C INTONATION: sounding polite Listen to the expressions in Exercise 7A. Notice how the speaker begins the expression with a high pitch to sound friendly. Listen again and repeat.

SPEAKING

8 Role-play an interview in pairs. Follow instructions 1–5.

1 Choose an interview type in Exercise 1A or Student A: turn to page 158 and Student B: turn to page 162.
2 Decide on your roles.
3 Interviewer: think of questions. You can make notes if you wish. Interviewee: guess what type of questions the interviewer will ask and prepare answers.
4 Practice your role-play.
5 Perform it in front of other students.

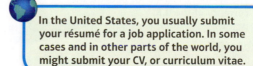

In the United States, you usually submit your résumé for a job application. In some cases and in other parts of the world, you might submit your CV, or curriculum vitae.

practice / counselor / at summer camp / question(s)   practise / tutor / on the summer camp / query(ies)

DVD PREVIEW

1 A Work in pairs and discuss the questions.

1 What creative or athletic activities are important to you? How would you feel if you couldn't do them any more?

2 Which creative or athletic activities would be particularly difficult if you were blind? What problems do you think a blind person would have?

B Read about the program. What caused Sargy Mann to go blind? What happened after he went totally blind?

▶ The Blind Painter

Sargy Mann painted all of his professional life, first as a teacher and later as a professional artist. In his mid-30s, he developed cataracts in both eyes, eventually leading to total blindness. He continued to paint. Twenty-five years later, Sargy's work was very popular with art collectors, with paintings regularly selling for more than $80,000 (£50,000). He spoke to BBC News about his life and how he continued to work.

DVD VIEW

2 Watch the DVD. What does Sargy use to help him paint? What do you think of his paintings?

3 A Answer the questions.

1 What do you know about Sargy Mann after watching the clip?

2 Why did Sargy start to paint again after he went blind?

3 How does he use Blu-Tack™ to help him paint?

4 Who buys his artwork?

B Look at the quotes from the DVD. Try to complete the phrases using the words in the box.

> sensation   go   edgy   coordinates   landscape   nonsense

1 The idea of painting when you were totally blind seemed a _____ to me.

2 I wonder what would happen if I give that a _____.

3 I had the most extraordinary _____.

4 Pre total blindness, I would say I was a _____ painter.

5 Now the thing about these bits of Blu-Tack™, of course, is that what they are actually is _____.

6 They are _____, dangerous. They tell stories, they're full of impact through color.

C Watch the DVD again to check your answers.

D Match the words and expressions from Exercise 3B with a)–f) below.

a) a very strange or unusual feeling

b) an artist who paints the countryside and scenery

c) experimental or avant-garde

d) numbers or information used to indicate a point

e) looked like a silly idea

f) (to) try something

4 Discuss the questions.

1 Do you think that Sargy Mann would be such a successful artist if he were not blind?

2 Can you think of other people who have achieved great things despite physical disabilities?

The symbol for dollars, as well as some other currencies, is $.
The symbol £ is used for pounds, the currency of the U.K.

nonsense / color   a nonsense / colour

American Speakout 60 sec. about you

5 A Listen to Monica talking about herself. Which questions does she answer from the questionnaire below? What does she say?

Who are you?

1. What three words best describe you?
2. What is your idea of perfect happiness?
3. What possession is most important to you?
4. What is your greatest achievement?
5. What do you like most/least about your lifestyle?
6. What are your favorite sound, smell and taste?
7. What do you always carry with you?
8. Who would be your perfect dinner date? Why?
9. What's your favorite month and why?
10. If you could change one thing about the past, what would it be?

B Listen again. Complete the phrases Monica uses.

KEYPHRASES

I'm going to tell you _____ about myself.

I think three words that describe me would be _____, talkative and hard-working.

One of the things I _____ about my lifestyle …

I suppose that's one _____ I don't like.

In the summer, I love to _____ to the coast …

It makes me feel _____.

C Prepare to talk about yourself for 60 seconds. Choose two or three questions from the questionnaire in Exercise 5A. Plan your answers. Practice and time your presentation to check you can say it all in just 60 seconds.

D Work in pairs and take turns to give your presentation. Take notes on your partner's presentation. What do you have in common?

writeback a personal description

6 A Read the text. What do you think Stephan's main achievements are?

Stephan Wilding in 100 Words:

Stephan decided to change his major from pharmacology to Thai. When he finished college, he spent six months in Thailand teaching English before going back to the U.S. Unsure of his next move, he spent his evenings and weekends teaching himself how to code. He then got together with some friends to start up their own software business. It was a huge adventure, and they learned a lot very quickly. They have recently won a contract to build a computer platform for a design company, so the future is looking good.

B Work in pairs. You are going to write a short description of your partner. Check your notes from Exercise 5D and ask your partner questions if you think you need more information. Then use the text in Exercise 6A to help you write your description (100 words).

favorite   favourite

17

V LANGUAGE

1 A Read the advice from a 1950s English textbook. Complete the sentences with the words in the box.

> foreign   strategy   jargon   bilingual
> native speakers   ~~fluency~~   slang   accuracy
> skill   mother tongue

1 Using the right method, _fluency_ in the target language is possible after just a few weeks.

2 Students should talk with _____ _____ only. Exposure to other learners will result in new errors.

3 To improve _____, the student should copy out several pages from the textbook every day.

4 The student's biggest problem is translating every word of English into his _____ _____.

5 The best _____ is for the student to imitate the recordings for an hour at a time.

6 It is unnecessary to learn _____ words unless the learner needs them for a specific job.

7 It is impossible to become _____ unless the second language was learned in childhood.

8 Students should avoid _____ because it isn't proper English.

9 To improve the listening _____, the student should listen daily to the radio.

10 The _____ student needs to be corrected every time he makes a mistake.

G QUESTION FORMS

2 A Find and correct the mistakes in the questions below. Four of the questions are correct.

1 When you started studying English?

2 Who did helped you to learn English?

3 What annoys you about your job or your studies?

4 Did you to learn anything important at school?

5 Do you be enjoy learning languages?

6 In your job or studies, is there anything you are not happy with?

7 When you imagine the perfect career, what do you think of?

8 What keeps you awake at night?

B Ask your partner four of the questions.

V RELATIONSHIPS

3 A Put the letters in the correct order to find the names of twelve types of people.

1 tomdogher	5 ceanife	9 sobs
2 niface	6 breemm	10 emeyloep
3 eeemnt	7 stamcasel	11 trenom
4 nraterp	8 dethagorf	12 maatteme

B Work in pairs. Which of these people do you know or have in your life? Which of these are you?

G REVIEW OF VERB TENSES

4 A Find and correct the mistakes. Five of the underlined verbs are incorrect.

> **12/10/09**
>
> I ¹was walking to work this morning when I ²was seeing Mr. Gonzalez, my old Spanish teacher. He ³was wearing a leather jacket and carrying a guitar. I ⁴ask him how he was. He said, "Fine. I ⁵go to my band practice." I said, "What band?" He replied, "I ⁶don't teach anymore. It ⁷wasn't really the best job for me. A few years ago I ⁸was starting a band called The Big Easy. We ⁹don't make much money, but I ¹⁰'m liking the lifestyle." I asked him where he lived, and he said, "I ¹¹'m living in my van at the moment. I ¹²travel a lot. I'm a child of the sixties!"

B Write a short journal entry about an interesting or unusual day.

F TALKING ABOUT YOURSELF

5 A Complete the conversations. Write an expression from the box in the correct place in the sentence.

> ~~question about~~   like to   to say   you about
> I ask   thing I'd

> _question about_

1 A: I have a / the class. Do I have to bring a pen?
   B: No, it's a computer class.

2 A: Could a question? Where does the tennis class meet?
   B: At the tennis courts.

3 A: I'd have I'm not sure you're qualified. Why should we employ you for the library position?
   B: Because I'm good with children and animals.

4 A: There are a couple of things I'd ask. First, can you work on Saturdays?
   B: Is that on the weekend?

5 A: One like to say is that you look good for your age. How old are you?
   B: Thirty.

6 A: Can I ask your latest film, *Philadelphia*? Where is it set?
   B: In Philadelphia.

B Work in pairs. Write an interview (for a job, a college, a magazine). Use the expressions in Exercises 5 and 7 on page 15 to help.

C Work in groups and take turns to role-play your interviews.

Mr. / on the weekend   Mr / at the weekend

2 tales

When is it OK to tell a lie?

INTERVIEWS

2.1)) FACT OR FICTION?

G present perfect and past simple

P weak forms: *have*

V types of story; prepositions

SPEAKING

1 A Work in groups and discuss. Can you think of a movie you have seen that has taught you about a person/event in history?

B Work in pairs and do the quiz. Decide if the information is fact, fiction or partly true. Then check your answers on page 158.

C Discuss. Do you think it is all right for filmmakers to change the facts of a story? Why?/Why not?

HOLLYWOOD versus History

Can you tell your facts from fiction?

1 In the film *The Last Samurai*, Tom Cruise plays a U.S. army captain who joins the samurai warriors in Japan in 1876. Was Captain Nathan Algren a real figure from history?

2 In *Shakespeare in Love*, William Shakespeare is inspired to write *Romeo and Juliet* by his real-life relationship with a young actress. Did this happen in real life?

3 In the film *Braveheart*, Mel Gibson plays the character William Wallace, leading an army of men with painted faces and wearing kilts* as he battles to free Scotland from the English. How much truth is there in the story?

4 In the 1995 adventure *Apollo 13,* we hear the pilot saying the famous words "Houston, we have a problem." But were these his exact words?

* kilt—a type of skirt traditionally worn by Scottish men

VOCABULARY
TYPES OF STORY

2 A Look at the types of movie stories in the box below. Match the **types of story** with the **descriptions** a)—i).

> a biopic   a docudrama   a disaster movie
> a romantic comedy   a period drama
> a fantasy film   a science fiction movie
> a psychological thriller   an action/adventure movie
> a mystery   a crime movie

a) Heroes chase and fight each other.

b) The main character has mental problems.

c) A story about the science of the future.

d) Things that happen in the life of a real person.

e) The good guy (the detective) finds the bad guy (the criminal).

f) People dressed up in old-fashioned costumes.

g) Funny things happen. Two people fall in love.

h) Terrible things happen, but people survive.

i) A documentary made more interesting with some parts acted.

j) Strange things happen in an imaginary world.

k) Somebody gets murdered, and a clever detective tries to find out who did it.

B Read the opinion below. What type of movies does the writer enjoy? Why?

> "I love watching romantic comedies. I enjoy sitting down and watching a couple find each other and fall in love. It's really easy watching. I find it relaxing because I don't have to think. It's funny how my taste in movies has changed. When I was younger, I enjoyed action movies, like *Terminator 2.* But now I guess my interests are different."

C Work in pairs and answer the questions.

1 Which types of movie do you enjoy watching? Have your tastes changed over the years?

2 Can you name movies that match each type of story? Have both of you seen them? Are your opinions about them the same or different?

LISTENING

3 A Listen to the first part of a radio program about movies and answer the questions.

1 What type of movie does the program talk about?

2 Why are these movies so popular?

B Work in pairs and discuss. Look at the photos of actors who have played the roles of famous people in movies. How do you think they prepared for the roles?

C Listen to the second part of the radio program. Are the sentences true (T) or false (F)?

1 Helen Mirren won an Oscar for her role as the Queen.

2 Will Smith met Muhammad Ali, but they didn't get along.

3 Josh Brolin talked to himself in a Texas accent all day.

4 Audrey Tautou watched movies of Coco Chanel.

4 A Listen to the whole program and complete the information.

1 Hollywood has always used _____ _____ in its films.

2 Hollywood began making movies in the _____s.

3 Some of the best movies in recent years have been based on _____ _____.

4 From these movies we've learned about the _____ lives of some of the biggest music legends.

5 Many of these actors have won _____ for their roles.

6 Helen Mirren met the Queen for _____ .

7 Josh Brolin phoned hotels in Texas to listen to their _____ .

8 Tautou wanted to look like Coco Chanel so that we would recognize her _____ .

B Check your answers in the audio script on page 164.

> In American English, you almost always say you're going to the movies (not the cinema) or to see a movie (not a film).

U.S. / learned / recognize   US / learnt / recognise

A | Helen Mirren

B | Queen Elizabeth I

C | Will Smith

D | Muhammad Ali

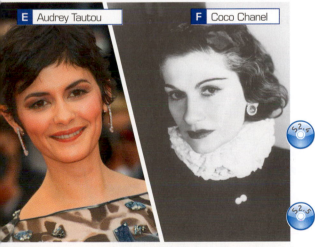

E | Audrey Tautou

F | Coco Chanel

G | Josh Brolin

H | George Bush

GRAMMAR

PRESENT PERFECT AND PAST SIMPLE

5 A Read the sentences in Exercise 4A and underline examples of the present perfect and past simple.

B Complete the rules with present perfect or past simple.

> **RULES**
>
> 1 Use the _____ to talk about experiences or things that happened before now. The time is not specified or important.
>
> 2 Use the _____ to talk about recent events or an action that started in the past and continues now.
>
> 3 Use the _____ to talk about a specific event in the past (we know when the event happened).
>
> 4 Use the _____ to talk about an action that started and finished at a specific time in the past.

C Look at the sentences in Exercise 4A again and match them with one of the rules above.

▶ page 130 LANGUAGEBANK

6 A Read the text. What changed Chris Gardner's life?

> Chris Gardner is a successful businessman and a millionaire. But things [1]_____ always _____ (not be) easy. He [2]_____ (not meet) his father until he was twenty-eight years old. This experience made him sure about one thing: he was determined to be a good father to his own children. As a young man, Gardner [3]_____ (experience) hard times. His wife [4]_____ (leave) him; he [5]_____ (lose) his job; and, at one stage, he and his two-year-old son [6]_____ (sleep) in train stations and airports. He [7]_____ (come) a long way since then. His life changed when he [8]_____ (meet) a man driving a red Ferrari and asked him what job he did. The man was a stockbroker, so Gardner asked him out to lunch. The Ferrari driver introduced Gardner to the world of finance. Since he has become successful, he [9]_____ (spend) a lot of money helping homeless people, and he [10]_____ also _____ (write) books about his experiences. His story was told in the movie *The Pursuit of Happyness*, starring Will Smith.

B Complete the text with the correct form of the verbs in parentheses.

7 A WEAK FORMS: *have* Listen to the pairs of phrases. Notice the difference.

1 I lived / I've lived

2 we met / we've met

3 he decided / he's decided

4 they spent / they've spent

B Listen and write the sentences.

C Listen again and check. Then listen and repeat.

8 A Work in pairs. Student A: write *Have you ever ... ?* questions using the prompts in the box below. Student B: turn to page 158.

> be on TV/in a newspaper   watch a movie at an outdoor movie theater
> do something embarrassing in public   write a poem/story
> go to a country on a different continent
> collect something as a hobby   see someone commit a crime

B Take turns asking and answering questions. Try to find five things that you have done and your partner hasn't done.

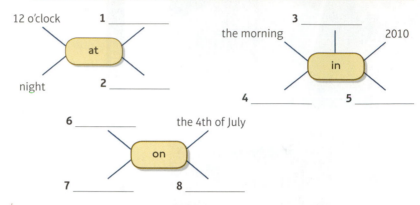

SPEAKING

9 A Imagine you are going to make a movie about your life. Choose five events you would like to include. Write some notes in the film strip below.

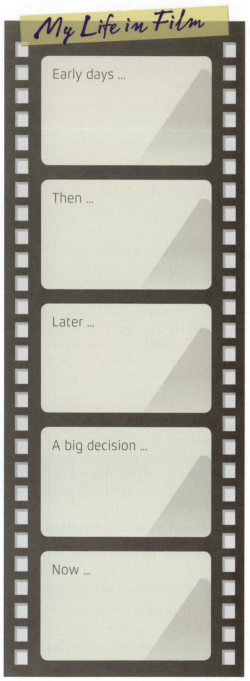

My Life in Film

Early days ...

Then ...

Later ...

A big decision ...

Now ...

B Work in pairs. Take turns talking about the film of your life.

C Think of three questions to ask your partner about the film of their life. Ask and answer the questions

Why did you choose to ... ?

What happened when you ... ?

What did you enjoy best about ... ?

VOCABULARY *PLUS*

PREPOSITIONS

10 PREPOSITION + EXPRESSIONS OF TIME Complete the word webs with expressions in the box.

> Saturday   the weekend   quarter to one   New Year's Day
> July   the winter/the summer   the twenty-first century   lunchtime

12 o'clock   **1** _____

at

night   **2** _____

the morning   **3** _____   2010

in

4 _____   **5** _____

6 _____   the 4th of July

on

7 _____   **8** _____

American Speak out TIP

To help you remember which preposition of time to use, try to memorize this: on Monday; in winter; at that time.
on = for specific days, in = for time periods, at = for specific times

▶ page 149 **VOCABULARYBANK**

11 PREPOSITION + NOUN Complete the phrases with the correct preposition: *on*, *for* or *by*.

1 It's a book ____ Dan Brown, a movie ____ Steven Spielberg, a song ____ Amy Winehouse.

2 I saw it ____ TV. I heard it ____ the radio. I spoke to him ____ the phone.

3 We went ____ a walk, ____ a drive, ____ a run, ____ a swim.

4 They traveled ____ boat, ____ plane, ____ bus, ____ train.

12 A FIXED EXPRESSIONS Match the fixed expressions in bold in sentences 1–10 with meanings a)–j).

1 I dropped it *by mistake*.	**a)** finally
2 I saw the movie *on my own*.	**b)** cannot wait
3 He's here *on business*.	**c)** by a person, not a machine
4 We met *by chance*.	**d)** it was not a mistake
5 It was made *by hand*.	**e)** alone, not with other people
6 We got there *in the end*.	**f)** not early, not late
7 She said it *on purpose*.	**g)** in a very short time
8 We arrived *on time*.	**h)** accidentally
9 I'll do that *in a moment*.	**i)** not on vacation, but for work
10 They're *in a hurry*.	**j)** it was not planned

B Look at Exercise 12A again. Write 6–8 questions with phrases with prepositions.

Do you usually arrive on time, or are you sometimes late?

Do you prefer to live with someone or live on your own?

C Work in pairs. Take turns asking and answering the questions.

on the weekend / memorize / bus   at the weekend / memorise / coach

2.2)) WHAT REALLY HAPPENED?

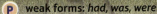

G narrative tenses
P weak forms: *had, was, were*
V the news

SPEAKING

1 A Discuss the questions.

1 How do you keep up-to-date with the news?
2 What have been the most important stories in the last five years?

B Listen to the excerpts from news reports. Which stories can you see in the photos?

READING

2 A Work in pairs. Read the definition and look at the photos below. Then answer the questions.

> **a conspiracy theory:** /kən'spɪrəsi 'θɪəri/ a theory or belief that there was a secret plan behind a major event

from Longman Active Study Dictionary

1 What do you think the conspiracy theories were about (the events in the photos)?
2 Which story do you think involved a real conspiracy according to official reports?

B Read the article to check your answers.

3 A Read the article again and answer the questions.

1 Who died in their bathroom?
2 Who was shot?
3 Who was arrested?
4 Who was murdered?
5 Who were the suspects?
6 Who was photographed?

B How are these words and phrases related to the stories?

> shadows   fans   stars   painkillers
> photographs   a studio   hospital
> the FBI (Federal Bureau of Investigation)
> a man with a gun   a flag

C Work in pairs. Answer the questions.

1 What do you think? Do you believe the official reports or the conspiracy theorists?
2 Do you know any other conspiracy theories? What happened?

The World's Best-known Conspiracy Theories

Man on the Moon We've seen the photos, but many people claim that Neil Armstrong's "giant leap for mankind" never really happened. They suspect that the astronauts Neil Armstrong and Buzz Aldrin never left Earth, but acted out the scene and took photographs in a studio. Conspiracy theorists say there were strange shadows falling in the photos, and surprisingly no stars are visible. They point out that the U.S. flag, planted by Buzz Aldrin, was apparently waving, although there is no wind on the moon. However, these doubts can be explained logically. The lighting conditions on the moon were complicated, and the flag only appears to "flutter" because the astronauts moved it.

The King Is Dead When Elvis Presley was found lying unconscious on his bathroom floor at his home, Graceland, his family and friends desperately tried to save him. An ambulance was called, and Elvis was rushed to the hospital where a special room had been prepared for him. However, the "King of Rock'n'Roll" was already dead when he arrived there. At first, doctors said that Elvis died because his heart had stopped, but later they claimed that drugs were involved. Elvis had taken painkillers because he had a toothache and he couldn't sleep. However, for years his fans refused to believe that Elvis was gone, and there were numerous sightings of "Elvis" around the world. There is even a website, elvis-is-alive.com, dedicated to finding out the truth.

The Death of a President President John F. Kennedy was assassinated on November 22, 1963. He was riding through crowds in his car when a gunman shot him once in the head. Lee Harvey Oswald was arrested almost immediately after Kennedy's death and charged with killing him. He was murdered two days later. A report in 1964 concluded that Oswald had acted alone. But conspiracy theorists have doubts and believe more people were involved. Suspects include the CIA, the FBI and the Cuban leader Fidel Castro. In 1979, a new report agreed that Oswald had killed Kennedy, but also concluded that the President was killed "as a result of conspiracy" by unknown people.

> You might write November 22, 1963 in American English, but 22nd November 1963 in British English. Be especially carefully with purely numeric dates. Depending where you are, 02/09/2016 could be September 2, 2016 or Februrary 9, 2016!

to the hospital /
had a toothache

to hospital /
had toothache

GRAMMAR
NARRATIVE TENSES

4 A Read the summary. Find and underline examples of the past simple and the past continuous and answer the questions.

> In 1963, President Kennedy and his team were preparing for the next presidential campaign. In Dallas, he was riding through crowds in his car when a gunman shot him.

1 Which tense is used to talk about the main events in a story?

2 Which tense is used to give background information in a story?

B Read the conclusion and answer the questions.

> Lee Harvey Oswald was arrested for the crime. A report later <u>agreed</u> that Oswald <u>had killed</u> Kennedy, but also <u>concluded</u> that there <u>had been</u> a conspiracy by a number of unknown people.

1 Which of the <u>underlined</u> verbs is in the past simple?

2 Which of the <u>underlined</u> verbs is in the past perfect?

3 Which tense describes the event(s) that happened first?

C Underline the correct alternative to complete the rule.

> **RULES**
>
> Use the past perfect to talk about actions that happened *before the past time event we are talking about/a very long time ago.*

D WEAK FORMS: *had, was, were* Listen to the news summary. Notice how *was*, *were* and *had* are pronounced. Listen again. Try to shadow read the text (read at the same time as the recording).

▶ page 130 LANGUAGEBANK

5 Read an account of an important news event. Complete the text with phrases a)–h).

a) He had been in prison

b) one of the branches broke

c) we heard some shots

d) 50,000 people were waiting

e) to hear what Mandela was saying

f) When he finally arrived

g) were talking to each other

h) many people had climbed onto it

> **February 11, 2000: Nelson Mandela's Release from Prison**
>
> I was in the crowd in the town square in Cape Town that day. It was a hot day, and ¹_____ to see Mandela walk free from the prison. ²_____ for twenty-seven years. At one point, ³_____, but most people stayed calm. People ⁴_____ and singing songs. There was a great feeling of solidarity. There was a large tree in the middle of the town square, and ⁵___ to get a better view. Suddenly, ⁶_____, and people fell to the ground. But nobody wanted to leave. Nobody wanted to miss the chance of seeing Mandela for the first time. ⁷_____, there was a huge cheer. From where I was standing, it was difficult ⁸_____, but I knew I was there for an important moment in our history.

VOCABULARY
THE NEWS

6 A Match the headlines 1–8 with the explanations a)–h).

1 Actress Survives **Crash**

2 Politicians **Attacked** by Angry Crowd

3 Student Demonstration Turns **Violent**

4 Workers to **Strike over Pay**

5 Massive **Earthquake** Hits Italy

6 Most Wanted **Fugitive** Arrested

7 Floods **Destroy** Crops

8 **Hostages** Released after Talks with Rebels

a) Lots of angry people shout and throw things at some politicians.

b) People who were kept as prisoners are allowed to go free.

c) Police catch a man who they suspect committed a serious crime.

d) A natural disaster destroys part of a country.

e) A woman is involved in a car accident but doesn't die.

f) A lot of farmland is now underwater.

g) Many people might refuse to go to work.

h) People who are protesting begin to fight on the streets.

B Work in pairs. Describe some stories that have recently been in the news using the vocabulary in bold above.

American Speak out TIP Headlines can be difficult. They contain incomplete sentences: articles and auxiliaries can be dropped, simple tenses are used instead of continuous or perfect tenses and the infinitive is used to talk about the future. Find examples in the headlines.

▶ page 149 VOCABULARYBANK

SPEAKING

7 A Choose one of the news stories in the lesson or another important news story. Make notes to answer the questions below.

1 What was the news story? Where were you when you heard the news?
2 What were you doing? Whom were you with?
3 What did you think at first? How did you feel?
4 Did the news change things for you in any way?

B Work with other students. Tell them about your story.

WRITING

A NEWS REPORT; LEARN TO USE TIME LINKERS

8 A Read the news report and answer the questions. Underline the parts of the news report that help you to answer.

1 Whom is the story about?
2 What happened?
3 Why did it happen?
4 Where did it happen?
5 When did it happen?
6 What is the situation now?

Fraud Fugitive in Facebook Trap

A man who was on the run from police in the U.S. revealed where he was hiding through a series of Facebook updates.

Cameroon-born Maxi Sopo falsely obtained credit from banks while he was living in the U.S. By the time he had finished, he had stolen more than $200,000. He then escaped to Cancun, in Mexico, where he was happily spending the money, until he made posts on his Facebook page telling the world that he was "living in paradise."

"He was posting about how beautiful life is and how he was having a good time with his buddies," said Assistant U.S. Attorney Michael Scoville. "He was definitely not living the way we wanted him to be living, given the charges he was facing," he added.

However, during his time in Cancun, Mr. Sopo also befriended a former justice department official on the networking site. This man, who had only met Mr. Sopo a few times, was able to discover exactly where Mr. Sopo was living. As soon as he had this information, he passed it to the Mexican authorities who arrested Sopo last month.

The twenty-six-year-old is currently in custody in Mexico City.

B Read the news report again. Find examples of the following:

1 quotes used to give someone's opinion
2 a concluding statement that gives us information about the current situation
3 an introductory statement that explains in one sentence what happened
4 more information about the background to the story

9 A Look at the news report and find examples of the time linkers in the box.

> as soon as   while   during
> until   by the time

B Look at the words/phrases in the box above. Which time linker do we use to link an action that:

1 happened previously?   _by the time_
2 continues up to that point and then stops?
   _____
3 happens at the same time as another action?
   _____
4 happens at some point in a period of time?
   _____
5 happens immediately after something else has happened?
   _____

C Complete the sentences with the correct time linker.

1 I came _____ I heard the news.
2 They arrived _____ we were having dinner.
3 Her cat died _____ the night.
4 We waited _____ the lights had gone out.
5 _____ the fire engines arrived, the house was destroyed.

10 A Work in pairs. Choose a headline and write six questions asking for information about the story.

> Actress Survives Crash

> Politicians Attacked by Angry Crowd

> Man Shot Outside His House

B Give your questions to another pair of students.

C Look at the questions and use them to write a short news report (100—150 words). Use the ideas in Exercise 8B to help you.

D Compare your stories with other students. Who has the best story?

G telling a story
P intonation: sounding interested
V say/tell

VOCABULARY
SAY/TELL

1 A Work in pairs and discuss. How do you know when someone is lying? Do you think their behavior changes?

B Read the text to check your answers.

How do you know if someone is lying?

From little white lies to lies that can destroy nations, people have lied for as long as they have told the truth. Some people are very good at it. So, how do we know if someone is lying?

Here are the things to look out for:

1 The guilty hand: when someone is telling the truth, they usually use more body language. They move their hands and their face more. When someone lies, their hands are still.

2 The lying eye: people find it very hard to tell you a lie if they're looking you straight in the eyes. Normally, they look away just at the moment that they tell the lie.

3 The "Me": when people tell a story about themselves, they tend to use a lot of "me" words, like *I, me,* and *my.* When they tell a lie, they don't use the "me" words as much.

2 A Match 1–6 with a)–f) to make sentences.

1 I'm terrible at telling

2 My brother told me

3 I think you should say

4 Sometimes it's better to tell

5 You should just say

6 I said

a) "hello," but she didn't answer.

b) a white lie than to upset someone.

c) what you mean.

d) a funny story yesterday.

e) sorry.

f) jokes. I always forget the punch line!

B Add the phrases with say and tell from Exercise 2A to the table.

Say	Tell
"hello"	a story

C Work with other students. Do you agree/disagree with the statements? Why?

1 A lie can travel halfway around the world while the truth is putting on its shoes.

2 A good storyteller should mix fiction with truth to make their stories interesting.

3 It's OK to tell lies sometimes.

A

FUNCTION
TELLING A STORY

3 A Look at the pictures above, which tell a story. They are not in the correct order. What do you think is happening in each picture?

B Listen to a woman telling her story. Number the pictures in the correct order.

4 A Look at the phrases we can use to help tell the sequence in a story. Add the sequencers from the box to the correct place in the table.

This happened when   The next thing I knew
Anyway,   In the end,   Before long,
And then,   all of a sudden

beginning
In the beginning, …
This happened when
describing what happened
Well, …
So, …
ending
So, …
Finally, …

B Listen to the story again, and check (✔) the phrases you hear. Check your answers in the audio script on page 165.

▶ page 130 **VOCABULARY**BANK

5 A Work in pairs. Practice telling the story using the sequencers and the pictures to help you. Start like this:

This happened when the woman had an important interview and …

B Do you think the woman was telling a true or false story? Listen to find out.

behavior   behaviour

LEARN TO
SHOW INTEREST

6 A Look at phrases a)–j). Which phrases complete extracts 1–6?

a) what happened then?

b) What did you do?

c) Then what?

d) Oh, no!

e) Oh, dear.

f) How embarrassing!

g) That's really funny.

h) Really?

i) You're joking!

j) You're kidding!

1 **W:** So, anyway, er … I then got on the subway, um … to go for my interview.

    M: OK, and ____*a*____

2 **W:** I'd woken up shouting the word, "Mom."

    M: No! _____

3 **W:** At the top of my voice, in a packed, quiet subway car.

    M: _____

4 **W:** … they're looking at me in a rather strange way.

    M: OK … _____

5 **W:** My face had swollen up! … And it was bright red, … and covered in blotches, spots…

    M: Oh! _____

6 **W:** Yes, and the pills that my mother had given me were so out-of-date that they had caused an allergic reaction …

    M: Oh! … _____

American
Speak
TIP

> When someone tells a story, try to use comments and questions to show that you are interested, e.g., How amazing! Remember to check your intonation. Do you sound interested?

B INTONATION: sounding interested Listen and check your answers. Notice how intonation is used to sound interested. Is it high or low?

C Listen again and repeat the phrases. Try to sound interested. Then repeat, but try to sound bored. Can you hear the difference?

SPEAKING

7 A Prepare to tell a story. It can be a true story or a lie. Choose one of the situations below. Talk about when you:

- got stuck in an elevator
- missed (or nearly missed) a flight
- lost something valuable
- spoke to someone famous
- got a tattoo
- went swimming at night
- were mistaken for someone else
- slept outside
- tried a very dangerous sport
- found something unusual

B Think about the details of your story. Think about the questions below and make some notes or practice telling your story. Try to use some of the sequencers from Exercise 4.

- Where were you?
- Why were you there?
- What were you doing?
- What happened?
- How did you feel?

C Work with other students. Take turns telling your stories and listening and responding. Ask questions to decide if it is a true story or a lie.

A: I once got stuck in an elevator.
B: Really?
A: Yes. I was …

D Tell the other students if it is a true story or a lie.

subway (train) / "Mom!" / elevator tube / 'Mum!' / lift

DVD PREVIEW

1 Work in pairs. Discuss the questions.

1 Which famous fictional thieves/investigators/detectives do you know about?

2 Which are famous in your country?

3 Do you watch any crime dramas? Which ones? What do you like/dislike about them?

4 What are the features of good detective dramas, e.g., interesting characters?

2 Look at the pictures and read about the program. What problems do you think Finch had when he stole the painting?

 **Hustle**

Hustle is a drama series about a team of criminals who try to obtain and sell things in an illegal or dishonest way. In this program, we meet Finch, a burglar. He's in trouble with Customs, which believes that he has stolen a valuable piece of art. Unfortunately for Finch, when he stole the painting, things didn't go quite according to plan.

DVD VIEW

3 A Watch the program. What problems did Finch encounter?

B Match the words in the two columns to make common crime collocations. Work with your partner. What do these words mean?

1 guard	a) thief
2 art	b) guard
3 valuable	c) weapon
4 burglar	d) officer
5 customs	e) dog
6 loaded	f) alarm
7 security	g) painting

C Check (✔) the things above that you see in the clip. Which of the above do you not see?

4 A Work in pairs and answer the questions.

1 How does Finch get onto the grounds of the mansion?

2 What is the security guard doing?

3 What does Finch do when he breaks into the house?

4 Why does Finch have to run with the artwork?

5 How does Finch escape?

6 What happens at the airport?

7 Why do customs officers search Finch? Do they find anything?

8 What does Customs plan to do?

B Watch the DVD again to check.

C Discuss what you think Finch does next. What do you think will happen?

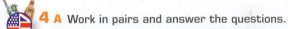

Customs, which believes / into the grounds
does Customs plan

Customs, who believe / onto the grounds
do customs plan

American Speakout a narrative

5 A Work in groups. Look at the pictures. What do you think happened?

B Listen to someone telling the story. Do you think the story is true?

C Listen again and check (✔) the key phrases you hear.

> **KEYPHRASES**
>
> This story is about …
>
> The problem was that …
>
> In fact, …
>
> What he didn't realize/know was that …
>
> However, …
>
> Later, …
>
> Because of this, …
>
> In the end, …

6 A Work in pairs. Take turns to retell the story using the key phrases.

B Work in pairs. Student A: look at the picture story on page 159. Student B: look at the picture story on page 160. Use the phrases in Exercise 5C to tell your partner what happens in your story.

writeback a newspaper article

7 A Read about a famous art theft. Who stole the painting? Why did he steal it? What happened in the end?

Famous Painting Stolen

On August 21, 1911, Leonardo da Vinci's *Mona Lisa*, one of the most famous paintings in the world, was stolen from the wall of the Louvre Museum, in Paris. At first, the police thought one of the guards might have stolen the painting, but seventeen days after the theft, they arrested poet Guillaume Apollinaire. However, he was released when police could find no evidence that he had committed the crime. Two years later, the real thief, Vincenzo Peruggia, was arrested in Italy. Peruggia had worked at the museum and had stolen the painting because he was angry about how many Italian paintings were on display in France. He had planned to return the painting to the Uffizi gallery, in Florence, Italy. The public was so excited at the news of finding the *Mona Lisa* that the painting was displayed throughout Italy before it was returned to France in 1913.

B Write up the story of Finch's art theft as a newspaper article, using the article above and the key phrases to help you.

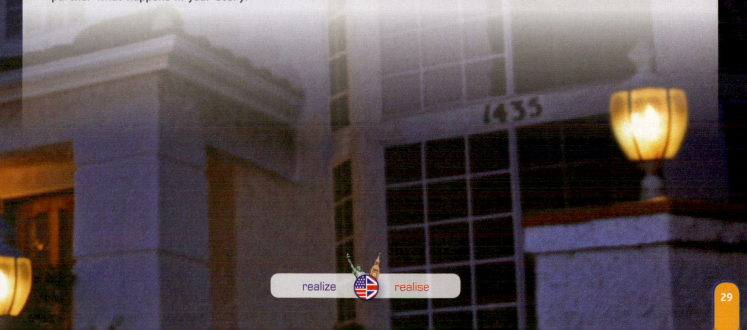

realize 🏴 realise

29

V TYPES OF STORY

1 A Add the missing letters to complete the types of story.

1 One of my favorite a_ _ _ _ _ films of all time is *The Terminator*.

2 Jamie Foxx stars in *Ray*, a great b_ _ _ _ _ of Ray Charles.

3 *Pretty Woman*, starring Julia Roberts and Richard Gere, is my favorite r_ _ _ _ _ _ _ c_ _ _ _.

4 I'm not a great fan of p_ _ _ _ _ d_ _ _ _ _, but I thought this production of *Jane Eyre* was brilliant.

5 I loved the p_ _ _ _ _ _ _ _ _ _ _- t_ _ _ _ _ _, *Silence of the Lambs*, but I found it very scary.

6 I still enjoy Agatha Christie's *Murder on the Orient Express*. It's one of the best ever d_ _ _ _ _ _ _ movies.

7 I can't watch s_ _ _ _ _ _ f_ _ _ _ _ films, like *Star Wars* and *Alien*. I can't stand them.

8 I think d_ _ _ _ _ _ _ _, films like *Nixon*, are a great way to learn about what really happened during important events.

B Choose your three favorite film genres. Find other students who like the same genres and work together to make "best ever" lists of the movies in those genres.

G PRESENT PERFECT AND PAST SIMPLE

2 A Look at the phrases below. Have you done any of these things? Write sentences using *I've* ... , *I haven't* ... and *I have never* ... .

- see a famous band
- ride a horse
- visit another country
- run a marathon
- start a business
- travel on your own
- write a diary/blog
- organize a big family party
- play in a band/write a song
- walk in the mountains/go skiing
- swim with dolphins/go scuba diving
- meet someone famous
- go to college/change your job

B Choose one thing you have/haven't done and tell your partner more about it.

I've played in a band. When I was in college, I played in a band called The Hooligans.

G NARRATIVE TENSES

3 A Put the verbs in the correct tense to complete the story.

Sasha [1]_____ (wake) up late because she [2]_____ (forget) to set her alarm clock. She [3]_____ (have) breakfast when the telephone [4]_____ (ring). It was her boss. He wanted to know why she [5]_____ (not finish) the report that he [6]_____ (ask) her to do. She quickly [7]_____ (leave) the house to go to work. She [8]_____ (stand) on the bus when she noticed that lots of people [9]_____ (look) at her feet. Then, she [10]_____ (realize) that she [11]_____ (forget) to put her shoes on. She [12]_____ (wear) her slippers.

B Can you remember a day when you woke up late? Why did you wake up late? What happened? Tell your partner.

V THE NEWS

4 A Underline the correct option to complete the headlines.

1 Postal *Destroy/Strike* Causes Huge Delays

2 Police Attacked During Student *Demonstration/Crash*

3 *Fugitives/Hostages* Released after Negotiation with Rebel Leader

4 Hundreds Homeless after *Earthquake/Violent* Hits

5 *Fugitive/Flood* Found Hiding in Forest

6 Train *Strike/Crash* Kills Sixty People

7 House *Attacked/Crashed* with Gas Bomb

B Work in pairs. Choose two or three of the headlines in Exercise 3A. Write mini news stories giving more details about each story.

F TELLING A STORY

5 A Add a word to each speaker's part to correct the conversations.

happened

1 **A:** This/when I was living in Hong Kong.

   B: Oh, really? happened?

2 **A:** I was taking a shower, when, all a sudden, I saw a huge spider.

   B: Oh, no. What you do?

3 **A:** Anyway, before I knew it, someone called the police.

   B: Really? What next?

4 **A:** The next I knew, the man was running toward me and shouting.

   B: don't believe it!

5 **A:** , anyway I was going up the ski-lift, and I fell off.

   B: embarrassing!

6 **A:** So, in end, I had to pay all the money back.

   B: , dear.

B Work in pairs. Choose three of the conversations above and expand the stories.

C Work in groups. Take turns role-playing your conversations

gas / taking a shower / toward   petrol / having a shower / towards

3 future

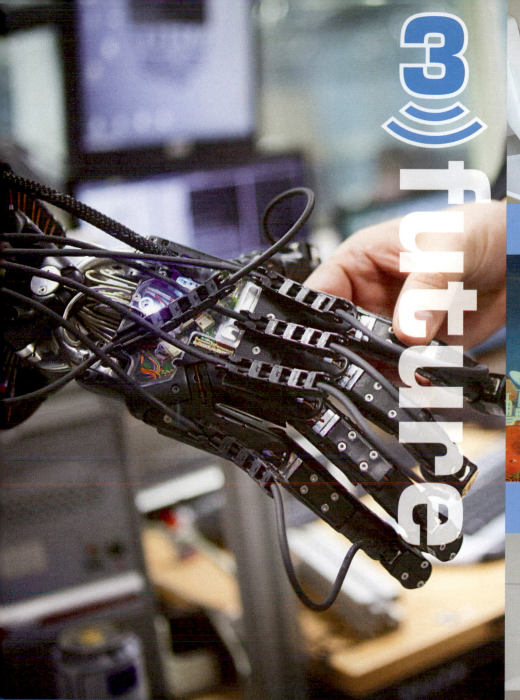

SPEAKING
3.1 Discuss your plans and arrangements
3.2 Talk about predictions
3.3 Explain misunderstandings
3.4 Discuss how to create a video channel

LISTENING
3.1 Listen to people discussing making plans
3.3 Listen to a series of misunderstandings
3.4 Watch a documentary about the rise of YouTube

READING
3.2 Read an article about the future

WRITING
3.1 Write a series of messages
3.4 Write a proposal

Can new technology help communication?

INTERVIEWS

G the future (plans)

P fast speech: *going to*

V organization

VOCABULARY
ORGANIZATION

1 A Work in pairs. Read the introduction to the questionnaire. Are you a planner or a procrastinator?

B In pairs, ask and answer questions 1—4 in the questionnaire. Do you have similar answers?

C Find phrases in bold to match the definitions below.

1 not pay attention to the things you are supposed to be doing

2 delay (a job)

3 spend time doing things that aren't important

4 put jobs in order of importance

5 do lots of different jobs at the same time

6 complete tasks

7 do jobs just before they need to be done

8 do things in advance

9 be careful with your time

10 begin a job

D Work in groups. Answer the questions.

1 When was the last time you left something until the last minute?

2 Can you think of a job that you have put off for a while? When do you plan to do it?

3 What do you get distracted by when you're working? How do you try to avoid distractions?

4 Do you think it's a good idea to write to-do lists?

▶ page 150 **VOCABULARY**BANK

LISTENING

2 Listen to three people discussing the questionnaire. Which of the following topics do they not talk about?

> making plans   vacations   writing lists   work arrangements for tonight

3 A Work in pairs. Can you complete these sentences from the listening?

1 You generally like to do things ahead of _____.

2 It's the only way to get _____ done.

3 You might need to change your _____, so why bother making plans in the first place?

4 I much prefer to _____ and see what happens.

5 This evening a _____ of mine's coming over.

6 I'm going to try out a new _____ recipe.

7 I'll see how I _____. I might go out, or I might just stay at home and _____.

8 I do get jobs done, but I never get started _____ away.

B Listen again to check your answers.

C Discuss. Whom would you prefer to work with, Laurie, Kenna or Javier? Why?

Are you a planner or a procrastinator?

Do you plan your day, or do you prefer to see what happens? A planner will spend the night before work making lists, prioritizing, and making sure everything is under control. Planners arrive early and get started on their first task. A procrastinator, on the other hand, is more likely to arrive at work just on time, with a coffee and breakfast in their hand and a stressed look on their face.

When you have a job to do, or you need to **meet a deadline**, do you:

1 generally **do things ahead of time** or **leave things until the last minute**?

2 prefer to **get started** on a difficult job or **put off** doing difficult jobs until later?

3 tend to **get distracted** easily and **waste time**, or do you **use your time wisely** and **get things done**?

4 write to-do lists and **prioritize tasks**, or do you prefer to **multitask**?

prioritizing(tize)   prioritising(tise)

GRAMMAR
THE FUTURE (PLANS)

4 Read the conversation and find examples of the structures described below.

Kenna: This evening a friend of mine's coming over. We're eating at my house—I'm going to try out a new pasta recipe. And then we're going to the movies to see that new Argentinian movie.

Laurie: Javier?

Javier: Uhhh ... I don't really know. I'll see how I feel. I might go out, or I might just stay at home and relax. I told you, I really don't like to plan.

RULES

1 Use the present continuous to talk about plans or arrangements that have already been made, e.g., *A friend of mine is coming over.*

2 Use *going to* + infinitive without *to* to talk about a plan or intention. You have decided that you want to do this, but you may not have made the arrangements, e.g., _____

3 Use *might* + infinitive without *to* when you are undecided or not sure what the plan is, e.g., _____

4 Use *will* + infinitive without *to* to talk about the future when you have no specific plan or you make the decision at the time of speaking, e.g., _____

▶ page 132 **LANGUAGEBANK**

5 A Listen and complete the sentences.

1 What _____ on the weekend?
2 We _____ my brother and his family.
3 Where _____ for them?
4 They _____ a party on Friday.
5 _____ with us tomorrow?
6 I'll ask Marion when she _____.

B **FAST SPEECH: GOING TO** Listen again. Notice how the speakers sometimes pronounce *going to* /ɡənə/ in fast speech. Check (✔) the sentences where *going to* is pronounced /ɡənə/.

C Listen again and practice saying the sentences fast.

What are you going to do on the weekend?

6 Underline the best alternatives to complete the conversation.

Pete: Hey Dax. What ¹*are you two doing/will you two do* on Saturday night?

Dax: I don't know. We ²*might/will* go to the Death City Dread concert. What about you?

Pete: ³*I'll have/I'm going to have* a small party. My parents ⁴*are going/will go* away for the weekend, so I've asked a few people to come over to my place. Kris ⁵*will bring/is bringing* his DJ equipment over, so ⁶*we're having/we'll have* music. And everyone ⁷*is going to bring/might bring* some food and drinks. Evan ⁸*will come/is coming* with a few friends. Do you think you can make it?

Dax: It sounds great. ⁹*I'm going to text/I'll text* Leyla to ask her what she thinks. Then ¹⁰*I'm calling/I'll call* you back to let you know. Is that OK?

Pete: That's fine. ¹¹*I'll talk/I'm going to talk* to you later. Bye.

7 A Write sentences for situations 1–6 below. Think about whether you have made arrangements already. Then decide which tenses to use.

1 something you plan to do on the weekend

Some friends are coming to stay. (I've already arranged this.)

I might go out for a pizza on Friday night. (I don't know yet.)

2 something you are going to do after class
3 something you might buy in the near future
4 something that someone in your family is planning to do
5 a plan or ambition you have related to your work/studies
6 something that you plan to do for your next vacation

B Work in pairs. Compare your ideas. Ask and answer questions to find out more information.

A: My sister's moving to Poland.
B: Really? That sounds exciting. Which city?

SPEAKING

8 A Think about two or three plans or arrangements with other people that you have made recently. Use the questions below to make some notes.

1 What is the plan?

2 Who is involved?

3 How did you communicate to make the arrangements?

B Work in groups. Tell the other students about your plans and how you made the arrangements. Do you have similar or different ways of organizing yourselves?

WRITING
MESSAGES; LEARN TO USE NOTE FORM

9 Work in pairs. Look at messages 1–4 and answer the questions.

1 What do you think the relationship is between the writer and the person they're writing to?

2 Are the messages formal or informal?

Leyla
Gone to the dentist.
Be back at 4 p.m.
Jen

Pete
Please call Tricia at
(076) 943-7562 asap.
Lucy

Hope you enjoyed
the concert.
Dinner's in the oven.
F x

Pick us up from
practice tonight?
See you later
Ben + Max

American Speak out TIP Leave it out! When we write notes and messages, we don't always write complete sentences. We often leave out small grammatical words to make the message shorter.

10 A Look at messages 1–4 in Exercise 9. The words in the box have been left out. Which message, do they belong to?

> I   We'll   Your   I've   Can you   I'll

B Rewrite messages 1–4 below using fewer words.

1 Are you feeling hungry? Do you want to meet me for lunch at Pavarotti's at 1 p.m.? Rx

2 We're going to see Elton John in concert. Would you like me to get you a ticket? Tonya

3 Pete called to say that he won't be able to come to dinner. Do you think you could call him back at (195) 162-7823? Thanks. Jayne

4 I'm really sorry, but I can't go to the movies tonight because I have too much work to do. I hope you enjoy the movie. Bess

11 Write short messages for the situations below.

1 You're going away for the weekend and would like your roommate to water the plants.

2 You want to invite a classmate to the movies.

3 You need to apologize to a work colleague for missing a meeting.

> Phone numbers in the U.S. are usually written: xxx-xxxx. When used, the area code is included in parentheses preceding the phone number: (xxx) xxx-xxxx.

roommate / apologize   flatmate / apologise

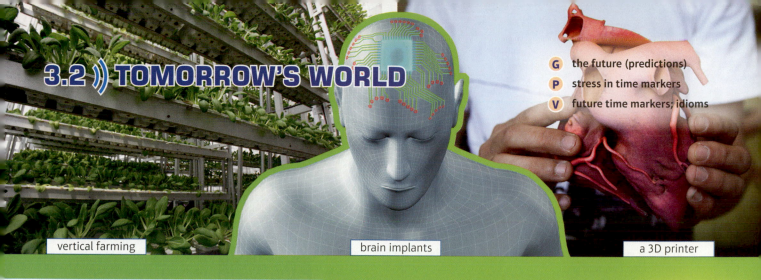

3.2)) TOMORROW'S WORLD

vertical farming

brain implants

a 3D printer

G the future (predictions)
P stress in time markers
V future time markers; idioms

READING

1 Look at the photos and answer the questions.

1 What inventions or developments do the pictures show?

2 How do you think they can benefit people?

2 A Read the article. What does it tell us about the things shown in Exercise 1? What predictions does it make about translating machines and nano monitors?

B Complete the summary of the article with words from the text. Use one word in each space.

The writer believes a machine will be able to ¹_____ our words into different languages. She thinks we'll use monitors in our ²_____ to check our health, and 3D printers will make perfect ³_____ of human organs like the heart. We will entertain ourselves with virtual reality, as computers learn to interact with the ⁴_____. The problems caused by ⁵_____ change will mean vertical farming becomes popular.

C Discuss with other students.

1 Which ideas in the article do you like? Can you think of other uses for these inventions?

2 Which ideas don't you like? Why not?

3 Which ideas do you agree will probably come true?

In the U.S., heights are typically measured in feet and inches, whereas, in much of the rest of the world, heights are measured in meters and centimeters.

A better world?

Communication

In the near future, we may be able to communicate in any language we choose. A number of companies are working on translating machines that use the voice frequencies of the speaker. This makes it sound as though the user is speaking the foreign language. We already have translating machines, but they are slow and inaccurate and sound like robots. In only a year or two, this new machine, which will be a headset, could come onto the market and allow us to speak every language under the sun.

Health

The future of health is going to be a tale of big and small. Tiny nano monitors will be placed inside our bodies, and these will produce big data—enormous amounts of information—that allow us to check our health and help us predict illnesses. Another big development probably won't be ready in the short term, but, in the long term, there is hope that 3D printers will make copies of body parts, such as hearts, livers and kidneys. If it happens, it is likely to save millions of lives. Using 3D printers, we can already make copies of plastic and metal objects. The next step is to copy living tissue.

Entertainment

Full immersion virtual reality will be with us in perhaps ten to twenty years' time. We will be able to plant tiny microchips in the brain, allowing a person to experience games, movies and virtual life as if they were real. As computers interact with the brain, we will have the sensation of touching, seeing, hearing and smelling virtual objects in virtual worlds. Instead of just watching heroes in movies, signals to the brain will let us feel what our heroes feel and see what they see. Fortunately, if things get too terrifying, we will be able to switch it off with the push of a button!

Global Problems

In the next thirty years, climate change is going to seriously affect traditional farming. Floods and droughts will disrupt farming patterns that have existed for thousands of years. Because of this, cities will have to start producing food, and vertical farming will become common. Apartment buildings and skyscrapers will have gardens built into them. Each floor will grow different plants, fruits and vegetables, and the water will be recycled. Instead of stretching out for miles across the landscape, farmland will now rise hundreds of feet into the air.

Apartment buildings   Tower blocks

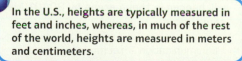

VOCABULARY
FUTURE TIME MARKERS

3 A Read sentences 1—6 from the article in Exercise 2A and underline the time markers.

1 **In the near future**, we may be able to communicate in any language we choose.

2 **In only a year or two**, the machine, which will be a headset, could come onto the market …

3 Another big development probably won't be ready **in the short term**,

4 … **in the long term**, there is hope that 3D printers will make copies of body parts …

5 Full immersion virtual reality will be with us **in perhaps ten to twenty years' time**.

6 **In the next thirty years**, climate change is going to seriously affect traditional farming.

B Look at the time markers again. Which of them mean *soon*? Which mean *in a long time*? Which name a future date or time period? Group them.

C STRESS IN TIME MARKERS Listen to the underlined expressions in 3A. Which words in these expressions are stressed? Which words are the most important to the meaning of each expression?

D Work in pairs. Ask and answer the questions using both the time markers given.

1 Will you still live in the same place: a) in the near future? b) in ten years' time?

2 What projects will you work on: a) in the short term? b) in the long term?

3 Will your working life/life as a student change: a) in the next five to ten years? b) in a year or two?

GRAMMAR
THE FUTURE (PREDICTIONS)

4 A Read the extracts from the article. Are the predictions certain (C) or possible (P)?

1 We <u>may</u> be able to communicate in any language we choose. *P*

2 In only a year or two, the headset <u>could</u> come onto the market.

3 It <u>is likely</u> to save millions of lives.

4 Climate change <u>is going to</u> seriously affect traditional farming.

5 Apartment buildings and skyscrapers <u>will</u> have gardens.

B Look at the underlined words above. Complete the rules with *will*, *could*, *to* or *be*.

> **RULES**
>
> 1 We use ___will___ + infinitive without *to* to make predictions about the future.
>
> 2 We use _____ *going to* + infinitive without *to* to make predictions when there is present evidence.
>
> 3 We use *may* or _____ + infinitive without *to* to say something is possible but not certain.
>
> 4 We use *likely* + infinitive with _____ to say something will probably happen.

▶ page 132 **LANGUAGE**BANK

---

5 A Circle the correct alternative to complete the text.

Dr. Michio Kaku is a physicist who makes TV programs about the future. He believes we [1]*will be design/will design* new worlds that look like our own, and that virtual reality is [2]*become/going to become* more like our reality. In one program, Kaku jumps into a remote-controlled car and tells us the car is so intelligent that the words "traffic jam" and "traffic accident" [3]*are going to disappear/going to disappear* from the language. He also says that, in a few years' time, microchips will be so cheap they [4]*are could be built/could be built* into every product we buy—our walls, our furniture, even our clothes. And they [5]*likely/are likely* to be so small we [6]*won't know/won't to know* they exist. Kaku also believes our sunglasses [7]*may become/may becoming* our future home entertainment centers. He then does a virtual dance using 3D technology (his dance partner is hundreds of miles away) and explains that, one day in the near future, 3D technology [8]*is could replace/could replace* the telephone and [9]*reduce might/might reduce* air travel. Finally, he investigates robots and concludes that, in the long term, some of our closest friends [10]*might not be/might be not* people.

B Discuss. Which predictions, if they come true, will be good/bad for the world? Why?

SPEAKING

6 A Look at the illustration about the world in 2040. What information did you already know? Is there anything you find surprising or unlikely?

B Imagine you are a "futurist" and it's your job to predict the future. Think about the topics in the box. What changes do you think will happen in these areas by 2040? Make some notes.

> communication   technology   food
> work habits   cities   the environment

C Work in pairs and discuss your ideas.

Communication: I think we will probably have video conference calls with people's holograms. There probably won't be …

 Dr. / center   Dr / centre

THE WORLD IN 2040

ENERGY green energy dominates: solar and wind power; no coal; nuclear plants

HEALTH AIDS eradicated; old cancers now curable, new forms of cancer incurable

INDIA **CHINA**

POPULATION 9 billion; India overtakes China as most populous country

EDUCATION 70% literacy

WEATHER hurricanes, droughts, flooding widespread

TRAVEL hydrogen-fueled transportation; electric cars common in developed countries; self-driving cars; hotel opens on the moon; first tourists go to Mars

POLITICS several countries cease to exist—30% of island nations submerged under water; United States of Europe a global superpower to rival China

American Speak TIP

Write new idioms in a special place in your vocabulary notebook. Record them in context and add your own examples. Do this for the idioms in Exercises 7 and 8. Then try them out. Make sure it's the right situation and you use the exact words.

VOCABULARY *PLUS*
IDIOMS

7 A Read comments 1—4. Which of the topics in the illustration are they referring to?

1 "I like that statistic. I teach reading, so it's an issue that's <u>close to my heart.</u>"

2 "If that statistic is correct, then coastal countries like mine are running out of time."

3 "This hits the nail on the head: we will eradicate old illnesses, but new ones will develop."

4 "Let's face it: the world will be completely overcrowded."

B Read the definition of an idiom and underline the idioms in sentences 1—4.

> **I idiom** /ˈɪdɪəm/ [C] a group of words that have a special meaning when they are used together: "On top of the world" is an idiom meaning "very happy."
>
> from Longman Active Study Dictionary

C Look at the underlined idioms in Exercise 7A and decide if these statements about idioms are true (T) or false (F)?

1 Idioms are usually formal.

2 You cannot usually change the order of words in an idiom.

3 You can sometimes change the verb tense and the subject of an idiom.

4 You can usually guess the meaning from one word in the idiom.

D Work in pairs and compare your answers. Then turn to page 159 to check your answers.

8 Work in pairs. Look at the idioms organized by topic. What do the underlined idioms **mean**?

Problems

1 We forgot to pay our taxes. Now we're <u>in hot water</u>.

2 I said the wrong thing again. I always <u>put my foot in my mouth</u>.

Time

3 We're <u>working against the clock</u>. We have two hours to finish the project.

4 I'm sure we can win this match, but we're <u>running out of time</u>.

9 Look at the idioms organized by key words. Match idioms 1—6 with meanings a)—f).

Body Parts

1 Keep an eye on him. *b*

2 Can you give me a hand?

Food and Drinks

3 It's not my cup of tea.

4 It was a piece of cake.

Animals

5 You're a dark horse!

6 I want to get out of the rat race.

a) I don't like it

b) watch

c) help me

d) the competitive world of work

e) you have good qualities that are not well-known

f) easy

10 A Find and correct the mistakes. There is a mistake in **each sentence**.

1 When was the last time you gave someone the hand?

2 Which student do you think is a horse dark?

3 When's the last time you put your feet in your mouth?

4 Which issues are close by your heart?

5 Do you often have to work against the clocks?

6 When were you last in warm water?

B Write an answer to each question. Then compare your answers.

▶ page 150 **VOCABULARY BANK**

fueled / transportation / put my foot in my mouth   fuelled / transport / put my foot in it

F dealing with misunderstandings
P linking in connected speech
V misunderstandings

VOCABULARY
MISUNDERSTANDINGS

1 Look at the photos. What is the situation in each one?

2 A Read sentences 1–8 and complete them with phrases a)–h). Which are about future arrangements?

1 When we meet later, make sure you go to the Judd Road downtown because …

2 We mistakenly left home at 5:30 because …

3 I was expecting to see Pete, my old school friend, but …

4 I didn't do the homework because …

5 I organized a party for tomorrow night! I thought her birthday was May 6th, but …

6 I ended up at the wrong house because …

7 I called Deb to invite her over, but she thought I was a stranger because …

8 I answered the phone, but …

a) it was a **wrong number**.

b) I **had** the **wrong address**.

c) I **had the date wrong**.

d) **we thought** it started at 6.

e) it was a **different** Peter Smith.

f) there are two streets **with the same name**.

g) she **didn't recognize** my voice.

h) I **didn't realize** it was due today.

B Which expressions in bold show misunderstandings about: a) people b) places c) times d) someone on the phone?

C Can you remember a misunderstanding in your life about a time, person, place, etc.? What happened? Tell other students.

FUNCTION
DEALING WITH MISUNDERSTANDINGS

3 A Listen to four telephone conversations involving misunderstandings. What was the misunderstanding in each conversation?

B Listen again and answer the questions.

Conversation 1

1 Whom did the woman want to speak to?

2 Whom did she speak to?

Conversation 2

3 How did David make his hotel reservation?

4 What hotel does he want to stay in?

Conversation 3

5 What time does the show finish?

6 What time did the show start?

Conversation 4

7 What does the woman want to rent?

8 What is the date?

C Complete expressions 1–7 with the words in the box.

> tell   that   me (x2)   saying   mean   name   again

1 I didn't catch any of _____.

2 You've lost _____.

3 Could you repeat the last _____?

4 Can you say that _____?

5 What exactly do you _____?

6 I don't get what you're _____.

7 Do you mean to _____ _____ … ?

D Listen and check. Then listen again and copy the intonation.

▶ page 132 **LANGUAGE**BANK

downtown / I had / realize   town centre / I'd got / realise

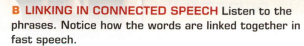

4 A Put the underlined words in the correct order to complete B's responses. Use capital letters where necessary.

1 **A:** Oh, no! I can't find the key.

 B: <u>do say mean to you</u> we're going to be locked out all night?

 Do you mean to say

2 **A:** And after Jimmy left Minnie, he married Millie, who used to be married to Billy.

 B: <u>lost me you've</u>. Who are all these people?

3 **A:** There was a little accident with the spaghetti bolognese and your sofa.

 B: <u>mean exactly what you do</u>?

4 **A:** The boss wants to see you. It's about the money that's missing from the accounts.

 B: <u>what don't saying get you're I</u>.

5 **A:** Um, er, I think my new phone number is, um, (654) 987-6743.

 B: <u>catch I that any of didn't</u>. What's the number?

6 **A:** My home address is 39 Oak Street, Phoenix, Arizona, 85923.

 B: <u>that you say again can</u>? I didn't hear.

7 **A:** We're leaving Los Angeles at 11 p.m. OK? Then we arrive in Sydney at 5:50 a.m.

 B: <u>part you the repeat could last</u>? I didn't hear you.

B Work in pairs. What does speaker A say next? Continue the conversations with your own words.

LEARN TO

REFORMULATE

5 A Read the extracts from audio S3.4. Underline five examples of how the speaker reformulates what he/she heard.

1 **A:** We don't have any reservations in the name of Cullinan, and we're fully booked tonight.

 B: <u>So you're saying</u> I can't stay here. This is the Sheldon Hotel, yes?

2 **C:** Didn't you say it starts at seven?

 D: No, it starts at five and finishes at seven!

 C: So what you mean is I've missed the whole show.

3 **E:** Yes, but today's a holiday and all the cars have been reserved already.

 F: Do you mean to tell me that there's nothing at all? No cars available?

 E: There's nothing until tomorrow, I'm afraid.

 F: But I definitely reserved a car for today, the third of July.

 E: It's the fourth of July today. In other words, your reservation was for yesterday.

B LINKING IN CONNECTED SPEECH Listen to the phrases. Notice how the words are linked together in fast speech.

So you're saying …

C Listen again and repeat the phrases.

SPEAKING

6 A Work in pairs and role-play the situation.

Student A

> You are a guest at a hotel. Twenty minutes ago you called reception, asking for some soap to be sent to your room. Room service brought you some tomato soup. You want them to take the soup back and bring some soap. Call reception to make your complaint.

Student B

> You are a receptionist at a hotel. A guest calls to make a complaint. Start the conversation by saying "*Reception. How can I help you?*"

> *Hello. Yes, I'm afraid I have a problem …* Explain the problem.

> Apologize for the misunderstanding and say you will send someone with soap.

> Check details and thank the receptionist for their help.

> Confirm details, apologize again and end the call.

B Change roles and turn to page 159.

C Work in pairs and take turns. Student A: call reception and make a complaint. Student B: apologize and offer a solution. Use the flow charts to help and role-play the situations.

> In American English, time may be variously written as 11 p.m., 11:00 p.m., 11 o'clock (a.m. or p.m.). In other places, you might see 11p.m. or 23:00, etc.

until / call   till / ring

3.4 YOUTUBE: THE FUTURE OF TV?

DVD PREVIEW

1 A Read six opinions about YouTube. What do the words in bold mean?

1 I love YouTube because the **creators** of the videos are often normal people like us, the **consumers**.

2 The thing I hate about YouTube is the **ads**, especially when you can't skip them.

3 The **audience** for some YouTube videos may be bigger than for some TV programs.

4 Most of the **content** on YouTube is terrible. The filming **techniques** are low quality.

5 I don't go on YouTube that much, and I'd never **subscribe** to a YouTube channel.

6 Making good quality YouTube videos requires a big **investment** of time and money.

B Work in pairs and discuss statements 1–6 above. Which ones do you agree with?

2 Read the program information. What is it about? Whom does the **host** speak to?

▶ The Culture Show YouTube: The Future of TV?

This documentary looks at the rise of YouTube and finds out what the company is doing to improve its online content. Jacques Peretti goes into the YouTube office and talks to some of the young creators who are changing the entertainment industry.

DVD VIEW

3 Watch the DVD. What is YouTube doing to improve its online content?

4 A Watch the DVD again and complete the fact file.

VALUE:	$1,000,000,000
FOUNDED:	in ¹_____
CREATORS:	for some, YouTube is a full-time job.
MAKING MONEY:	YouTube invites popular creators to put ²_____ on their videos.
STUDIO:	creators with 50,000 ³_____ can use the studio.
BIGGEST STUDIO:	Deep Focus
CRITICISM OF BUSINESS MODEL:	⁴_____ think content should be free.

B Work in pairs. Answer the questions.

1 Who has "some of the biggest audiences in Britain"?

2 Who makes more money: YouTube video creators or TV show producers?

3 What kind of techniques do creators learn in the YouTube studios?

4 What will "a better quality of content" bring to YouTube?

5 What does Andrew Keen say about the Internet and "the creative community"?

C Watch the DVD again to check your answers.

5 Discuss in groups.

1 Do you think the DVD clip is positive or negative about YouTube, or is it balanced?

2 What do you think of the type of short clips ("kids messing around in their bedrooms") in the program?

3 Do you think that YouTube is "the future of TV"? Do you think it will become more popular than mainstream TV, or is it only aimed at young people?

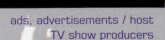

ads, advertisements / host
TV show producers

adverts, advertisements / presenter
TV program makers

American Speakout create a video channel

6 A You are going to create your own video channel. Think about the points below. Is there any other important information you should consider?

- name of channel
- type of video clips
- target audience
- what's special about the channel
- who will star in the videos
- competitors/rivals
- how frequently you will upload new videos

B Listen to two people planning a new YouTube channel. What do they say about each of the points in Exercise 6A?

C Listen again and check (✔) the key phrases you hear.

> **KEYPHRASES**
>
> The first thing [I think] is …
>
> We came up with this idea.
>
> It would be really [cool/interesting/fun] to …
>
> What's the angle?
>
> So the target audience is …
>
> Who will the presenters, or hosts, be?
>
> Who are our competitors or rivals?
>
> How often will we upload new videos?
>
> What about a name?

7 A Work in groups. Think of an idea for the task in Exercise 6A. Make sure you discuss all the points and take notes.

B Work with another group and take turns presenting your ideas. What are the advantages and disadvantages of each idea?

writeback a proposal

8 A A new company is looking for funding to make videos. Read the company's proposal. Do you think it will get funding? Why?/Why not?

FUTURE SHOCK VIDEOS

We are looking for funding to make exciting and innovative videos about a topic that is close to everyone's heart: the environment. In the long term, there will be big changes to the natural world, including floods and major earthquakes. As a group of environmental scientists, we intend to predict the effects of these changes and, ultimately, to help prevent them.

We will combine straight reporting, docudrama and science fiction. The videos will be presented by some of the nation's leading scientists and thinkers as well as actors. We will upload new videos once a month.

Our target audience is anyone interested in how the world will look in the next 30–100 years. It could be other scientists, students or anyone from the general public.

We thank you for your attention and look forward to hearing from you soon.

James Toffler

Please see the attachment for funding scales and further details of our financial plan.

B Use the sentence openers below to write a proposal for your idea from Exercise 7A. Invent any additional details you want to.

We are looking for …

We intend to …

The videos will be presented by …

We will upload new videos …

Our target audience is …

We thank you for …

C Work with a different group from the one you worked with in Exercise 7B and exchange proposals. Do you think the other group's proposal is worth funding? Why?/Why not?

V ORGANIZATION

1 A Complete the sentences with words from the box.

wisely   ahead   minute   time
prioritize   multitask   off
distracted   done   started
deadline

1 It's late. I really think we should get _____.

2 Why do you always have to leave things until the last _____?

3 Sorry, I got _____ by the football game on TV.

4 You have so many things to do. You'll have to _____ and start with the most important.

5 I worked hard and got a lot of things _____ this morning.

6 I'm afraid they're just wasting your _____.

7 I'd like to get this done _____ of time so we can go on vacation.

8 I keep putting _____ writing my essay.

9 I'm going to have to stay up all night, or I'll never meet the _____ for this work.

10 We won't be here for long, so use your time _____.

11 I think it's better not to _____ but to focus on doing one job at a time.

B Work in pairs. Choose two or three of the phrases from Exercise 1A and use them to make short dialogues.

A: We need to get a lot of things done, but we don't have much time.
B: Right. We'd better get started.

G THE FUTURE (PLANS)

2 A Complete the paragraphs with phrases from the box.

'm going to have   having
'm organizing   might
'm leaving   are going   I'll be
are coming   will   going to

I ¹_____ work at the end of the month. I've been a teacher here for nearly twenty years, so ²_____ sad when I leave the school for the last time. But in the future, I ³_____ more time to do some of the things I enjoy. My wife and I ⁴_____ to travel. We ⁵_____ visit Australia, which I've always wanted to do.

I'm ⁶_____ be forty next month, so I'm ⁷_____ a big party. Lots of people ⁸_____ I don't see very often, so I'm really looking forward to it. I ⁹_____ a band and lots of delicious food and drinks, so everyone ¹⁰_____ have a good time.

B Write a short paragraph describing a plan you have for the future. Then compare your ideas with a partner.

V FUTURE TIME MARKERS

3 A Choose the correct ending in each case, a), b) or c).

1 I might live in a *foreign country* in the long a) time b) term c) days.

2 I hope to *be retired* in twenty years' a) future b) ahead c) time.

3 I will finish *this course* in a month a) or two b) coming c) time.

4 I hope to *write my autobiography* a long time a) ago b) ahead c) from now.

5 I want to buy a *new car* in the near a) time b) future c) term.

6 I'm going to *travel* next a) year b) years c) future.

B Choose four of the sentences above. Change the words in italics so they are true for you.

G THE FUTURE (PREDICTIONS)

4 A Find and correct the grammatical mistakes. One sentence is correct.

1 Man not will fly for fifty years. (1901)

2 There isn't going be any German reunification this century. (1984)

3 Democracy will to be dead by 1950. (1936)

4 By 1980, all power (electric, atomic, solar) is likely be almost free. (1956)

5 The Japanese car industry isn't likely to be successful in the U.S. market. (1968)

6 Man will be never reach the moon. (1957)

7 Television won't very matter in your lifetime or mine. (1936)

8 The Internet may to become useful for business but never for the general public. (1989)

B Change the verbs so they mean the opposite and become intelligent predictions. You may need to change some other words.

Man will fly within fifty years.

F DEALING WITH MISUNDERSTANDINGS

5 A Complete B's responses using the words in the box.

lost   mean   to   say
saying   don't   do

1 A: I've heard that a lot of our employees like you.
  B: I ¹_____ get what you're ²_____.
  A: And I'm looking for someone to take over the business when I retire.
  B: What exactly ³_____ you ⁴_____?

2 A: David Johnson and Johnny Thomson are going to meet Tommy Davies tonight.
  B: You've ⁵_____ me.
  A: Johnson, Thomson and Davies are the company directors. They're meeting to discuss the company's future.
  B: Do you mean ⁶_____ ⁷_____ they're meeting without me?

B Work in pairs. Write a dialogue that uses three of the phrases in Exercise 5A. Act out your dialogues.

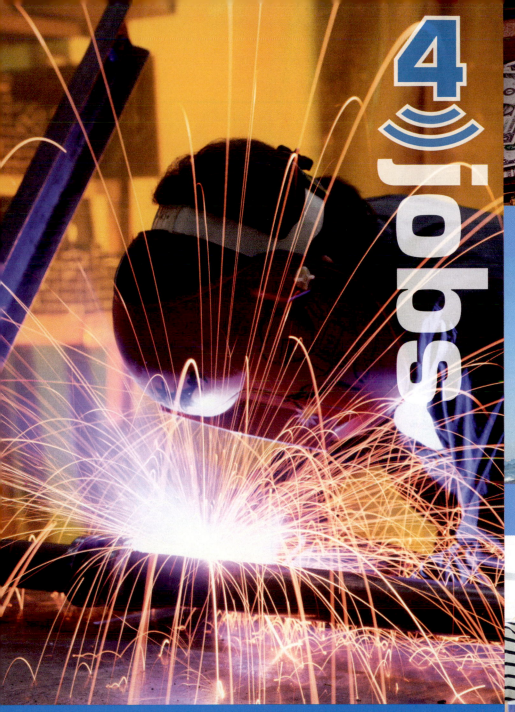

4 jobs

SPEAKING	4.1 Discuss how important becoming a millionaire is for you
	4.2 Talk about past habits
	4.3 Participate in a meeting
	4.4 Describe a day in your life
LISTENING	4.2 Listen to people describing dream jobs gone wrong
	4.3 Listen to people making decisions in a meeting
	4.4 Watch a comedy about a man's first day in a new job
READING	4.1 Read an article about millionaires
	4.2 Read a cover letter
WRITING	4.2 Write a cover letter
	4.4 Write about your daily routine

Is your job a "dream job"?

INTERVIEWS

VOCABULARY
PERSONAL QUALITIES

1 A Read about the qualities people need to do their jobs. Which jobs do you think they are talking about?

" Winning is the most important thing for me. I've always been **competitive**, so I love my job. I think I'm **a good leader**. It's important that all the players know what they're doing, and it's my job to tell them. The decisions I make are important for the whole team, so I can't be **indecisive**. "

" I have classes of 80 to 100 children, so I have to be **hard working**. I do my best because education is so important for the children. You need to be **a good communicator** in my job so that you can get the children interested in what they have to learn. Often, we don't have very many resources, so we also need to be creative and be able to **think outside the box**. "

" I'm **a risk taker**, so starting my own business wasn't difficult for me. I've always been very **motivated** and **ambitious**. I start work at 4:30 a.m. every day. I don't enjoy sleep. You can't afford to be lazy if you want to make money. "

B Match the words and phrases in bold above with the definitions 1–9.

1 work with a lot of effort

2 have problems making a decision

3 think differently or in a new way

4 want to be more successful than others

5 eager to be successful or powerful

6 willing to work hard to achieve something

7 person who does things that are dangerous

8 person who has the qualities to manage a group of people

9 person who can express ideas or feelings clearly to others

C Which qualities do you think you have? Work in pairs and compare your answers.

▶ page 151 VOCABULARYBANK

READING

2 A Which of the personal qualities discussed in Exercise 1 do you think are qualities you need to become a millionaire?

B Are the statements 1–6 about millionaires true (T) or false (F)?

1 Most millionaires are born rich.

2 Millionaires think that money is more important than love or marriage.

3 They work more than sixty hours a week.

4 They don't like to work when they're in college.

5 They do well at school and usually go to college.

6 They like spending money on designer goods.

C Read the article and check your answers.

D Work in pairs. Do you agree with the article? Do any of the facts surprise you? Why?

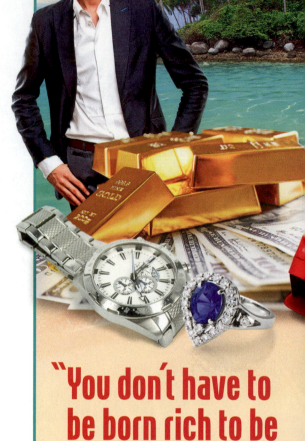

"You don't have to be born rich to be a millionaire."

1 So you want to be a millionaire, but have you got what it takes? To find out what millionaires are really like and what motivates them, the program *Mind of a Millionaire* did a survey. Psychologists looked at self-made millionaires to try and understand what qualities are needed to make a million. So, what is really important to a millionaire?

2 The answer, not surprisingly, is money, money and more money. Money is more important than love or marriage. And if you give a millionaire money, they won't spend it, they'll invest it to make more money. But you don't have to be born rich to be a millionaire. Most millionaires come from relatively poor backgrounds. And you don't have to work hard at school either. A lot of successful entrepreneurs were lazy at school and didn't get good grades. However, you have to have a clear idea of what you want to do (get rich), and you really should start early. A lot of millionaires left school early to start their own businesses.

have to / should   must / ought to

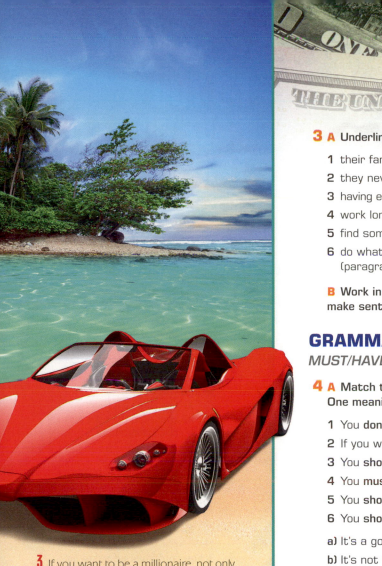

3 If you want to be a millionaire, not only do you have to work hard, but you should enjoy your work. And you shouldn't take too many vacations. Most millionaires work more than sixty hours a week. Half stay in contact with the office while they're on vacation, and fourteen percent of them refuse to switch off. Having a good work-life balance is fine for people who only want to be moderately successful, but if you're really ambitious, you have to put in the hours.

4 What are millionaires like as people? The survey found that they are competitive, they like taking risks, and they are aggressive and self-confident. They'll do anything they can to get what they want.

 5 Millionaires can break all sorts of rules. The only thing they must not do is break the law. Surprisingly, most millionaires are careful spenders. They prefer Gap to Gucci. Many of them choose not to spend money on expensive designer clothes—they would rather find a bargain on Main Street. And they don't spend lots of money on expensive meals in restaurants either. They prefer to eat at home. However, they do like to drive Mercedes and go on at least three expensive vacations a year. One last thing: millionaires don't care what other people think of them. So, if you want to be a millionaire, you shouldn't worry about what other people think of you. Just do your own thing.

3 A Underline words or phrases in the article that match meanings 1–6.

1 their family didn't have much money (paragraph 2)

2 they never stop thinking about work (paragraph 3)

3 having enough time for work and for the things you enjoy (paragraph 3)

4 work long hours (paragraph 3)

5 find something for a good price (paragraph 5)

6 do what you want without worrying about what other people think (paragraph 5)

B Work in pairs. Choose two or three of the expressions. Use them to make sentences about yourself or people you know.

GRAMMAR
MUST/HAVE TO/SHOULD (OBLIGATION)

4 A Match the words in bold in sentences 1–6 with the meanings a)–e). One meaning matches with **two** sentences.

1 You **don't have to** be born rich to be a millionaire.

2 If you want to be a millionaire, you **have to** work hard.

3 You **should** have a clear idea of what you want to do.

4 You **must not** break the law.

5 You **shouldn't** take too many vacations.

6 You **shouldn't** worry about what other people think of you.

a) It's a good idea.

b) It's not necessary. You don't need to be/do this.

c) It's necessary. You have no choice.

d) It's important that you don't do this.

e) It's not a good idea.

 B FAST SPEECH: *have to* Listen to the pronunciation of *have to* /hæftə/ in fast speech. Listen and repeat the sentences.

▶ page 134 LANGUAGEBANK

5 A Make sentences with the prompts. Use the positive or negative form of the word in parentheses.

1 mailmen / get up early in the morning (have)

   Mailmen have to get up early in the morning.

2 window cleaners / be afraid of heights (must)

3 nurses / be patient and care about other people (should)

4 businessmen often / travel a lot (have)

5 politicians / do their job because they want fame (should)

6 teachers / enjoy working with children (should)

7 doctors / train for several years before they can work (have)

8 teachers / work at school during vacations (have)

9 police officers / be good communicators (have)

▶ page 151 VOCABULARYBANK

B Work in pairs. Think about three different jobs. Make sentences to describe what qualities are/aren't important for these jobs. Read your sentences to your partner. Can they guess which job it is?

A: These people have to be motivated. They should be good communicators, especially when talking to children. And they have to be very patient.
B: Teachers?

Main Street / mailmen   the high street / postmen

SPEAKING

6 A Work in pairs. Take the quiz. Then check your score on page 160.

B Discuss. How many of the questions did you answer like a millionaire? Do you agree with the results on page 160? Is getting rich something that concerns you? Why?/Why not?

VOCABULARY *PLUS*
CONFUSING WORDS

7 Read the vocabulary notes and complete sentences 1 and 2.

> ### Job • Work
>
> **Work** is what you do to earn money:
> *What kind of **work** does he do?*
>
> A **job** is the particular type of work that you do:
> *Sam's got a **job** as a waiter.*
>
> **Job** can be plural, but **work** cannot.

1 I've finished my degree, so I'm looking for a _____.

2 It's not easy to find _____ when you're my age.

8 A Underline the correct alternative in the sentences below. What is the difference between these words?

1 He suddenly *remembered/reminded* that he had to go to the bank.

2 I have to call my boss later. Can you *remember/remind* me?

3 I've *forgotten/left* my door open. I really should close it.

4 Did you *hear/listen* that noise?

5 Can you say that again? I'm sorry, I wasn't *listening/hearing*.

6 Being sick on vacation isn't much *fun/funny*.

B Turn to page 160 to check your answers.

▶ page 151 VOCABULARY**BANK**

American Speak out TIP To help you remember confusing words and vocabulary, write them in personalized sentences in your notebook. Write sentences about your life using some of the words from Exercise 8.

9 A Complete questions 1–6 with a suitable word from Exercises 7 and 8.

1 What are the best paid _____ in your country?

2 Is there anything you often _____, like phone numbers or someone's name?

3 If you _____ carefully, what noises can you hear at the moment?

4 Do you write notes to _____ yourself about important things?

5 Do you _____ your first job? What did you do?

6 What do you like doing for _____ ? Do you like playing games?

B Work in pairs. Take turns asking and answering the questions above.

DO YOU HAVE WHAT IT TAKES TO BE A MILLIONAIRE?

Do you answer these questions like a millionaire would?

1 Would you like to be …
- a) a bit richer
- b) a lot richer
- c) mega rich

2 If you wanted a pair of shoes that you couldn't afford, would you …
- a) buy them anyway
- b) wait until the sales and risk losing them
- c) walk away

3 How many credit cards do you carry with you?
- a) One or none
- b) Two
- c) More than two

4 If you could just afford to pay for it, would you splurge on on …
- a) a heated swimming pool
- b) a racehorse
- c) a big party for all your friends

5 Do you most enjoy stories about …
- a) romance
- b) adventure
- c) mystery

6 Do you check that your bill is correct after a meal out?
- a) Yes
- b) No
- c) Only if I'm alone

7 What is 9 multiplied by 8?
- a) Did you get the answer right instantly?
- b) Or only after doing the math in your head?
- c) Did you get the wrong answer?

8 If a favorite relative left you a watch that was not your style, would you …
- a) sell it
- b) keep it to sell on a rainy day
- c) keep it to help you remember them

personalized / splurge / doing the math   personalised / splash out / doing little sums

4.2)) DREAM JOB

G *used to, would*
P intonation: emphasis; linking: *used to*
V extreme adjectives

LISTENING

1 Work in pairs. Look at the photos and answer the questions.

1 What are these jobs? Would you like to do them? Why?/Why not?
2 What is your idea of a dream job?

2 A Listen to people talking about their dream jobs. Match the speaker to the photos.

B What problem does each speaker talk about?

C Listen again and answer questions 1–8. Write Nicola (N), Luca (L) or Amy (A).

1 Who had a boss who worked in the media?
2 Who worked for a big company?
3 Who spent a lot of time by the ocean as a child?
4 Who had to try and invent new ideas for the job?
5 Who decided to do this job because they saw someone else doing it?
6 Who had a different job in the summer and in the winter?
7 Who had a difficult relationship with their boss?
8 Who started to find their job boring?

D Check your answers by reading audio script S4.2 on page 167.

VOCABULARY
EXTREME ADJECTIVES

3 Find the extreme adjectives in bold in audio script S4.2 on page 167. Match them to the gradable adjectives below.

1 good: wonderful, amazing, _____
2 bad: awful, _____
3 big: enormous
4 small: tiny
5 tasty: _____
6 hot: _____
7 cold: freezing
8 tired: exhausted
9 angry: _____
10 interesting: _____
11 pretty: _____
12 difficult: _____

4 A Complete conversations 1–6 with extreme adjectives.

1 **A:** The food here tastes so good.
  B: Yes, it's _____.

2 **A:** It's over ninety degrees outside today.
  B: I know. It's absolutely _____.

3 **A:** Was your girlfriend angry about you being late?
  B: Yes, she was really _____.

4 **A:** The view of the lake is really pretty.
  B: Yes, it's _____, isn't it?

5 **A:** Do you find the job interesting?
  B: I think it's absolutely _____.

6 **A:** It's hard to understand what he's saying.
  B: I know. It's _____.

B INTONATION: emphasis Listen and mark the stress on the adjectives. Notice how speaker B emphasizes the stressed syllable in their intonation.

C Listen again and shadow speaker B's response.

ocean / emphasizes sea / emphasises

A Amy

B Nicola

C Luca

In many English-speaking countries, temperature is usually given in degrees Celsius. In the U.S., temperature is given in degrees Fahrenheit. Thirty degrees Celsius is about 86 degrees Fahrenheit.

GRAMMAR
USED TO, WOULD

5 A Read the texts. What did the children dream of doing? Have they achieved their dreams?

Childhood Dreams

When I was young, I spent afternoons imagining that I had my own rocket ship. I would invite my cousins and my friends to join my crew, and we would lie on our backs inside a very large cardboard box and go through a countdown, blast off into space, spend the whole day exploring other planets and be back in time for dinner. So that was sort of the beginning—my earliest memories of being fascinated by space.

Chang Diaz, rocket scientist

We used to live in France, and, as a child, I always used to collect small insects that I found in the fields near my house. One day, I found a butterfly. It couldn't fly, so I put it in a jar and looked after it. The next morning, when I opened the jar, the butterfly opened its wings and flew away. That was when I realized what I wanted to do with my life.

Lowri Davies, veterinary surgeon

B Look at the underlined words in sentences a)—d) and match them with rules 1—3.

a) I would invite my cousins and my friends to join my crew.

b) We used to live in France.

c) I always used to collect small insects.

d) One day I found a butterfly.

RULES

1 Use the past simple, not *used to* or *would*, to talk about specific events in the past. _____

2 Use *used to* or *would* to talk about a past habit. You can also use the past simple. _____ and _____

3 Use *used to* to talk about a past state. You cannot use *would* to talk about a past state. _____

▶ page 134 LANGUAGEBANK

6 A Complete the texts. Where possible, use *would*. Where neither *used to* or *would* are possible, use the past simple.

It's every young girl's dream to be an actress when she grows up. I ¹_____ (love) watching beautiful actresses on television. I was so sure that was what I wanted to do that I ²_____ (practice) my Oscar speech in front of the mirror in the bathroom. I ³_____ (use) a shampoo bottle instead of a microphone, and I ⁴_____ (thank) all my family and friends, even my three cats, for helping me!

My family ⁵_____ (live) in Sheffield, just near the soccer stadium, so as a child, I ⁶_____ (go) to soccer games most weekends. I remember the first game I went to. My grandpa ⁷_____ (take) me. I was very young, and I had never seen so many people in one place at one time. It was quite frightening, and I don't think I ⁸_____ (watch) the game very much. But I remember that we won, and the crowd went crazy. After that, every week I ⁹_____ (ask) Grandpa if he had tickets, and usually he did.

B LINKING: used to Listen and repeat. Notice the pronunciation of *used to* /juːstə/. Practice saying the sentences.

1 I used to play football when I was a kid.

2 I used to practice every day.

3 We used to live in Ohio.

4 I didn't use to like classical music.

5 My father used to take me fishing.

6 I used to ski, but now I snowboard.

7 We used to go to the movies a lot.

C Did you use to do any of the things mentioned above? Tell your partner.

SPEAKING

7 Work in pairs and discuss.

1 What were your childhood dreams? Have you achieved them?

2 Did you have any interests or hobbies in the past that relate to your life (job/studies) now? What were they?

3 How have your ideas, opinions, hobbies, etc., changed? (Think about food you liked/hated as a child, television programs you enjoyed, etc.) Are there any things that you used to do that you don't do now? Why did you stop? Would you do these things again?

As a child, I always used to dream about being an artist …

A "soccer game" in the United States is a "football match" in most other English-speaking countries.

WRITING

A COVER LETTER; LEARN TO ORGANIZE YOUR IDEAS

8 Read the text below and answer the questions.

1 What kind of person would be good at this job?
2 Would you like to do this job? Why?/Why not?

> Would you like to travel the world staying in some of the world's top holiday resorts for free? A luxury travel company is looking for a reviewer to try out top hotels and vacation resorts for one year. The lucky applicant will be expected to stay in a variety of locations that include: Caribbean islands, waterside hotels in Venice, some of the world's top ski destinations as well as Las Vegas and Buenos Aires. They will be expected to write about their experiences on the company blog. No formal qualifications are needed. However, the successful applicant will be sociable, have great communication skills and, of course, a passion for travel.

9 A Read the cover letter. Do you think this person would be good for the job? Why?/Why not?

> **1** Dear Matthew Ray,
>
> **2** I'm writing to you regarding your advertisement for a professional travel reviewer, which I saw on www.findajob.com. I would like to submit an application for the position. Please find my résumé attached.
>
> **3** As an experienced travel blogger who has spent the last five years traveling around the world, I believe that I meet all the requirements you outline in your advertisement.
>
> Good communicator with excellent language skills: As a regular travel blogger, over the last few years, I have built and maintained a wide audience of readers. I have also published newspaper and magazine articles and given radio interviews about my travel experiences. I am fluent in English and French and also speak a little Russian.
>
> Interest in travel and tourism: In addition to my own travels, I worked for six months for a tour bus company in Australia, where I had hands-on experience guiding tours.
>
> Proven ability in website management: As well as maintaining my own website, consisting of a journal and video weblog with up-to-date photos and stories of my travels, I have helped to manage the website for a youth hostel in Ireland.
>
> **4** If you require any further information or would like to arrange an interview, please call me at (077) 886-5842 or email me at mjdaley@yahoo.com. I look forward to hearing from you at your earliest convenience.
>
> **5** Sincerely yours,
>
> Megan Daley

B Is the wording of the letter formal or informal? Find examples of expressions that tell you this.

C Underline phrases in the letter that match meanings 1–6.

1 about (paragraph 2)
2 I want to apply for the job (paragraph 2)
3 I think I would be good for the job (paragraph 3)
4 practical experience of doing the job (paragraph 3)
5 I have shown that I am able to do this (paragraph 3)
6 as soon as you have the opportunity (paragraph 4)

D Underline any other useful phrases.

10 Match the parts of the letter 1–5 with notes a)–e).

Preparing a Cover Letter

A What qualities are they looking for? Write three to four points that show you have these qualities. Use the same words as they use in the advertisement.

B Address your letter to an individual. Only use "Dear Sir/Madam" when you can't find out the recipient's name.

C Finish with a call to action. What is going to happen next? Are you going to call them or should they call you?

D Explain why you are contacting them. What is the job? Where have you seen it?

E Use "Sincerely," if you know their name or "Yours faithfully" if you don't.

11 Look at the job advertisements on page 161 and write a cover letter for one of the jobs. Use the sample letter and useful phrases to help you.

cover letter / call me at   covering letter / call me on

4.3)) THAT'S A GOOD IDEA

F reaching agreement
P sentence stress
V business

VOCABULARY
BUSINESS

1 A Work in pairs. Discuss. Would you consider starting your own business? What kind of business would you start? Is there anything stopping you from doing it?

B Complete the questions with words from the box.

> fired   salary   work   compete   runs   idea
> interview   charge

1 Do you know anyone who _____ their own company?
2 Have you ever been in _____ of a team of people?
3 Have you ever been out of _____?
4 When did you last go for a job _____?
5 Have you ever had to _____ with others for a job?
6 Which jobs earn a high _____?
7 What kinds of things does someone have to do to get _____ from their job?
8 Can you think of reasons a business _____ might fail?

C Take turns asking and answering the questions above.

FUNCTION
REACHING AGREEMENT

2 Listen to a team having a meeting to decide how to set up a new café. Write some notes about their decisions.

Setting up a new café:

Type of food?   Name?   Location?

3 A Look at the phrases in the table. Listen to the conversation again and check (✔) any of the phrases you hear.

Giving Opinions
I (really) feel that …
The way I see things, …
The way I see it, …
Commenting on Other Opinions
I (don't) see what you mean.
Exactly!
I'm not sure that I agree. ✔
I'm not sure (that's a good idea).
I'm not sure about that.
I think that's a great idea.
That's a good point.
That sounds good.
That's OK by me.
Suggestions
What about … ? / How about … ?
Let's focus on …
I suggest we think about …
I think we should think about …
How about if we (call it) … ?
Why don't we (call it) … ?

B Check your answers in the audio script on page 167.

▶ page 134 **LANGUAGE**BANK

4 A Put the words in the correct order to make sentences and questions.

1 decide / I / on / name / we / think / a / should
2 good / a / that's / point
3 you / see / mean / what / I
4 suggest / location / the / on / I / focus / we
5 fine / that's / me / by
6 sure / I'm / that / agree / not / I
7 we / about / don't / it / why / think / ?
8 business / a / the / about / what / for / name / ?

B SENTENCE STRESS Listen to the phrases. Which words are stressed?

C Listen again and repeat.

LEARN TO
MANAGE A DISCUSSION

5 A Complete the underlined phrases for managing a discussion.

1 <u>First of</u> _____, we need to <u>decide on the location</u>.
2 <u>Let's</u> _____ on the ideas we had for the <u>location</u>.
3 So, <u>moving on to the next</u> _____, what kind of food are we going to serve?
4 _____ recap: a Portuguese café selling cakes and lunches, located near the station.
5 <u>I think we need to come</u> _____ to the type of café we're establishing.
6 <u>Let's</u> _____ up what we've decided.

B Listen and check your answers.

C Cover up Exercise 5A. Which phrase would you use for these situations?

1 the end of a meeting to go over everything that has been discussed?
2 when you want to discuss the next issue?
3 to review what has been discussed so far?
4 to start a meeting and talk about the first point?
5 to get everybody to talk about the same thing?
6 to return to a point that was discussed previously?

SPEAKING

6 A Read the task and write down some ideas.

> ### SET UP A COMPANY TO PROMOTE TOURISM
>
> You are going to set up a tour company to promote tourism in your town/city/country (or the town/country where you are studying). You need to decide the following:
>
> ○ the name and location of the company
> ○ what type of tours you will organize (themed tours/language tours/sports tours, etc.) and where they will go
> ○ how you will promote tourism
> ○ how the company will be different from other tour companies

B Work in groups. Read your roles and come up with a plan for the business. You have five minutes.

Student A: It's your job to keep the meeting focused. Try to cover all the points.

Student B: Make sure you take notes about any decisions that are made. You will be the group's spokesperson and will have to sum up at the end of the meeting.

Student C: Try to come up with as many ideas as possible.

C When you are ready, start the discussion like this.

A: Shall we start? First of all, ...

D Tell the other groups about your business plan. Which group do you think has the best plan?

4.4  GAVIN AND STACEY

DVD PREVIEW

1 Work in pairs. Answer the questions.

1 Do you enjoy watching comedy programs? Why?/Why not?

2 Which ones are popular in your country?

3 Which comedy programs do you enjoy watching?

2 Read about the programs. What type of things do you think Gavin needs to learn on his first day at work? Whom do you think he will meet?

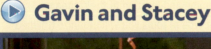 Gavin and Stacey

Gavin and Stacey is a program about a young couple. Gavin comes from Essex, near London, and Stacey comes from Cardiff, Wales. After a long-distance relationship conducted online and by telephone, they eventually get married, and Gavin moves to Wales. In this episode, Gavin starts a new job. On his first day, his family wants him to do well and be happy at work.

DVD VIEW

3 A Watch the DVD. What is the main problem Gavin has during his first day at work?

B Match DVD extracts 1–5 to the correct responses a)–e).

1 Mr. Davies, good to see you again. *b*

2 Did you get your welcome pack?

3 Ready when you are.

4 Now here's somebody you've not met yet.

5 Parcel for you.

a) Oh, thanks.

b) Oh, please, call me Huw.

c) Hi. Nice to meet you.

d) Er… yeah. I think so.

e) OK. Let's show you around.

4 A Answer the questions.

1 What does Huw, the boss, give Gavin?

2 When does Gavin say he will call his mother?

3 How many phone calls does Gavin receive?

4 What does Uncle Bryn bring for Gavin?

5 What is the message on the balloon? Who do you think sent it to him?

B Watch the DVD again to check.

C Discuss. How do you think Gavin will feel at the end of his first day at work?

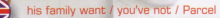
his family wants / you haven't / Package   his family want / you've not / Parcel

American Speakout a day in the life … writeback your daily routine

5 A Listen to someone describing a typical day in her life. Do you think she likes her job?

B Read the key phrases below. Complete each phrase by adding one word.

KEYPHRASES

I usually wake up _____ (about) 6:30.

I have to leave home by 8:30 at the _____.

The first _____ I do when I get to work/school is …

In the afternoon, I _____ to catch up on …

I usually [make some deliveries/do some shopping/ …] on my _____ home.

I try to be _____ by (about) 7 o'clock.

I _____ just cook dinner and watch some television.

C Listen again to check.

D Prepare to tell other students about a normal day in your life. Write notes about your typical day. What do you have in common?

• hours of work/studying

• tasks you have to do

• people you spend your day with

• problems and challenges

• how you relax

• the best parts of your day

6 A Read about a day in the life of a gym instructor. Is his daily routine similar to yours? How is it different?

I work as a gym instructor in a recreation center. **I get up at** 5 a.m. every morning and make a cup of coffee. I can't function until I've had my coffee! I drive to work—it takes about fifteen minutes on a good day—**usually getting there at about** 5:40. **The first thing I do is** switch on the lights and the air conditioning if it's summer (heating if it's winter) and then the radio. We have the radio on all day because our clients like listening to the news and the music. The recreation center opens at 6 a.m.

I work in a team of four, although only two of us are ever in the gym at the same time. The instructors all wear sports clothes. **It's important to be** comfortable because we sometimes need to show new clients how to use the machines. Apart from this, **our other tasks are** quite simple: we check that everyone has their membership card when they come in, and we check that the machines are clean and safe.

I have a one-hour break for lunch, and I usually do two more hours after lunch. **I go home at about** 2:30.

The best part of the job is meeting people. Our clients range from eighteen-year-old body builders to eighty-year-olds who come to exercise and chat. I've never had any problems at the recreation center. It's a really good job, though it doesn't pay very well. In the evenings **I relax by** reading a book and cooking for myself, and I'm usually in bed by 9:30 p.m.

Frank Carduna

B Write about a typical day in your life using the sentence starters in bold in the text and the key phrases to help. Try to include two or three pieces of information that make your day different from everybody else's. Alternatively, look at the pictures on page 47. Imagine what a day in the life of this person would be like and write about it.

recreation, rec center / good job   sports centre / nice job

V PERSONAL QUALITIES

1 Work in pairs. Student A: describe a word/phrase from the box in your own words, starting with *I am/like/enjoy*, etc. Don't say the word/phrase. Student B: listen and try to guess the word or phrase.

> hard working   indecisive
> a risk taker   a good leader
> ambitious   competitive
> think outside the box
> a good communicator

A: I enjoy working and want to succeed in what I do.
B: You're motivated?
A: Correct. Your turn to describe a word.

G MUST/HAVE TO/SHOULD (OBLIGATION)

2 A Underline the correct alternative to complete the sentences.

1 I *have to/mustn't* call my mother today. It's her birthday.

2 I really *should/shouldn't* do more exercise. I'm so out of shape.

3 I'm lucky because I *don't have to/shouldn't* get up early in the morning. I'm a student.

4 I think you *should/shouldn't* study harder. Your test results weren't very good.

5 You *must not/should* be afraid of taking risks, or you will never live your dreams.

6 I *shouldn't/don't have to* waste so much time on the computer. I'll never finish my work.

B Complete the sentences so that they are true for you.

1 I have to … this evening.

2 I really should do more …

3 I'm lucky because I don't have to …

4 I think you should … because …

5 You shouldn't worry about …

6 I shouldn't waste so much time …

C Compare your ideas in pairs.

V EXTREME ADJECTIVES

3 A Replace the underlined words in the sentences below with extreme adjectives in the box.

> great   fascinating   awful
> exhausted   tiny   boiling
> impossible   delicious   furious

1 I'm very tired. I didn't sleep well.

2 Should we open a window? It's very hot in here.

3 My boss just called. He's very angry.

4 I find phrasal verbs very difficult to remember.

5 The vacation was very good, but the weather was very bad.

6 How can you work in this office? It's very small.

7 I find astronomy very interesting.

8 Did you cook this? It's very tasty.

B Work in pairs and take turns testing each other.

A: Very big.
B: Enormous.
A: Correct. Your turn.

G USED TO, WOULD

4 A Replace the past simple with *used to* or *would* where possible. Where both are possible, choose *would*.

1 My family lived in Paris, but we moved when I was a teenager.

2 I spent a lot of time with my grandparents when I was younger.

3 For my first job, I washed dishes in a restaurant.

4 I didn't think money was important. Now I have lots of bills to pay.

5 We had a lot more free time before we had children.

6 My best friend at school lived just across the road from me.

B Change four of the sentences so that they are true for you.

C Compare with a partner. Find three things that you both used to do as children but you don't do now.

F REACHING AGREEMENT

5 A Complete the conversations.

1 A: The way I s_____ things, all cars should be banned from downtown.

   B: E_____.

2 A: I really f_____ that we need to look at immigration.

   B: That's a good p_____.

3 A: The w_____ I see it, the company is making too much money.

   B: I don't see what you m_____.

4 A: I th_____ we should ask for more money.

   B: I'm not s_____ I agree.

5 A: I s_____ we try to meet again next week.

   B: T_____ fine by me.

B Work in pairs and practice the conversations.

6 Work in groups. Look at the questions below and discuss. Try to reach agreement on each answer.

> **1** Should there be a limit to the number of hours people can work in one week?

> **2** Should there be a minimum wage? What should it be?

> **3** How long should men/women be allowed to stay home from work after they have children?

> **4** Should everyone be allowed to work from home at least once a week?

> **5** Should employees be allowed to wear whatever clothes they want to work?

great / stay home from work   brilliant / stay off work

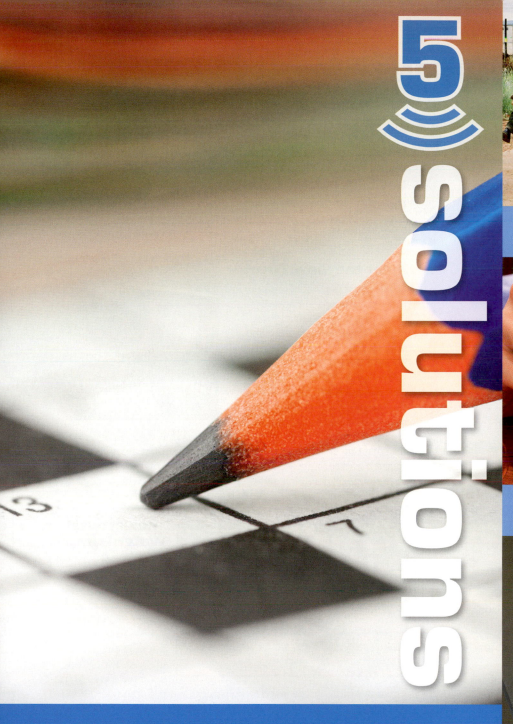

5)) solutions

WE REGRET THAT THIS
TERMINAL IS TEMPORARILY
OUT OF SERVICE
DO NOT RE ENTER YOUR PIN

SPEAKING

5.1 Talk about inventions over the last 100 years
5.2 Present and answer questions about your area of expertise
5.3 Explain/Solve problems
5.4 Present a new machine

LISTENING

5.2 Listen to people answering difficult questions
5.3 Listen to conversations about technical problems
5.4 Watch a program about a race between a car and two people

READING

5.1 Read about some low-tech solutions
5.2 Read a book review

WRITING

5.1 Write an advantages/disadvantages essay
5.4 Write an advertisement

Are you good at solving problems?

INTERVIEWS

5.1)) LOW-TECH SOLUTIONS

G comparatives/superlatives
P syllable stress
V technology

READING

1 Work in pairs. Discuss the questions.

1 In general, do you like or dislike new technology and gadgets like ebooks, tablets and phones?

2 Can you think of ways in which technology has made our lives better/worse?

3 Are there any problems that technology has helped to solve? Give examples.

2 A Look at the prompts below. What information do you think could go in the blanks to describe the problems? Use the pictures to help you.

1 New _____ tends to make things faster and more efficient.

2 Popular entertainment (theater, movies, music concerts, exhibits) is often _____ and based in cities.

3 In many villages in Asia and Africa, access to _____ is still a huge problem.

4 The citizens of Bogotá, Colombia wanted young people to have more access to _____.

B Read the text to check your answers.

3 A Work in pairs. Answer the questions.

1 How is the Rural Academy (slow theater) different from other theater companies?

2 Why might people living in rural areas appreciate this type of theater?

3 How does the PlayPump help children to solve the problem of access to water?

4 How has the pump changed the lives of the young girls in particular?

5 How has the invention of the ebook changed how people read?

6 Where have they put the new libraries in Bogotá?

B Discuss. What do you think of the solutions suggested? Which idea do you like best? Can you think of some other solutions to these problems?

Why is it that people seem to think that the newest technology is always the best? From high-speed trains to high-speed Internet, you could be forgiven for thinking that faster is always better (not to mention, more efficient and more economical). We decided to investigate a few simpler, more low-tech solutions to the world's problems.

Meet the Slow Theater

Much of our popular entertainment these days is action-packed, expensive and based in cities. So, the Rural Academy decided they wanted to offer an alternative. Touring the United States, they take a horse-drawn theater and a bicycle-powered silent movie on the road with them. They want to celebrate and call attention to

life in more rural locations, in opposition to what they see as the global urbanization of our culture, economy, media and art. By using a carriage pulled by horses, rather than a vehicle that runs on gas, they offer less expensive, low-tech alternative entertainment, which they hope will include more people and move at a slightly slower pace.

The Carousel Water Pump

Access to a clean water supply is still one of the biggest problems for people living in rural villages in Asia and Africa. To try to solve the problem, a company in South Africa has invented a way to use children's high energy levels to help pump water from underground. The PlayPump is a water pump that is powered when the children use the carousel. As they play, the water is pumped from below the ground into a storage tank. Before the pumps were installed, many young girls had to spend hours of their day walking to collect water, rather than going to school. With the new pumps, however, the girls don't need to miss school, so they get a much better education.

Bus Stop Libraries in Bogotá

The invention of the ebook has meant that books are now slightly cheaper and a lot lighter to carry. But in Bogotá, Colombia, they had a far better idea for helping people to read on the go. The city wanted to improve the access that young people had to books, but not by buying new tablets. They decided to install colorful book libraries around the city, in the parks and at bus stops. What could be better than to sit in the sunshine and read a book while waiting for your bus?

urbanization / carousel   urbanisation / roundabout

GRAMMAR
COMPARATIVES AND SUPERLATIVES

4 A Read the article again. Underline examples of comparatives and superlatives.

B Look at your examples and complete the rules. How do we form the comparatives and superlatives of common adjectives?

> **RULES**
>
> **1** Adjectives with one syllable
>
> comparatives: add _____
>
> superlatives: add _____
>
> **2** Adjectives with two or more syllables
>
> comparatives: add _____
>
> superlatives: add _____

C Look at the sentences below and complete the rules with *small* or *big*.

a) Entertainment has become a lot/much/far more expensive.

b) Technology has made books a little/a little bit/slightly cheaper.

> **RULES**
>
> **1** Use quantifiers *a lot/much/far* to talk about _____ differences.
>
> **2** Use quantifiers *a little/a little bit/slightly* to talk about _____ differences.

▶ page 136 **LANGUAGEBANK**

5 Complete the statements with the prompts in parentheses.

1 The invention of the bicycle made it _____ (lot/easy) for people to travel from one village to another and meet new people.

2 The world has become a _____ (much/safe) place to live since the invention of antibiotics. People are _____ (far/healthy) now than 100 years ago.

3 The invention of the washing machine has meant that it is _____ (lot/quick) for people to wash their clothes. I think it's _____ (good) invention of the last century.

4 Although we have computers, paper is still _____ (cheap) and _____ (flexible) way to record the written word.

5 Electricity is _____ (important) invention because, without it, many of the other things we have would not have been possible.

6 The invention of the telephone and the computer have meant that we are _____ (much/busy) now than we were in the past.

VOCABULARY
TECHNOLOGY

6 A Work in pairs. Put the words/phrases in the box into the correct word web.

> ~~electricity~~   nuclear power   antibiotics
> vaccinations   computer networks   motorcycle
> genetic engineering   washing machine
> vacuum cleaner   space travel   solar power
> commercial airplanes   communications satellites

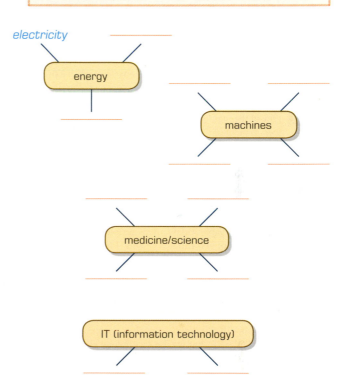

electricity

energy

machines

medicine/science

IT (information technology)

B Work in pairs. Can you add any more words to each word web?

C SYLLABLE STRESS Look at the words/phrases above and underline the main stress(es). Sometimes there can be more than one per word/phrase.

electricity   nuclear power

D Listen and check. Then listen again and repeat.

▶ page 152 **VOCABULARYBANK**

SPEAKING

7 A Work in pairs. Choose an invention from the last 100 years. Write two or three sentences to describe how this invention has changed our lives. Don't say what the invention is.

This invention made it much easier to travel from one place to another. Even people in poor societies can use this invention because it does not need gas.

B Read your sentences to other students. Can they guess the invention?

C Discuss which invention you think has been the best/worst? Why?

WRITING

AN ADVANTAGES/DISADVANTAGES ESSAY; LEARN TO USE DISCOURSE MARKERS

8 **A** What do you think are the main advantages and disadvantages of technology in everyday life? Write a list.

B Read the model essay. Does it mention any of your ideas?

The Advantages and Disadvantages of Modern Technology

1 It is easy to see the advantages of modern technology in our everyday lives. Technology has given us cell phones, computers, televisions and many other useful things. However, most modern inventions come with a price— maybe social or environmental—so we need to look at both sides of the story.

2 One of the main advantages of modern technology can be seen in medical science. The discoveries of antibiotics and vaccinations have saved millions of lives around the world. In addition to this, modern technology has made industry more efficient.

3 On the other hand, modern technology is responsible for the development of weapons, which have caused a lot of destruction. Another disadvantage is that technology makes us lazy. Nowadays, many people spend their lives sitting in front of computer screens. This is a development that clearly has negative effects on our mental and physical health, making us more isolated and less active.

4 In my opinion, modern technology is a good thing. In general, the advantages outweigh the disadvantages. Of course there are drawbacks, but it is important to remember that technology itself is not the problem. The problem is that we use technology without always thinking about the harmful consequences.

C Match paragraphs 1—4 with descriptions a)—d).

a) discussion of disadvantages _____

b) conclusion _____

c) introduction ___1___

d) discussion of advantages _____

D Work in pairs. Complete the guidelines for writing an essay with the expressions in the box.

personal opinions   examples   notes   beginning   logical order

1 Sort out the facts: make _____ on all the relevant information you have on the subject.

2 Plan your argument: organize your notes and arrange the ideas in a _____.

3 Give your essay an appropriate _____. Describe what you are planning to say.

4 Decide how many paragraphs you need for your argument. Each paragraph should discuss one point. Use _____ to support your arguments.

5 Write a logical conclusion. Though the style of the essay is generally formal and impersonal, this might be the place to include some _____.

9 **A** Look at the underlined words and phrases in the essay. Put them in the correct place in the table.

introduce advantages
The most important advantage is …

introduce disadvantages
The main disadvantage is …

contrasting ideas
Although, …

additional reasons
Besides that, …
And another thing, …

personal opinion/conclusion
In general, …
As far as I'm concerned, …

B Underline the correct alternatives.

Satellite TV: good or bad?
More and more people are watching satellite television.
[1]*The main advantage / Besides that* is that you can choose exactly what you want to watch, and, [2]*in addition to this, / however,* you can watch programs in other languages.
[3]*However, / Although* this means that, whereas people used to talk about programs with colleagues and friends, now they usually don't watch the same programs.
[4]*On the other hand, / And another thing,* there is too much choice. There are so many programs to choose from that people can't decide what to watch. [5]*This means that / As far as I'm concerned,* they watch too much television.
[6]*In my opinion, / The problem is that* satellite television is a good thing, since it gives people more choice. [7]*However, / In general,* people need to choose their programs carefully.

10 Choose one of the topics below and write an essay about the advantages and disadvantages of it. Look back at Exercises 8 and 9 to help you.

• modern technology in everyday life

• owning a car/bicycle

• playing computer games

• using a digital camera

• using email/text messages

• cheap flights

5.2)) ASK THE EXPERTS

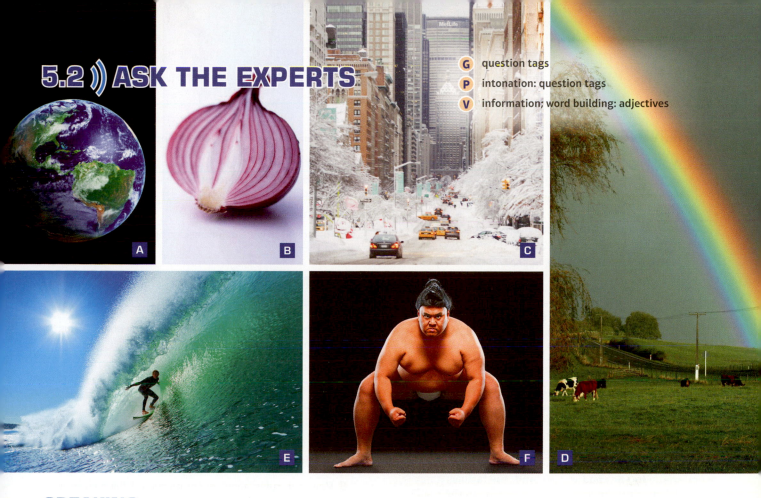

G question tags
P intonation: question tags
V information; word building: adjectives

SPEAKING

1 A Match photos A–F to the questions below.

1 Is it possible to surf a tidal wave?
2 Why is snow cold?
3 Is there an easy way to prove Earth is round?
4 Why do onions make you cry?
5 Is a rainbow hot or cold?
6 Why are sumo wrestlers so fat?

B Work in pairs. How many questions above can you answer in two minutes?

C Turn to page 161 and check your answers.

VOCABULARY
INFORMATION

2 A Match the pairs of verbs in the box with situations 1–5.

> ~~question/wonder~~   discuss/debate
> respond/reply   research/investigate
> inquire/look into   argue/quarrel

1 Someone tells you something. You are not sure you agree.

question/wonder

2 Someone writes you a letter.
3 There is an interesting topic in class.
4 You disagree with someone and talk angrily with them.
5 You are writing a thesis for your Master's degree.
6 You need to find some information, e.g., about movie times or to reserve a table.

B Read the sentences below. In which sentence is *wonder* a verb? In which sentence is it a noun?

a) I wonder if anyone has ever tried to surf a tidal wave.

b) I can name the seven wonders of the world.

C Underline the correct alternative to complete the sentences. Is the correct answer a noun or a verb?

1 The police officer continued his *investigation/wonder/inquire* of the robbery.
2 Didn't you get my email? You didn't *response/look into/reply*.
3 We had a very interesting *discuss/debate/wonder* about the death penalty.
4 I've nearly finished my *research/investigate/reply* on nuclear particles.
5 When I hear about all these social problems, I have to *inquire/question/respond* the education system.
6 You want a job here? No problem. My cousin is the boss. I'll *inquiry/debate/look into* it for you.
7 It was a silly *respond/quarrel/argue*. Now they are friends again.

LISTENING

3 A Work in groups and discuss.

1 How do you prefer to find information, on the Internet, in books or by asking people? What does it depend on?

2 What type of questions do children ask? Think of some examples.

They sometimes ask difficult questions like: "Why is snow cold?"

B Read a review of a book about questions children ask their parents. How did the author get the idea for the book? Are any of your questions included in the examples from the book?

Questions Daddy Can't Answer

It all began with a question asked by Dean, a four-year-old boy: "Why do ships have round windows?" His father didn't know. And when his sister started behaving badly, Dean asked another question: "Why can't we just cook her?" On a long drive, the boy wondered why the road was so loud. His father replied, "Because the people who live next to the road have their vacuum cleaners on." The boy's questions kept coming: "Why is the sky blue? Are rainbows hot or cold? What was it like living in the 1940s? What would hurt more—getting run over by a car or getting stung by a jellyfish? Why do police officers like donuts?"

Eventually, Jamieson decided to write down the questions. He thought it might be fun one day to show them to his son. Then he had a better idea: he'd research the answers. Some people might do their investigations on the Internet. Not Mr. Jamieson. He contacted experts ranging from astronomers to Buddhist monks, to scientists, to magicians, and asked lots of questions. He later turned these—and the experts' responses—into a book: *Father Knows Less.*

4 A Read five questions from the book *Father Knows Less.* Try to answer them. Compare your ideas with other students.

> How many hairs are there on the human head?
> Why are the windows on ships always round?
> Why is there war?
> Why did the Beatles break up?
> What happens when your plane flies over a volcano?

B Listen to some people trying to answer the questions in Exercise 4A. Are their answers the same as your ideas?

C Listen again and complete the notes.

1 Ships' round windows: _____
2 Number of hairs on a human head: _____
3 A plane flies over a volcano: _____
4 The Beatles broke up: _____
5 Reasons for war: different ideologies, a sense of honor, _____

GRAMMAR
QUESTION TAGS

5 A Complete questions 1–6. Then look at audio script S5.2 on page 168 to check.

1 Round windows are stronger, _____ they?
2 No, it's not that many, _____ it?
3 It depends whose head, _____ it?
4 Nothing happens, _____ it?
5 They got old, _____ they?
6 John Lennon went off with Yoko Ono, _____ he?

B Read the rules about question tags. Which rules are exemplified in 1–6 in Exercise 6A?

Rule 2 is shown in question number 3. It uses "doesn't."

> **RULES**
>
> **1** Use question tags to confirm information.
>
> **2** To form a question tag, repeat the auxiliary verb. For example, use *do* or *does* for the present. Use *will* or *won't* for the future.
>
> **3** After the auxiliary verb, use a pronoun (e.g., *he*, *she*, *it*, *they*).
>
> **4** If the sentence is positive, the question tag is negative.
>
> **5** If the sentence is negative, the question tag is positive.

▶ page 136 LANGUAGEBANK

6 Look at the statements below and complete the question tags.

1 You're Italian, *aren't* you?
2 You aren't a doctor, *are* you?
3 You don't smoke, _____ you?
4 You play a musical instrument, _____ you?
5 You didn't know any of the other students before, _____ you?
6 Our teacher hasn't taught you before, _____ she?
7 You will be here tomorrow, _____ you?
8 You went to bed late last night, _____ you?
9 You've traveled a lot, _____ you?
10 You were good at sports when you were a child, _____ you?

questions / honor   inquiries, queries / honour

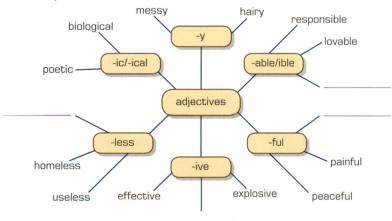

7 A INTONATION: question tags Listen to two questions. Notice how the intonation goes down when the speaker is sure of the answer. Notice how the intonation goes up when the speaker is not sure.

1 You're Italian, aren't you? (the speaker knows the answer)

2 You aren't a doctor, are you? (the speaker is not sure of the answer)

B Listen to the questions in Exercise 6. Which answers is the speaker sure about? Listen and repeat the questions, using the same intonation.

C Work in pairs. Choose six questions to ask your partner. Make sure your intonation is correct in the question tags.

A: You play guitar, don't you?
B: Yes, I do. I play bass in a band.

SPEAKING

8 Work in groups and follow instructions 1–4 below.

1 Think of one subject each that you know a lot about. Write your topics on a piece of paper.

tennis, Japanese cars, hip hop

2 Exchange papers with another group.

3 Think of statements about the subjects. Use question tags.

Rafael Nadal is the best tennis player in history, isn't he? The most popular Japanese car is the Toyota, isn't it?

4 Read your statements to the first group. Are they correct?

VOCABULARY *PLUS*
WORD BUILDING: ADJECTIVES

9 A Read the text below. How was the ice cream cone invented?

For over a hundred years, ice cream was sold mainly in dishes. Then, one day, a creative ice cream seller turned a hopeless situation into a profitable one. In 1904, at a festival, he ran out of spoons and dishes. He bought some wafers from a vendor next to him and put the ice cream into them. The customers loved them, and the idea spread quickly. The world has been thankful ever since!

B Underline four adjectives in the text and add them to the word web below. Can you think of other examples of adjectives that fit these patterns?

biological
messy
hairy
responsible
poetic
-ic/-ical
-y
-able/ible
lovable
_____
adjectives
_____
-less
-ive
-ful
painful
homeless
useless
effective
explosive
peaceful
_____

American **Speak** TIP

Use L1. L1 is your First Language. Some suffixes in your L1 might have similar meanings to suffixes in English. For example, the Italian *-ivo/a* means the same as the English *-ive*. Can you think of any examples from your language?

10 Complete the text. Add suffixes to the words in parentheses.

The city of Detroit, was famous for its ¹_____ (value) car industry. In the early days, the city was ²_____ (response) for the majority of cars in the U.S., and Detroit's streets were full of cars. A police officer called William Potts saw that the organization of the traffic was ³_____ (hope) and the traffic was very slow. So, in 1920, he developed an ⁴_____ (effect) system of lights to regulate the flow of cars. He used the same colors as the railway system and put the lights in a tower so that it would be ⁵_____ (ease) for drivers to see them even on ⁶_____ (rain) days. Potts's system was very ⁷_____ (success). When other countries realized how ⁸_____ (use) it was, the system spread all over the world.

11 A Complete the words by adding suffixes.

Find someone who:

1 has a peace*ful* neighborhood.

2 is hope_____ at math.

3 is a good, care_____ driver.

4 is quite mess_____at home.

5 thinks he/she is quite creat_____.

6 is quite knowledge_____ about politics.

B Work in groups. Ask and answer questions about the information above.

You live in a peaceful neighborhood, don't you?

▶ page 152 **VOCABULARY**BANK

color(s)   colour(s)

F polite requests
P intonation: polite requests
V problems and solutions

A

B

C

D

E

VOCABULARY
PROBLEMS AND SOLUTIONS

1 A Think of two pieces of technology you have used in the last twenty-four hours. Did you have any problems with them? What problems can you have with them?

B Work in pairs. Look at the photos. What is the problem in each case?

C Look at the phrases in bold. Are they problems (P) or solutions (S)? Which phrases can you use to talk about the problems in pictures A–E above?

1 It's **broken down**.
2 It **needs recharging**.
3 It's **out of order**.
4 It **needs fixing**.
5 There is no **reception** (for my phone).
6 **Try switching it off** (and on again).
7 It **keeps making this strange noise**.
8 It **crashed/froze**.
9 It **doesn't work** (any more).
10 We have to **sort it out**.
11 **Save it onto a memory stick**.
12 Should I **print it for you**?

D Work in pairs and answer the questions.

1 Have you or anyone you know had any of these problems recently?
2 How did you feel when it happened?
3 How did you try to solve the problem?

FUNCTION
POLITE REQUESTS

2 A Listen to four conversations. What is the problem in each case?

B Read questions 1–8. Which can you answer? Listen again to check.

1 In conversation 1, what question does the man ask?
2 Where does the woman suggest that he go?
3 In conversation 2, what does the woman "keep losing"?
4 What does the man suggest?
5 In conversation 3, what does the vacuum cleaner "keep making"?
6 Does the woman give the man instructions about what to do to fix his vacuum cleaner?
7 In conversation 4, what does the man ask for?
8 Whom does the man need to speak to?

C Complete the extracts in the table with the correct words.

Could you	[1]_____ the line, please? [2]_____ me a refund?
Could you tell me	whom I should [3]_____ to? what the [4]_____ is?
Do you know	what the problem is? if there's another [5]_____ somewhere?
Would you mind	[6]_____ at it for me? [7]_____ him for me?

D Listen and repeat the requests.

▶ page 136 **LANGUAGE**BANK

LEARN TO
RESPOND TO REQUESTS

3 A Read some conversation extracts from Exercise 2. Complete the responses with the phrases in the box.

> Yes, I can   I'm not sure   I'm afraid I can't
> Yes, of course (x2)   Of course not   Sure/OK
> Let me have a look

1 M: Do you know if there's another ATM somewhere? I really need to get some money.

 W: Hmm … _____. Try the shopping mall.

2 W: Would you mind looking at it for me?

 M: _____.

3 W: Do you know what the problem is?

 M: _____.

4 W: Could you tell me what the problem is, sir?

 M: _____. It keeps making a funny noise.

5 W: Could you hold the line, please?

 M: _____.

6 M: Could you give me a refund?

 W: _____ do that.

 M: Well, could you tell me whom I should speak to?

 W: _____. You need to speak to the manager.

 M: OK. Would you mind calling him for me?

 W: _____. I'll just call him.

B Read audio script S5.5 on page 168 to check.

4 A Make polite requests and responses with the prompts in parentheses.

1 A: I can't think. (Would / mind / turn / music down)?

 B: Sure. Sorry about that.

2 A: I need to speak to the manager. (Do / know / if / anyone in the office)?

 B: Let me have a look.

3 A: I'm afraid Mr. Soul isn't here at the moment.

 B: (Do / know / when / coming back)?

 A: (not / sure). Do you want me to check?

 B: Thank you.

4 A: (Could / tell / how / machine works)? I don't know how to turn it on.

 B: (Yes / course).

5 A: I need to take this machine to the sevice department. (Would / mind / help / me)?

 B: (course / not). Leave it here.

6 A: My computer has frozen. (Could / tell / whom / I / speak / to)?

 B: OK. (Let / have / look).

B Listen to check your answers.

C INTONATION: polite requests Does the speaker's voice start high or low? Listen again and repeat the requests copying the polite intonation.

SPEAKING

5 A Work in pairs. Read your role and think about the phrases you are going to use. Then role-play the situation below.

Student A

> Tell Student B that you have reception on your phone. Suggest that he/she try standing outside.

> Tell Student B he/she can borrow your phone to make the phone call.

Student B

> You need to call your sister, but you can't get any reception on your phone. Ask Student A if he/she knows where you can get reception.

> You still can't get any reception. Ask Student A if you can borrow his/her phone to send a text message.

> Thank Student A for his/her help.

B Change roles and role-play the situation below.

Student A

> You can't get the printer to work. Ask Student B if he/she can help you.

> It still doesn't work. Ask Student B if he/she knows of other printers in the building.

> Thank Student B for his/her help.

Student B

> Suggest Student A try turning it off and then on again. Ask if that has worked.

> Tell Student A he/she can use your printer.

C Choose one or two situations from Exercises 4 and 5. Write a conversation using the flow charts above to help. Then role-play it with a partner.

shopping mall   shopping centre

DVD PREVIEW

1 Work in pairs and answer the questions.

1 Look at the person on page 65. What type of sport is he playing?

2 Would you like to try this sport? Why?/Why not?

2 Read about the program. Who do you think will win the race? Why?

▶ Top Gear

Top Gear is an international award-winning television series about motor vehicles, mainly cars. More than 350 million viewers worldwide enjoy watching the hosts with their quirky, humorous style. On the show, they compare and test-drive cars and organize all kinds of crazy races. In this program, James May, possibly the slowest driver in Great Britain, challenges two freerunners to a race in downtown Liverpool. James has to drive six miles toward the Liver building in the center of the city in a Peugeot 207. The two teenagers who try to beat him will run and jump over buildings, taking a much more direct route. Who do you think will get there first?

3 Watch the DVD to see if you were right. Number the events in the correct order.

a) The men jump over James's car. _____

b) James arrives at the Liver building. _____

c) James checks his speed. _____

d) The men jump over people eating at a restaurant. _____

e) James stops at a red traffic light. _____

4 Watch the DVD again. What does James May say? Complete the phrases.

1 As we can see, it's a very pretty car, but is it any _____?

2 I'm going to have a race, and it's against the latest French development in urban transportation solutions: a couple of young men in silly _____.

3 Parkour: that's a French invention and involves that sort of thing. Running around the _____ leaping across buildings and benches.

4 Come on, we're not all _____!

5 I must have averaged ten or twelve miles an hour. I should _____.

6 They are not here. No sign of combat trousers man. I've _____!

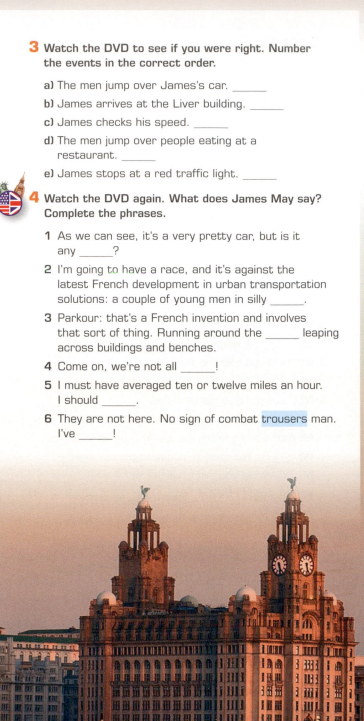

humorous / pants   humourous / trousers

American Speakout present a new machine

5 A Work in pairs. Answer the questions and complete the tasks.

1 Write a list of things you have to do every day.

2 Are there any things on this list that you don't enjoy? Could a machine do them for you?

3 Invent a machine that would help you do one of the things. Draw a picture of your machine.

B Listen to someone talking about a new machine. What is the invention? What does it do?

C Listen again and check (✔) the key phrases he uses.

> **KEYPHRASES**
>
> I'm going to tell you about …
>
> Basically, …
>
> The way it works is this.
>
> It works like this …
>
> First of all, ….
>
> Then/Also, you can …
>
> All you have to do is …
>
> Make sure you …
>
> The best thing about it is that …

D Prepare and practice a short presentation about your new machine. Use your picture and the useful phrases to explain how it works.

E Present your ideas to the class. Which invention do you think is the best?

writeback an advertisement

6 A Read the advertisement and answer the questions. What is the musical shower? How does it work?

The Musical Shower

If you like listening to music when you have a shower, then you might already have a stereo in your bathroom. But imagine how much better it would be if your shower-head also had an MP3 player attached to it.

It will download your favorite tunes or radio programs at night. Then in the morning, your shower will automatically play your favorite tunes for you. Try our musical shower.

There's no better way to start the day.

B Write an advertisement (ad) for your invention (120–180 words). Use the ad above and the key phrases to help.

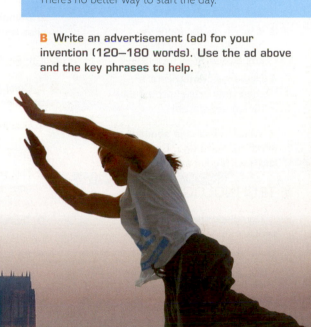

G COMPARATIVES/ SUPERLATIVES

1 A Look at the information and complete sentences (1–4) using the prompts in parentheses.

100 years ago in the U.S.: the average life expectancy was forty-seven years, only eight percent of homes had a phone, the maximum speed limit in most cities was ten miles per hour, the average wage was twenty-two cents per hour, and ninety percent of all doctors had no college education.

1 100 years ago, people didn't live _____ as they do today. (long)

2 It used to be _____ to communicate with people on the other side of the world. (far, difficult)

3 It is _____ for modern businesses to pay their employees. (far, expensive)

4 Nowadays, doctors are _____ than they were in the past. (much, educated)

B Write sentences about a hundred years ago. Compare them with your partner.

V TECHNOLOGY

2 A Complete the words in sentences 1–6.

1 I don't agree with nu_____ po_____. I think it's a dangerous way of making el_____.

2 Sp_____ tr_____ is a waste of money. Why do we need to send people to the moon?

3 I couldn't live without my wa_____ ma_____. I hate dirty clothes.

4 I had to have lots of va_____ when I went to Malawi. I didn't want to get sick.

5 I think ge_____ en_____ is terrible. People might start to want only babies who are beautiful.

6 Doctors give people too many an_____. So now, some medicines don't work any more.

B Work in pairs. Choose three sentences you disagree with. Tell your partner why.

G INFORMATION

3 A Put the letters in italics in the correct order to find words related to questions.

1 In class last week, we *useddiscs* …

In class last week, we discussed …

2 I can't answer *nosequits* about …

3 I try to *penrods* quickly to …

4 In the next few months I'm going to *took lion* … (2 words)

5 I recently *quidrein* about …

6 I *ownred* what happened to …

7 I enjoy a good *teabed* especially about …

8 It would be interesting to *sitnegative* a crime like …

B Complete the sentences so that they are true for you.

G QUESTION TAGS

4 A Complete the sentences with the correct question tag.

1 She wrote the first *Harry Potter* book in a café, *didn't she*?

2 This man, who is U2's singer, does a lot of humanitarian work, _____?

3 This actor won an Oscar for *Forrest Gump*, _____?

4 He was probably the greatest basketball player in history, _____?

5 She lived in Calcutta, where she helped street children, but she wasn't from India, _____?

6 He became Cuba's leader in 1959, and he didn't transfer power to his brother until 2006, _____?

7 Her full name is Madonna Louise Ciccone, _____?

8 Her husband was a U.S. President. If she becomes President, she would be as famous as he is, _____?

B Whom are these sentences about?

1 J. K. Rowling

C Work in groups. One student thinks of a famous person. The others ask tag questions to find out who it is.

A: It's a man, isn't it?
B: Yes.

F POLITE REQUESTS

5 A Match requests 1–5 with responses a)–e).

1 Excuse me, could you tell me where I can find the bathroom?

2 Could you call me a taxi?

3 Would you mind helping me with my bags? They're very heavy.

4 Would you mind opening the window?

5 Could you tell me what time the restaurant opens?

a) Sure. It's very hot in here, isn't it?

b) Yes, of course. It's just over there, down the stairs and on the left.

c) Yes, of course. Where do you want to go to?

d) I'm not sure. Let me have a look. Yes, it opens at 11 a.m.

e) Of course not. Let me take your suitcase.

B Work in pairs. Take turns practicing the conversations using the prompts below.

Student A:
• where/ restroom?
• call/taxi?
• store/close?
• get/door?

Student B
• open/window?
• restaurant/open?
• help/shopping?
• tell/platform the train leaves from?

Other ways to say "bathroom" include "restroom," "WC," "washroom," "toilet" and "loo."

6)))) emotion

How are you feeling today?

INTERVIEWS

G real conditionals

P weak forms: pronouns + 'll

V -ing/-ed adjectives; multi-word verbs

SPEAKING

1 A Look at photos A–F. What emotions do you think these people are feeling? Why are they feeling them?

B Read the text and match photos A–F with the emotions.

C When was the last time you felt these emotions? Give some examples.

Did you know that there are actually only six basic emotions that all humans experience and that we recognize by our facial expressions? The six emotions are:

1 JOY—that wonderful feeling of happiness when something brings a smile to your face. We all love and recognize this one. It's a motivator, too. We keep doing things that make us feel happy.

2 ANGER—when something goes wrong and you lose your temper. This emotion allows you to deal with difficult situations and not just run away.

3 SADNESS—often experienced when we lose someone or something important to us. If we see someone who's feeling sad, we may start to feel sad, too.

4 FEAR—this is probably the most basic emotion. We can experience this from a very early age, and it helps us to escape from danger.

5 SURPRISE—when something unexpected happens, you raise your eyebrows and actually open your eyes wider to help you see what it is.

6 DISGUST—this is an important emotion that helped our ancestors to survive. If you eat something disgusting or poisonous, your face warns others what has happened.

VOCABULARY
-ING/-ED ADJECTIVES

2 A Work in pairs and discuss the questions.

1 What makes you angry or **annoyed**?
2 What sorts of things do you find **relaxing**?
3 Is there anything you are **frightened** of?
4 What kinds of things make you **worried**?
5 Have you ever been really **embarrassed**?
6 What makes you feel **exhausted**?
7 What sorts of things do you find **confusing**?
8 Do you find your job/life **satisfying**?

B Look at the quiz again and answer the questions.

1 Which ending is used to talk about feelings: *-ed* or *-ing*?
2 Which ending is used to talk about the cause of feelings: *-ed* or *-ing*?

C Complete the sentences with the correct form of the adjectives in Exercise 2A. Remember to use *-ed* or *-ing* endings.

1 It's very *frightening* watching the news at the moment. I think there's going to be another war.
2 I'm going to bed. I'm _____ because I've been working late every night this week.
3 My face went bright red when I realized what I'd said. It was really _____.
4 I love it when I see people enjoying the food I've cooked. I find it very _____.
5 I don't understand the grammar. I'm completely _____.
6 I go to yoga every week because it makes me feel so _____.

▶ page 153 **VOCABULARYBANK**

E

F

LISTENING

3 Read the definition and listen to the radio program. Answer the questions.

> **T** **therapy** /ˈθerəpi/ *n [C,U] plural* **therapies** the treatment of a mental or physical illness over a long period of time, especially without using drugs or operations: *He's having therapy to help with alcohol addiction.*

from Longman Active Study Dictionary

1 Which two therapies does the program talk about?

2 The therapies are used in different situations. Which situations are mentioned in the show?

4 A Are the statements true (T) or false (F)?

1 Eight out of ten people have trouble controlling their anger.

2 With destruction therapy, you use your anger to destroy something in a controlled way.

3 If you think about a situation in which you were angry, the therapy will be more enjoyable.

4 In Spain, some companies pay for their workers to build hotels.

5 In Mexico, they use destruction therapy in hospitals.

6 Laughter therapy can help people to feel less pain.

7 On average, children laugh 100 times a day, and adults laugh seventeen times.

B Listen again to check. Correct the false statements.

C Discuss the questions.

1 Do you think destruction therapy and laughter therapy are good ideas? Why?/Why not?

2 Would you try any of the ideas in the program?

GRAMMAR
REAL CONDITIONALS

5 A Look at four sentences from the program. Which talk about a general situation (GS) and which talk about a specific/future situation (FS)?

a) When people get angry, they don't know what to do with their anger.

b) When we get there, I'll give you a hammer.

c) If I smash the car to pieces, will I feel better?

d) If people laugh about something, they feel better.

B Underline the correct alternative to complete the rules.

> **RULES**
>
> **1** Use the zero (0) conditional (*If/When* + present simple + present simple) to talk about a *general/specific* situation (fact), or something that is always true.
>
> **2** Use the first (1) conditional (*If/When* + present simple + *will/might/could*) to talk about a *general/specific* (possible) situation in the future.

▶ page 138 LANGUAGE**BANK**

6 A Listen and underline the words you hear.

1 If he shouts, *I get/I'll get* angry.

2 If I see him, *I tell/I'll tell* him.

3 When they arrive, *we eat/we'll eat*.

4 When we get there, *we phone/we'll phone* you.

5 If I finish early, *I go/I'll go* home.

B WEAK FORMS: pronouns + 'll Listen again and repeat. Pay attention to the weak form of 'll /əl/ in the contraction *I'll* /ɪəl/ *or we'll* /wɪəl/.

7 A Complete the sentences with the correct form of the verbs in parentheses. Mark each sentence zero (0) or first (1st) conditional.

1 a) If I go running every day, it _____ (make) me feel good.

b) I'm feeling down. If I go for a run, I _____ (feel) better.

2 a) When I finish reading this book, I _____ (give) it to you to read.

b) When I _____ (finish) reading a book, I usually feel disappointed.

3 a) I'm meeting my boss later. If I tell him about my new job, he _____ (get) angry.

b) If I _____ (get) angry, I take a deep breath and count to ten.

4 a) If I'm tired, I _____ (like) to eat in front of the television and go to bed early.

b) I'm planning to drive through the night. If I get tired, I _____ (stop) and sleep.

B Complete the sentences so that they are true for you. Compare your ideas with a partner. Can you find any similarities?

When I get older, …

When my English gets better, I …

If I'm happy, I usually …

When I get home this evening, …

If I'm stressed, I usually …

SPEAKING

8 A Work in pairs. What do you do in situations 1–7? Write three pieces of advice to give to someone in one of these situations.

1 You're nervous about a job interview/test.
2 You're annoyed with someone in your family.
3 It's the weekend, and you're bored.
4 You're stressed about your work/studies.
5 You have too many things to do.
6 You get home from English class and realize you've left your backpack behind.
7 When you get home, you're hungry, but there's nothing to eat.

B Work in groups and compare your ideas. Which is the best idea for each situation?

If you have too many things to do, you should try to prioritize your tasks.

If you get stressed about your work, try to exercise more to help you relax.

VOCABULARY PLUS
MULTI-WORD VERBS

9 A Match the following topics: *Clothes, Computers* and *Love and Friendship* with paragraphs 1–3.

> **1** _____ : I met my ex-boyfriend when he **hit on me** in a bar. We **got off** to a good start. We were together for two years, and we were planning to **settle down**. Then I got bored and **gave up** on him!

> **2** _____ : It's a bit confusing. You have to **scroll up** and then **click on** the arrow icon. If you want, you can **log off** before you **shut down**.

> **3** _____ : I love **dressing up,** so, when I **tried on** that purple suit, I thought it was perfect for my first day at work. I was so embarrassed when I arrived and the receptionist told me to **take off** my tie because everyone **dresses down** at the company!

B Match the multi-word verbs in bold in Exercise 9A with the correct definition in the word webs. You will need to use the infinitive form.

put the computer mouse on a specific place and press _click on_

on — talk to someone you like so they'll go out with you _____

wear clothes to see if you want to buy them _____

off — to begin something _____

remove (clothes) _____

exit from a website _____

up — to lose interest in or no longer bother with _____

wear especially nice or colorful clothes, e.g., for a party _____

move the computer mouse to see text above _____

down — choose to live a calm life, e.g., at home with a partner _____

switch off the computer _____

wear clothes (to work) that are not nice, e.g., old jeans _____

10 A Look at the dictionary definitions below and answer the questions.

1 Which verb needs an object?
2 Which verb does not need an object?
3 Which verb can be followed by another preposition?

> **T** **try** *sth* ↔ **on** *phr v* to put on a piece of clothing to find out if it fits or if you like it: *Can I try these jeans on, please?*

> **G** **get along** *phr v* **1** if people get along, they have a friendly relationship: + **with** *She doesn't get along with my mom very well.*

> **S** **shut down** *phr v* if a company, factory, machine etc. shuts down, or if you shut it down, it stops operating: *Hundreds of local post offices have shut down.* | **shut** *sth* ↔ **down** *Did you shut the computer down?*

from Longman Active Study Dictionary

B Use the dictionary definitions to help you decide which sentences are possible. Mark the sentences with a check (✔) or an ✘.

1 I **tried** the suit **on**. / I **tried on** the suit.
2 I **get along** really well with Simon. / I **get** Simon **along** really well.
3 You need to **shut down** the computer. / You need to **shut** the computer **down**.

> **American Speak out TIP**
> There are different ways to group multi-word verbs (including phrasal verbs) in your notebook. For example, you can group them by topic (e.g., weather, travel, work) or by preposition (e.g., multi-word verbs with *on, over, by*). Decide how you want to group them and then add the phrases to your notebook.

C Choose three or four verbs from above and write your own example sentences. Use a dictionary to help. Then compare them with a partner. Are the sentences correct?

▶ page 153 **VOCABULARYBANK**

> While in the U.S. you say you "get along" with someone, in Britain, you might say you "get on" with someone.

6.2)) THE PEOPLE WATCHERS

G hypothetical conditional present/future
P connected speech: would
V verb-noun collocations

If you wanted to persuade someone to dress up as a tree in public, what would you do? If you wanted to raise money for charity on the streets, whom would you ask to help you? What would you do if you wanted to sell cake and nobody was buying it? What would you do if you needed to think creatively but didn't have any ideas?

One thing you could do is watch a program from the TV series *The People Watchers*. The show asks the question "Why do we do what we do?" Through twenty episodes, Professor Richard Wiseman, two psychologists and a neuroscientist do experiments involving members of the public, secretly filming them with a hidden camera. The experiments show why we behave the way we do in everyday situations. If you wanted to know how to get a seat on a crowded train, stop people from cutting in line, get someone to do you a favor, work out if someone is lying, and get a complete stranger to lend you a cell phone, you could find out by watching.

In one experiment, two of Wiseman's psychologists pretended to sell cake. They set up a stand on the street and tried to sell pieces of cake for a pound each. No one bought any. So they did what stores do: they held a sale. But it wasn't a real sale. They pretended that one piece cost two pounds, and, if you bought a piece, you would get another one free. People started buying! Later they told people that the pieces of cake usually cost two pounds, but they were offering a deal and selling them for just one pound. Again, people bought the cake. It seems that everyone loves the idea of a bargain even if they aren't really getting one.

Another experiment looked at "experts" who aren't. Emma, a psychologist, pretended to be a hairdresser. While "cutting" three people's hair, she talked like a hairdresser, saying all the right things, and dropped a few bits of fake hair. The three volunteers later said they were very happy with their haircuts. In reality, Emma hadn't cut any hair. Richard Wiseman's conclusion? People would do better if they didn't always listen to "experts." Instead, they should trust their own eyes.

In another experiment, Jack, a psychologist, had to persuade ordinary people to dress up as a tree. The trick was to "start small." First, Jack asked a man to wear a badge; then he asked him to wear a cap; and finally the tree suit. This, Wiseman says, is called "The foot-in-the-door technique": if you want a big favor from someone, first ask for a small favor!

READING

1 A Read the first paragraph of the article. How would you answer the four questions in that paragraph? Discuss with other students.

B Now read the rest of the article to find out what researchers did to answer the questions.

2 A Work in pairs and answer the questions.

1 What question does the program try to answer?
2 How did Wiseman's team carry out its research?
3 What was the "trick" to get people to buy cake?
4 What "trick" did Emma, the fake hairdresser, use?
5 What is "the foot-in-the-door technique"?

B Read the article again. Make notes under these headings.

1 People Involved in the Program
2 Situations
3 Conclusions from the Experiments

C Think of a question about human behavior that you would like answered. What could researchers in this program do to answer it?

VOCABULARY
VERB—NOUN COLLOCATIONS

3 A Match verbs 1—6 with nouns a)—f).

1 hold   a) money (for something)
2 raise   b) experiments
3 do   c) a program
4 get   d) hair
5 cut   e) a seat
6 watch   f) a sale

B Which do you do:

1 to sell something cheaply?
2 to avoid standing up in a train/bus/waiting room, etc.?
3 to help a charity?
4 to be informed or entertained?
5 to make someone look more beautiful?
6 to obtain new scientific information?

cutting in line, butting in line   jumping the queue

GRAMMAR

HYPOTHETICAL CONDITIONAL: PRESENT/FUTURE

4 **A** Read a review of *The People Watchers*. Why does the reviewer like the program?

▶ Pick of the Month

My own favorite show this month? *The People Watchers*. Hosted by Professor Richard Wiseman and his really attractive psychologist friends, the show asks some very interesting questions. <u>If no one saw you, would you take something without paying for it?</u> <u>How close to someone would you stand if you didn't know them?</u> It's all good stuff, but <u>maybe the program could be even better if we heard from more experts.</u> Unfortunately, for most of the series, we only hear Professor Wiseman's voice. And <u>it would also be nice if we had more statistics.</u> Some of the experiments using hidden cameras show only one or two people in action, which is not enough to come to big conclusions about human nature. But, overall, this is good TV: light, easy on the eye, and fun.

B Look at the four underlined sentences above and complete the rules with the words in the box.

would could hypothetical subjunctive

RULES

1 We use the hypothetical conditional to describe a _____ situation.

2 In the *if* clause, we use the _____.

3 In the result clause, we use _____ or *'d*.

4 If we are not sure of the result, we can also use _____.

C Find other examples of the hypothetical conditional in the article on page 71.

▶ page 138 **LANGUAGEBANK**

▶ page 138 **LANGUAGEBANK**

5 **A** **CONNECTED SPEECH:** *would* Listen and complete the conversations.

1 **A:** What _____ _____ _____ if your laptop exploded?
   B: If my laptop exploded, I'd call for help!

2 **A:** What would you do if you lost your house keys?
   B: If I lost my house keys, _____ climb through the window!

3 **A:** How would you feel if your car broke down?
   B: If my car broke down, I _____ _____ happy!

B Listen again and answer questions 1–3.

1 How do we pronounce *would* in the question form?

2 How do we pronounce *would* in fast spoken English in positive sentences?

3 How do we pronounce the negative of *would*?

6 Complete the sentences with the correct form of the verbs in the box.

~~write~~ do can fail not/rain see (x2) go like ~~not/have~~ not/be tell

1 I would ___*write*___ my autobiography if I *didn't have* so much work to do.

2 What _____ if you _____ a UFO?

3 If I _____ go anywhere in the world, I _____ to the Caribbean.

4 If it _____ so much, I _____ to live in Norway.

5 You _____ very happy if you _____ your test.

6 If you _____ a friend shoplifting, would you _____ the police?

7 **A** Complete the sentences about your classmates.

1 If _____ could go anywhere, he/she …

2 If _____ weren't so busy, he/she …

3 If _____ were able to speak to his/her President, he/she …

4 If _____ knew how to, he/she …

5 _____ would feel very happy if …

6 _____ 's life would be easier if …

7 _____ wouldn't like it if …

8 _____ wouldn't care if …

B Ask your classmates if your sentences are true.

SPEAKING

8 **A** What would you do if …

1 someone asked you to dress up as a tree for charity?

2 a stranger asked to borrow your cell phone?

3 someone cut in line ahead of you?

4 you had to think of a way to raise money in the street for a charity?

5 someone asked you to take part in a TV program?

6 you heard someone saying bad things about your friend?

7 you saw someone stealing bread in the supermarket?

8 you found a bag of money in the street?

I'd take the bag of money to the police.

B Choose five or six of the situations. Work in groups and tell other students what you would do.

WRITING

AN EMAIL OF ADVICE; LEARN TO QUALIFY WHAT YOU SAY

9 Look at the first photo and discuss. What do you do when you need advice? Do you look for help online or perhaps ask a relative/friend/experienced older person? What does it depend on?

10 A Read the dilemma. What do you think the person should do?

> My cousin has asked me to lend her some money to start an Internet business. She is intelligent and reliable, and I like her, but she is only twenty years old. Also, I know nothing about Internet businesses. Should I lend her the money?

B Read the responses. Which do you agree with? Why?

Yes

You have the money. She has the ideas, the energy and the expertise. If I were you, I wouldn't worry about her age. As a young person, she might know more about the Internet than you do. And she isn't asking for your advice, only your money. So, come on. You're a member of her family. What do you have to lose apart from a bit of money? And if you're really worried, maybe tell her you want fifty percent of the money back within two years. If she's reliable, you'll probably get it.

No

So your cousin wants money. Perhaps you really trust her, but at age twenty, she probably doesn't have much experience in business. If I were you, I'd ask a lot of questions first. I'd find out how much research she has done, how well she knows the market and who else is involved. It's possible that she will be successful, but over 90 percent of new companies disappear within the first year. The other thing is time. It might take her a few years to start making a profit. Can you wait that long to get your money back? And think about this: if it weren't your cousin asking, would you lend the money?

C Check (✔) the things an email of advice might include. Compare your ideas with other students.

1 a short summary of the situation
2 a few sentences describing your qualifications
3 some ideas about what the person should do
4 some background information explaining your ideas
5 a question for the reader to think about

D Find the things you checked (✔) in the responses in Exercise 10B.

11 A Look at the words/phrases in the box. Find and underline these in the emails in Exercise 10B. Then answer the questions.

| maybe   probably   perhaps   might   It's possible that |

1 Which words/phrases mean "there is a strong possibility"?
2 Which two words have the same meaning?

B How do you feel about statements 1–4? Qualify them, using the words and phrases above.

1 As life in the twenty-first century gets more complex, people will have more complex problems.
2 In the future, machines will "read" our emotions and "know" if we have a problem.
3 In the future, most young people will prefer to talk to strangers online about their problems rather than have face-to-face conversations with family and friends.
4 I'd never write to an advice column if I needed advice.

Most people ask their family and friends for advice. They don't need to write to advice columns.

*Most people **probably** ask their family and friends for advice. **Maybe** they don't need to write to advice columns.*

12 A Read the problem below. Work with other students and think of possible solutions.

> I have a problem. My twenty-six-year-old brother has always loved football, but now it's becoming an obsession. He goes to watch games every weekend even though the tickets are expensive, and he doesn't have much money. At his house, he sometimes watches three or four games on TV a day! His only friends are football fans, and his last girlfriend broke up with him because of his obsession. I want to help him, but he's older than I, and he thinks it's none of my business what he does in his free time. Please can you give me some advice?

B Write an email of advice to the writer above.

C Work in groups and take turns reading what you wrote. If you were in the person's situation, which letter would you like to receive?

advice column   problem page

6.3)) THAT'S GREAT NEWS!

F giving news
P intonation: giving bad news
V life events

VOCABULARY
LIFE EVENTS

1 A Look at phrases 1–8. Are they good news (G) or bad news (B)?

1 Fail your final exams
2 Be offered a job
3 Get accepted into college
4 Get engaged/married
5 Lose your job/money
6 Split up with a partner
7 Get promoted
8 Buy a house

B Work in pairs. Have any of the things above happened recently to you or anyone you know?

2 A Work in groups and discuss. What is the best way to give bad news?

B Complete the article with the phrases in the box.

> give a reason   tone of voice   prepare your listener
> bad news   making people too upset   good news

Good Ways to Give Bad News

It's easy to give someone good news, but what about when you have some [1]_____ to tell? Are there any good ways to give bad news without [2]_____ ? The following steps might help:

Say something positive: Try to start or end the conversation with some [3]_____ so that it's not all bad. For example, "You did very well in the interview, but unfortunately we've given the job to somebody else."

[4]_____ **for the news:** Use phrases to introduce what you're going to say, like "Unfortunately, ...," "I'm really sorry, but ..." or "I'm afraid I have some bad news." This gives the listener time to prepare for what you're going to say.

Try to [5]_____: People like to know why things go wrong. Try to explain the decision: if someone doesn't get the job, can you explain why? If you have to cancel an arrangement, try to give a reason.

Use a soft [6]_____: If you're giving someone bad news, try to use a soft, calm voice to make you sound kind. Say things to show you understand, like, "I'm really sorry" or "I know this must be disappointing."

C Read the article again. Do you agree with the advice? Why?/Why not?

FUNCTION
GIVING NEWS

3 A Listen to seven conversations. Match the conversations to the pictures A–G.

B Look at the pictures again. What is the good news or bad news in each situation?

4 A Look at the phrases the speakers use to introduce their news. Listen again and write the conversation number next to each phrase.

good news	I have some good news (for you). I'm really happy to tell you … You'll never guess what.
bad news	Bad news. I'm sorry to have to tell you, but … I'm afraid/Unfortunately, … I'm afraid I have some bad news … There's something I have to tell you.
good or bad news	You know … ? Well, … I have/We have something to tell you. *1*

B Listen to some of the phrases in the table again. Underline the stressed syllables.

C INTONATION: giving bad news Listen again. Is the speaker's voice high or low for good news? Is it high or low for bad news? Practice the phrases.

▶ page 138 LANGUAGEBANK

5 Put the words in the correct order to make sentences.

1 news / afraid / I'm / bad / the / we / game / lost
2 to / I'm / the / you / tell / got / pleased / you / really / job / that
3 going / I'm / to / late / we're / be / afraid
4 have / you / there's / tell / I / to / something
5 never / what / you'll / guess
6 have / news / I / for / good / you / some
7 was / concert / the / unfortunately, / canceled
8 lost? / you / the / we / cat / know / we / again / found / him / well,

get accepted into college   get a place at university

D   **E**   **F**   **G**

LEARN TO
RESPOND TO NEWS

6 How do the speakers respond to the news? Complete the conversations with the words in the box.

> joking   sorry   lucky   annoying   happy
> Congratulations great shame terrible

1 **A:** I've been offered a job.

    B: Wow! That's fantastic. _____!

2 **A:** We've offered the job to someone else.

    B: Oh. That's a _____. Thanks, anyway.

3 **A:** I just won some money in a creative writing competition.

    B: You're _____? … How much did you win?

    A: Two thousand dollars.

    B: You _____ dog!

4 **A:** We crashed the car.

    B: Oh, no. That's _____.

5 **A:** The college accepted me!

    B: That's wonderful news. That's _____! I'm so _____ for you.

6 **A:** Steve lost his job.

    B: Oh, no. That's awful. I'm really _____ to hear that.

7 **A:** And they want us to fill out another form.

    B: No! That's really _____.

> **American Speak TIP** Exaggerate! Sometimes when you speak in a foreign language, your intonation can sound flat. This can mean that you don't sound as polite or enthusiastic as you want to. Try to exaggerate the intonation pattern to sound enthusiastic or concerned. Say the responses in Exercise 7A with an exaggerated intonation.

 7 A Listen to responses 1–4. Notice the intonation patterns .

1 Congratulations!   **3** That's a shame.

2 That's fantastic news!   **4** That's awful.

B Practice saying the phrases with the correct intonation.

 C Mark the main stress on sentences 1–6. Which ones use a higher voice? Listen and check, then listen and repeat.

You lucky dog!

That's terrible.

That's great!

I'm so happy for you.

That's really annoying.

That's awful. I'm really sorry to hear that.

SPEAKING

8 A Work in pairs and role-play the situation. Student A: you just won some money in a lottery. Student B: listen and respond to Student A's news.

Student A

> Tell Student B you have some good news.

          Student B

> Ask Student A what the news is.

> Tell Student B that you won some money in the lottery.

> Respond to the news and ask Student A how much they won.

> Tell Student B how much money you won.

> Tell Student A how lucky you think they are. Ask Student A what they plan to do with the money.

> Tell Student B you are going to use the money to help send your brother and his young family on vacation because they have had a difficult year.

> Respond to the news.

B Work in pairs. First, think of three pieces of good/bad news to tell your partner. Then take turns giving and responding to each other's news using expressions in Exercises 4 and 6.

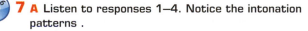

6.4 ⏽)) MY WORST WEEK

DVD PREVIEW

1 A Discuss. How do you think people usually feel the week before their wedding? What kind of things can go wrong when you are preparing for a wedding?

B Read about a TV comedy. Why is this week supposed to be special for Howard? What's the problem?

▶ My Worst Week

The week before a wedding can be a difficult time, but, for publisher Howard Steele, marrying the beautiful Mel, it becomes a complete nightmare. Everything that can possibly go wrong does go wrong, even though Howard tries desperately to do the right thing. During the week, Howard accidentally kills his in-laws' dog, puts Mel's grandma in the hospital, and loses the wedding ring (which has been in the family for many generations) twice. It's not a good start, and what should have been a very special week soon turns into the worst week of his life.

DVD VIEW

2 A Watch the DVD. What is the problem?

B Number the events in the correct order.

a) Mel calls Howard at his office.

b) Eve takes the ring off using soap in the bathroom.

c) Howard arrives at his office and shows his secretary, Eve, the ring. *1*

d) Howard's work colleagues organize a surprise party for him.

e) The ring gets stuck.

f) Eve bursts into tears, so Howard lets her try the ring on.

3 A What do they say? Complete the phrases using the words in the box.

> wedding   happiness   3 mm   a hundred and fifty
> plumber   secretary   luck

1 Howard: "It's been in Mel's family for _____ years. They have this rather charming tradition where they (uh) pass it down from generation to generation."

2 Eve: "I always wanted a fairy-tale _____ of my own."

3 Eve: "I can't do that. It's bad _____."

4 Howard: "I picked it up on my way in. They've reduced it by _____."

5 Howard: "When the vicar asks me to put the ring on my fiancée's finger, it would be very nice if my _____ was not attached."

6 Boss: "We'd like to wish you and Mel every _____ and hope you have a great day on Saturday."

7 Eve: "I'll get a _____."

B Watch the DVD again to check.

4 A Complete the sentences about how the characters felt.

1 Eve is impressed when she sees …

2 Eve gets upset about …

3 Howard is annoyed when …

4 Eve is anxious about …

5 Howard is surprised when …

6 Howard is shocked when …

B Compare your ideas with another student.

> From the French, "fiancée" is a woman engaged to be married, and "fiancé" is a man engaged to be married.

in the hospital / arrive at the office   in hospital / arrive in the office

American Speakout memorable moments

5 A Listen to a man talking about a special weekend. Which of the following statements is not true?

1 His brother organized a surprise weekend away.

2 They went on a boat trip to a lighthouse and slept there.

3 They went shopping with his brother's money.

4 They went to the theater and then ate an expensive five-course meal.

B Listen again and check (✔) the key phrases you hear.

KEYPHRASES

One of the most memorable moments/events in my life was …

The happiest moment of my life was when …

It all started one day when …

I was so [embarrassed/delighted/shocked/terrified] when …

I had absolutely no idea.

The funniest thing that ever happened to me was …

The next thing/morning …

That weekend/day is one of my happiest memories.

C Choose one of the following questions. Plan your answer using some of the key phrases.

1 What are the strongest memories of your childhood?

2 Have you ever done anything you regret?

3 What's the most embarrassing/funniest/scariest thing that has ever happened to you?

4 What do you remember about the house you lived in as a child?

5 Can you remember a time when you felt very proud?

6 What is your happiest memory?

D Work in groups and tell your stories.

writeback a website entry

6 A Read the website entry. What kind of things do people write about on this website? What was special about Jess's trip?

100 Lives
real life, real people, real experiences

Join people from around the world who want to share their stories and experiences. Read true personal stories. Chat and get advice from the group.

Q: What's your happiest memory?

One of my happiest memories is of a trip I took to America when I'd just left school. My father told me that everyone should see New York once in their lifetime, and he helped me to save enough money to buy my plane ticket. I spent three weeks traveling around the U.S. on my own. I visited New York and Washington D.C. and traveled through the countryside on a bus. I met so many wonderful people on that trip and saw some amazing sights. I remember I had this great sense of freedom, like I was at the beginning of the whole adventure of my adult life. Everything was in front of me, and I would be able to do whatever I chose to do. When I think back to those days, it always brings a smile to my face.

Jess, U.K.

B Choose another question from Exercise 5C and write your story (150–200 words). Use the website entry above and the key phrases to help.

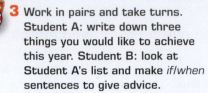

G -ING/-ED ADJECTIVES

1 **A** Work in pairs. Use adjectives to describe how you feel in the following situations.

1 You lose your bus/train ticket.

2 You get lost at night in a foreign city.

3 You wait for a delayed flight.

4 You forget someone's name (when you should know it).

B Write situations for the adjectives in the box.

> annoying   worried   boring
> embarrassing   relaxing
> confusing   exhausted
> frightening   satisfied

annoying: When you discover your phone has run out of power, it's …

worried: My final exams are tomorrow. I'm really …

C Work in pairs. Take turns reading your situations. Don't say the adjectives they describe. Can your partner guess the adjective?

G REAL CONDITIONALS

2 **A** Match 1–7 with a)–g) to make sentences.

1 If you drink too much coffee,

2 If you go to bed early,

3 If you always go to bed late,

4 If you listen to loud music when you study,

5 You won't get in shape if you

6 If you don't like your job,

7 You'll have problems at work if you

a) drive everywhere in your car.

b) you won't sleep tonight.

c) it's difficult to concentrate.

d) you'll exhaust yourself.

e) don't finish that report on time.

f) you'll feel better in the morning.

g) look for a new one.

B Look at the sentences in Exercise 2A. Can you think of other ways to complete them? Compare your ideas with a partner.

3 Work in pairs and take turns. Student A: write down three things you would like to achieve this year. Student B: look at Student A's list and make *if/when* sentences to give advice.

A: one: find a new job, two: get in shape, three: improve my English

B: one: find a new job: If you look on the Internet, you might find a new job.

V VERB—NOUN COLLOCATIONS

4 Rearrange the letters in bold to complete the sentences with collocations of *watch/hold/raise/do/get/cut*.

1 We should go to the concert early so we can **est gates**. *get seats*

2 They are going to **heal loads** to sell their old clothes.

3 The schoolchildren decided to **ease my iron** for cancer research.

4 I'm going home early because I want to **chat how was** on TV.

5 He gave up his job because he didn't want to **opened term six** on animals.

6 My cousin **i shut car** for a living.

G HYPOTHETICAL CONDITIONAL

5 Work in pairs. Student A: use an *if* clause with the phrases in your box. Student B: respond with the correct *would* clause from your box.

A

> I/be/rich   there/be/no war
> there/be/more hours in the day
> I/have/more/energy
> nobody/smoke   can/paint/well
> I/give up/coffee

B

> dance/all night   sleep/better
> people/be/healthier
> do/a portrait of you
> give/money/charity
> people/work/more
> the world/be/peaceful

A: If I were rich …
B: I'd give some money to charity.

F GIVING NEWS

6 **A** Each conversation has two words missing. Write in the missing words. You may have to change the punctuation.

1 A: Bad news a͟f͟raid. *I'm*

B: What's the matter?

A: The computers aren't working.

B: Not again! Annoying.

2 A: You'll never what.

B: What?

A: I got the job.

B: Congratulations! That's news.

3 A: I have some good news you.

B: What is it?

A: I've been promoted.

B: That's!

4 A: I'm to have to tell you, but I'm leaving the company.

B: What? Why?

A: The company has problems, so they're reducing the number of managers.

B: I'm sorry to that.

5 A: You that test I took last week?

B: Yes?

A: Well, I passed.

B: Congratulations! I'm so for you.

B Work in pairs and practice the conversations.

get in shape   get fit

7)) success

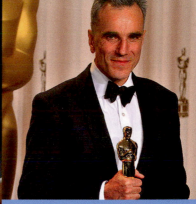

THE MEMORY MEN   p83

What has been your greatest achievement to date?

 INTERVIEWS

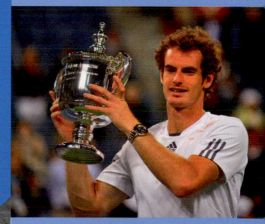

G present perfect simple versus continuous
P weak forms: *have*
V success; verb phrases

SPEAKING

1 A Write the names of three very successful people. Answer the questions.

1 How and why did these people become successful?
2 Do you think they have a special talent, or have they just been lucky?
3 What advice would you give to someone who wants to be as successful as these people?

B Work in pairs and read the quotes. What do they tell you about success? Do you agree or disagree?

> "I have not failed. I've just found 10,000 ways that won't work."
>
> Thomas Edison

> "Success doesn't come to you ... you go to it."
>
> Marva Collins

> "The secret of success in life is for a man to be ready for his opportunity when it comes."
>
> Benjamin Disraeli

C Can you recognize any of the people in the photos? Do you know why they are famous?

LISTENING

2 A Read the introduction to an article about success. What do you think the secret of success is?

What is the secret of success?

BBC Focus Magazine Investigates

What makes the most successful people on the planet different from the rest of us? If we were more like Albert Einstein or John Lennon, surely we could enjoy the same level of success. In his new book, Malcolm Gladwell reveals that there is one factor—so obvious that it's right under our noses—that all successful people share ...

B Listen to the radio program and complete the summary.

In this new book, *Outliers*, Gladwell argues that Beethoven, the Beatles and Bill Gates all have one thing in ¹_____. They ²_____ what they do, and they practiced a lot. In fact, Gladwell discovered that, in order to be truly ³_____ in anything, it is necessary to practice for more than ⁴_____ hours. These people have done that, which is why he believes they have been so ⁵_____.

3 A Are the statements true (T) or false (F)?

1 If we want to learn from Bill Gates' achievements, we need to look at where he came from and the opportunities he had.

2 If you're going to be world-class at something, you need to have parents who are high achievers.

3 The Beatles played all-night concerts in Hamburg, and this helped them to master their craft.

4 To become a successful tennis player, you need a very talented teacher and enough money to pay for your lessons.

B Listen again to check.

C Discuss. Do you agree that, if you practice something enough, you can become world-class at it, or do you think you need to have a natural talent for it?

VOCABULARY
SUCCESS

4 A Complete sentences 1–8 with the phrases in the box.

work hard (at something)   be a high achiever
have a natural talent for …   focus on
have the opportunity (to do something)
believe in yourself   master (a skill / a craft)
(be) world-class (at something)

1 You will never achieve anything if you don't _____ *work hard* _____ at it.

2 I don't _____ languages. I find them difficult to learn.

3 If you _____ and your abilities, then you can achieve anything.

4 It's amazing what children can achieve if they _____ to try different skills.

5 If you want to _____ any skill, you have to practice it regularly.

6 I'm sure she will _____. She is determined to do well at everything.

7 When I really want something, I try to _____ my goal.

8 She'll beat all the women in the world this year. She's a _____ gymnast.

B Find phrases above to match meanings 1–6.

1 be sure about your ideas/abilities
2 only think about one objective
3 become very skilled at something
4 have the chance to do something
5 be ambitious and successful in your work or studies
6 to be one of the best in the world

C Choose two of the phrases and make sentences that are true for you. Compare your ideas with a partner.

▶ page 154 **VOCABULARY**BANK

SPEAKING

5 Discuss the questions in groups.

1 Do you have a special skill/interest? How many hours do you think you have spent practicing it? (10,000 hours is approximately ten hours per week for twenty years.)

2 What things have you been successful at? What factors do you think contributed to that success?

3 Are there any particular skills you wish you had? Do you think you could master that skill if you worked hard at it?

GRAMMAR
PRESENT PERFECT SIMPLE VERSUS CONTINUOUS

6 A Read sentences a)—e). Underline examples of the present perfect simple and circle examples of the present perfect continuous.

a) Martina's been playing tennis since she was three years old.

b) Anya's been going to ballet lessons since she was a child.

c) I've known Max for years.

d) How long have you been studying French?

e) He's always enjoyed playing sports.

B Match sentences a)—e) with rules 1—3. Some sentences will match more than one rule.

RULES

1 Use the present perfect continuous to emphasize that an action has been long and repeated.

2 With state verbs (e.g., *like, love, understand, remember, know*, etc.), we cannot use the present perfect continuous, so we use the present perfect simple.

3 We often use *for, since* and *How long have you ...?* with the present perfect simple and the present perfect continuous. We choose the present perfect continuous where possible, unless the main verb is a state verb.

▶ page 140 LANGUAGEBANK

7 A Complete the sentences with the present perfect simple or continuous form of the verbs in parentheses and any other information you need.

1 I _____ (study) German for ... years, but I still find the grammar difficult!

2 I _____ (learn) Arabic for two years.

3 I _____ (live) on my own since I ... .

4 I _____ always _____ (love) art, but I'm not very good at it.

5 I _____ (have) my own car since I was ... .

6 I _____ always _____ (want) to ... . Maybe I'll learn one day.

B **WEAK FORMS:** *have* Listen to the sentences. Notice the pronunciation of *have*. Is it strong or weak? Practice saying the sentences.

C Change some of the sentences in Exercise 7A so they are true for you. Compare your ideas with a partner.

8 A Make questions with the prompts.

1 how long / you / know / best friend?

2 how long / you / do / your hobby?

3 how long / you / have / that ... (watch/phone/jacket)?

4 how long / you / live in this town/city?

5 how / you / spend / your days off recently?

B Work in pairs. Take turns asking and answering the questions above. Think of two or more follow-up questions for each question.

A: How long have you known your best friend?
B: For about fifteen years.
A: Where did you meet?

VOCABULARY *PLUS*
VERB PHRASES

9 A Choose the correct preposition to complete the verb phrases in sentences 1—7.

1 I don't have a lot in common *to/with/for* my sister.

2 We don't have access *with/at/to* the Internet at work.

3 She's world-class *in/for/at* playing the violin.

4 He works very hard. He puts *in/to/with* a lot of hours.

5 I have a lot to think *with/for/about* at the moment.

6 The movie picks up *on/to/at* the difficulties people experienced during the war.

7 She has a talent *about/for/in* finding a bargain.

B Add the verb phrases from Exercise 9A to the correct group below.

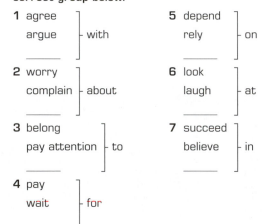

1 agree
  argue ⎱ with
  _____

2 worry
  complain ⎱ about
  _____

3 belong
  pay attention ⎱ to
  _____

4 pay
  wait ⎱ for
  _____

5 depend
  rely ⎱ on
  _____

6 look
  laugh ⎱ at
  _____

7 succeed
  believe ⎱ in
  _____

American Speak TIP
There are many verbs in English that use prepositions. Keep a record of which prepositions go with which verbs in your notebook. Can you add any more phrases to the diagram in Exercise 9B?

C Write three questions to ask a partner about his/her life, using the verb phrases above.

Would you think about learning a new skill?

Is there anyone you tend to rely on?

What kinds of things do you generally succeed in?

D Work in pairs. Ask and answer your questions.

▶ page 154 VOCABULARYBANK

G present and past ability
P word stress
V ability

VOCABULARY

ABILITY

1 Make a list of five things you are good at and three that you are bad at. Show the list to a partner. He/She asks questions to find out what you are good/bad at.

How long have you been playing the drums?
How often do you play? Do you …

2 A Read sentences a)–h), then discuss questions 1–3 with a partner.

a) He's **an expert in** Italian art.
   He's written several books about it.

b) He's **gifted at** painting. He had his first show when he was sixteen.

c) She **has a lot of ability as a** dancer.
   I think she could become a professional.

d) She's the most **skillful** soccer player I've ever seen. She can play in any position.

e) He **has an aptitude for** math.
   He learns new formulas very quickly.

f) He is a really **talented** musician.
   He can play six instruments.

g) I'm **hopeless at** geography. I failed my test three times.

h) I'm **useless at** sports. I can't play any.

1 Which of the words in bold are negative?

2 Which are nouns, and which are adjectives?

3 What do you think the words mean? Use the context of the sentences to help you.

B **WORD STRESS** Look at the words in bold in exercise 2A. Then listen to the sentences and answer the questions.

1 Which parts of the words in bold are stressed? Underline the stressed part.

2 Which five words have two syllables? Where do we normally put the stress on two-syllable words?

C Listen again and repeat the sentences. Focus on the stressed parts.

3 A Write the name of:

• an expert in your own area of interest.

• someone in the class who is talented.

• a gifted musician.

• something you are useless at.

• something you have an aptitude for.

B Work in groups. Ask each other to explain what they wrote and why.

READING

4 A Work in pairs. You are going to read about two men, one nicknamed the "Human Computer" and the other, the "Human Camera." What special abilities do you think they have?

B Student A: read the text below to see if your ideas are mentioned. Student B: turn to page 161.

THE HUMAN COMPUTER

Daniel Tammet says he was born on a blue day, January 31, 1979. He knows it was blue because Wednesdays are always blue, like the number nine or the sound of people arguing.

As a child, Daniel was diagnosed as autistic. He couldn't make friends. He was too different from the other children. At age eight, he was able to calculate 82 x 82 x 82 x 82 in his head, but he couldn't tie his own shoelaces or ride a bicycle.

The thing that makes Daniel special is that he has an incredible ability with numbers. He imagines them as shapes and colors ("289 is an ugly number," he says) and is able to do extremely difficult mathematical calculations. On the TV program that made him famous, he managed to recite 22,514 numbers from pi perfectly. If you tell Daniel your birth date, he can tell you what day of the week you were born on and what day of the week it will be on your 65th birthday.

Daniel counts everything. He eats exactly forty-five grams of oatmeal for breakfast each morning, and he brushes his teeth for exactly two minutes. He doesn't like walking on the beach near his home because there are too many pebbles to count.

Daniel's other great love, besides numbers (which he calls "his friends"), is learning languages. He speaks ten, and he managed to learn Icelandic in a week for a TV program in Iceland. He is now a bestselling author; his books include *Born on a Blue Day*, *Embracing the Wide Sky* and *Thinking in Numbers*.

C Student A: read the text above again and answer the questions.

1 How was his behavior different from that of other children?

2 What special talents does he have?

3 How did the public learn about his special talents?

4 What country/countries has he been to, and what did he do there?

5 What does he do now?

6 What has he published?

D Tell your partner about your text. Use questions 1–6 to help.

skillful / soccer player   skilful / footballer

GRAMMAR

PRESENT AND PAST ABILITY

5 Read sentences a)–i) and answer questions 1–3.

1 Which sentences describe present ability, and which describe past ability?

2 Which words are used to express past and present ability? Underline them.

3 Which three sentences are negative?

a) If you tell Daniel your birth date, he <u>can</u> tell you what day of the week you were born on. *present ability*

b) He could see a building just once and remember everything about it.

c) As a child, he couldn't make friends.

d) He is able to do extremely difficult calculations.

e) He was able to calculate 82 x 82 x 82 x 82.

f) He wasn't able to sit still.

g) He always manages to draw everything in the right place.

h) He managed to learn Icelandic in a week.

i) He didn't manage to pass his final exams.

▶ page 140 **LANGUAGEBANK**

6 A Read the text below quickly. What does Derek have in common with Daniel Tammet and Stephen Wiltshire?

B Complete the text with the words in the box.

> can   isn't   can't   managed   could   to
> couldn't   able

When four-year-old Derek Paravacini heard the sound of the piano, he ran toward it. Although he was blind, he ¹_____ to reach the instrument. He pushed the piano player—a small girl—off her stool and started to play. Adam Ockleford, a piano teacher, said, "It was … extraordinary. He was hitting the notes with his hands, his feet, his nose, even his elbows." Paravacini was ²_____ to play the tune he had just heard, and, at that moment, Ockleford realized the boy was a genius.

Paravacini was born blind and autistic and had great learning difficulties. As a child, he ³_____ do many things that ordinary children do. Even today, as an adult, he ⁴_____ count to ten, and he ⁵_____ able to dress or feed himself. But Paravacini has one incredible gift: music. Like Mozart, he ⁶_____ remember every piece of music he hears.

It started when his parents gave him a plastic organ when he was eighteen months old. He couldn't see the notes, but he managed ⁷_____ play tunes on it. By the time he was four, he ⁸_____ play many pieces on the piano. With Ockleford's help, Paravacini developed his technique and played his first major concert at the Barbican Hall in London, at age nine. He has performed all over Europe and the U.S. and, in 2006, recorded his first CD.

SPEAKING

7 A Look at the activities in the pictures and read the instructions below.

1 Put one check mark next to the things you can do now.

2 Put two check marks next to the things you could do when you were a child.

3 Put three check marks next to the activities you are very good at.

B Work in groups. Compare your abilities. Say how often you do these things and which of them you enjoy. Describe any special memories you have of any of these activities.

CHANGE THE TIRE ON A CAR

PAINT PICTURES

RUN FOR AN HOUR

Toc! Toc!

Qui est là?

TELL A JOKE IN A FOREIGN LANGUAGE

CLIMB A MOUNTAIN

WRITE WITH YOUR LEFT HAND

REMEMBER IMPORTANT DATES FROM HISTORY

1066 1666
1901 1837

PLAY TENNIS

RIDE A MOTORCYCLE

CATCH AND COOK A FISH

COOK A CHICKEN!

PLAY THE GUITAR

WRITING

A SUMMARY; LEARN TO MAKE NOTES FOR A SUMMARY

8 A When do we **summarize** information? Have you ever written a summary? Why might it be useful to make notes first?

B Read the summary and answer questions 1–3.

> Daniel Tammet and Stephen Wiltshire are two gifted young Englishmen who suffer from forms of autism. These men have one thing in common; they are able to remember large amounts of information. But, their talents are very different. Wiltshire has an ability to draw complicated images after seeing them only once, while Tammet has an amazing aptitude for remembering numbers. They have both appeared on television programs, which helped make them famous, and both have published books. While Tammet and Wiltshire experienced difficulties during their childhood, their great achievements are now recognized by the public. And best of all: they both seem happy with their lives.

1 Does the summary explain the main idea of the text(s) (who, what, where and why)?

2 Is the summary shorter or longer than the original text(s)?

3 Does the writer of the summary copy sentences from the original text(s) or does he/she use his/her own words?

C Work in pairs. Look at phrases 1–5 from the summary. What details do these phrases leave out? What information is missing?

1 Wiltshire has an ability to draw complicated images.

He drew a train station in London and pictures of other cities, including Rome, Hong Kong and New York.

2 Tammet has an amazing aptitude for remembering numbers.

3 They have both appeared on television programs.

4 Both have published books.

5 (They) experienced difficulties during their childhood.

9 A Read the notes and find examples of 1–6 below.

> ▶ **MEMORY MEN**
>
> Tammet & Wiltshire = very gifted. They are able 2 remember lots of info.
> Their Abilities → them becoming famous
> The Artist—Wiltshire remembers <mark>things he sees</mark>
> The Mathematician—Tammet remembers <mark>numbers</mark>, does math problems

1 an abbreviation

2 symbols for: a) *and* b) *resulted in*

3 a number to represent a word that sounds the same

4 a heading

5 a subheading

6 highlighted information

B Are 1–8 good or bad ideas for taking notes? Change the bad ones.

1 Use abbreviations and symbols.

2 Use diagrams or drawings.

3 Try to write down every word you hear/copy down every word you read.

4 Write fast. Don't worry about handwriting.

5 Don't worry about spelling. You can check later.

6 Highlight important information.

7 Don't use your own words—you might make mistakes.

8 Use a space or a new heading for a change of speaker or topic.

10 A Listen. Check (✔) the things in the box they talk about.

> names   faces   dates   words   birthdays   directions to places
> books you've read   places   movies   information about products
> things that happened to you when you were very young   jokes

B Read the notes about Peggy. Listen again and use the same headings to write notes about John and Tim.

> ▶ **PEGGY**
>
> Job—sales rep 4 publishing company
> Memory—needs 2 remember lots not good at directions; used to get lost all the time. has to remember names faces of people + product information

C Compare your notes with a partner. What else can you remember about what they say? Use the phrases below to help you.

> ~~Sally or Samantha?~~   makes mistakes   blocking
> all other students   after an hour of watching a movie

She spent an hour calling a woman Sally when her real name was Samantha.

D Work in pairs. Ask and answer the questions.

1 Do you have a good memory, generally?

2 Which things in Exercise 10A are you good at remembering?

3 Which would you like to be better at remembering?

4 Do you use any special strategies to remember things?

11 A Prepare to talk about an important memory, e.g. a good trip.

B Tell your partner about the memory. He/She takes notes as you speak. Then change roles.

C Write a summary (100–120 words) of what you learned from them.

summarize   summarise

7.3)) ARE YOU QUALIFIED?

F expressing uncertainty

P intonation: showing interest

V describing people

VOCABULARY
QUALIFICATIONS

1 A Work in pairs. What do the words in bold mean? Which words are shown in the photos?

1 What **qualifications** do you have? Apart from tests at school, what other tests have you taken or will you take in the future?

2 In your country, do you get a **certificate** when you leave school?

3 Do you have a **driver's license**? What other **licenses** can you get?

4 Have you ever taken an **online course**?

5 Is **distance learning** popular in your country? Is it more popular than **face-to-face learning**? Which do you prefer?

6 For which professions do you have to do an **apprenticeship**? Does the company usually pay you while you do your training?

7 Do you have a **degree**? From which college?

8 Do you know anyone with an **MA** or a **PhD**? In what subject and from which college did they get it?

B Discuss the questions in groups.

FUNCTION
CLARIFYING OPINIONS

2 A Work in pairs and discuss. Do you think people with a lot of degrees are usually intelligent?

When you are asked about your qualifications, you may be being asked about your skills and experience or about degrees or certificates you've earned.

B Listen to two people discussing intelligence. What do they talk about?

a) intelligent animals

b) intelligent people

c) "intelligent" technology

C Answer the questions. Then listen again to check.

1 Why does the man think the boy from Egypt is intelligent?

2 Why does he think his friend is intelligent? What did the friend do?

3 Why are degrees and certificates useful according to the woman?

4 What else, according to the woman, gives you an education?

3 A Complete the phrases in the table.

Offering Opinions	Giving Examples
The [1]_____ I say (he's intelligent) is (that) ... For me ... In [2]_____ view ... I do think ...	For example, ... Let me [3]_____ you (an/another) example. For [4]_____ thing ...

B STRESS PATTERNS: short phrases Listen to some three-word phrases from Exercise 3A. Which word is stressed?

C Listen to the full sentences. Copy the stress patterns.

▶ page 140 **LANGUAGEBANK**

driver's license driving licence

4 Complete the sentences with the words/phrases in the box. Do you agree with the statements? Use the phrases from 3A to offer your opinions and give examples.

> ~~have to say~~   In my   Let me give   The reason I
> For one   For example   I do   For

1 I _have to_ say many creative people are bad students. _____, most artists and musicians don't have many academic qualifications.

2 _____ me, degrees aren't that important. _____ thing, they don't show a person's character.

3 _____ view, face-to-face learning will disappear. _____ say that is that people want to study from home, so they prefer distance learning.

4 _____ think geniuses often have personal problems. _____ you an example: Van Gogh.

LEARN TO

REFER TO WHAT YOU SAID EARLIER

5 Read the phrases from audio script S7.5 and answer questions 1–3.

a) **Like I said,** he doesn't go to school, but, for me, he's super-intelligent.

b) **Having said that,** I do think degrees are useful.

c) Exactly. **That's what I was saying.** Like the boy from Egypt.

Which phrase shows that you:

1 have already given an opinion that someone else is now giving?

2 have already said something?

3 have said something but now want to give a different opinion?

6 A Complete the conversation using the phrases below.

> Like I said,   That's what I was saying.
> Having said that,

A: I think online classes are great if you can't travel to class. ¹_____ I prefer to have a real teacher.

B: I agree. You learn more with other people in the room.

A: ²_____ an online teacher is not the same.

B: I've taken some online classes, though. It was really convenient because I could study at home.

A: ³_____ They're great for people who can't travel.

B In pairs, practice the dialogue in Exercise 6A. Make sure you stress *said* and *saying* in the referring phrases, for emphasis. Then change roles.

SPEAKING

7 A Read the job advertisement. What type of person would be suitable for the job? Would you like this job? Why?/Why not?

GUIDES NEEDED FOR ECO-TOURS CRUISE SHIPS

▶ **Location:** along the River Nile

▶ **Salary:** $20,000

▶ **Duration:** 6 months (includes four 5-week tours)

Duties: introduce tourists to the plant and animal life of the Nile, organize day trips for tourists, write a blog. Candidate must: speak Arabic, English, plus other language; have tour guide license; have college degree, certificates and/or experience in biology and/or land management.

B Work in groups of three. Students A, B and C: read about your candidate. What benefits can they bring to the job? Are there any requirements they don't meet?

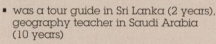

Candidate A
Suresh Perera, Sri Lanka, 42

- was a tour guide in Sri Lanka (2 years), geography teacher in Saudi Arabia (10 years)
- licensed tour guide, MA in Geography
- speaks English, Arabic, Tamil
- knows Egyptian culture and people
- hobbies: sailing and swimming

Candidate B
Dr. Ahmed Nasari, Egypt, 54

- biologist (20 years), experience in 11 countries.
- PhD in marine biology
- wrote 3 books on marine biology, writes for biology journals
- speaks Arabic, English, basic German
- will take tour guide exam next month
- wants to research Nile animal life

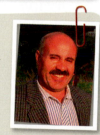

Candidate C
Delilah Olufunwa, Nigeria, 28

- former TV actress and model, then tour guide in Nigeria
- degree in performing arts
- excellent physical fitness (qualified scuba diver, strong swimmer)
- speaks English, Arabic, Spanish, Portuguese, French, is studying Japanese
- loves animals and nature

C Present your candidate to your group. Who should get the job? Why?

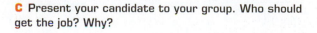

DVD PREVIEW

1 Work in groups. Discuss the questions.

1 Do you enjoy sports? Which ones?

2 Have you ever tried to learn a new sport? How successful were you? Why?

3 Have you ever won a sports competition or attempted a sports challenge? How did you feel?

2 Read the program information. Why is Andy Murray famous? What have been his biggest achievements?

▶ Andy Murray: The Man Behind the Racquet

This documentary follows tennis star Andy Murray, a U.S. Open, Olympic and Wimbledon champion, revealing just what it takes to be a global sports icon. The program looks at Murray's life off the court, filled with commitments and responsibilities. Cameras follow him as he takes an open-top bus ride in his hometown of Dunblane, in Scotland, and as he trains on the court in the U.S. A private and shy man, Murray won the hearts of many with his raw emotion on the court when he lost a Wimbledon final to Roger Federer. However, he later earned his own place in history by winning the U.S. Open, becoming Britain's first male Grand Slam champion in seventy-six years, and then eventually with a spectacular victory at Wimbledon.

DVD VIEW

3 A Watch the DVD. What do you now know about Andy Murray that you didn't know before? Is there anything in the program that surprises you?

B Are the following statements true or false?

1 Andy Murray returns home to find the streets are filled with people to welcome him.

2 Andy left home when he was fifteen years old to move to the U.S. and play tennis.

3 Andy picked up his first tennis racket when he was just three years old. Both he and his brother played tennis and began to win junior tournaments.

4 In Miami, Andy trains for 6–7 hours a day and sometimes with other tennis stars.

5 Andy's friends think he's very serious and not much fun to be around.

C Watch the DVD again to check. Correct any sentences which are false.

4 Discuss.

1 Would you enjoy the life of a professional athlete? Why?/Why not?

2 What do you think it takes to achieve success? Think about a sports, career or other challenge in life.

3 What ambitions do you hope to achieve in your own life? What achievements are you proud of?

Racket   Racquet

American Speakout an achievement

5 A Listen to someone talking about a recent challenge/achievement. Answer the questions.

1 What was her challenge?

2 Was it a good or bad experience?

3 What did she find easy?

4 What problem(s) did she have?

5 Did she succeed?

B Listen again and check (✔) the key phrases you hear.

C You are going to talk about a recent challenge/achievement. Before you talk, make some notes on the following:

• What was your challenge? (Were you learning a new sport/how to drive, etc.?)

• Where were you?

• How did you feel?

• What was the experience like?/What did the challenge involve?

• Who helped you?

• Did you try any special techniques?

• Did you succeed?

D Work in groups and take turns. Tell each other about your experiences. Who had the funniest/most interesting/most embarrassing experience?

writeback an on-line post

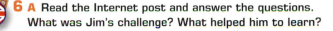

6 A Read the Internet post and answer the questions. What was Jim's challenge? What helped him to learn?

A Beautiful Language

I was never very good at languages when I was at school, so learning Welsh **was a huge challenge for me**. **I wanted to learn** Welsh because I was living in Wales and my wife spoke Welsh. **So, I decided** to enroll at the university and go to classes twice a week. I **soon** fell in love with the language—it's so gentle and musical. **I began to realize** how many people living around me loved and treasured their national language. Welsh has beautiful expressions, and has often been called the language of poets. **It's not an easy** language **to learn**, **but it's very satisfying**. I feel like **I've achieved a lot**. **Now**, when I go into my local store, I try to speak to people in Welsh. I'm sure **I make a lot of mistakes**, but everyone is very kind to me, and they always smile.

B The My Story website publishes stories from the public about their experiences and achievements. Write your own story (120–180 words) to submit to the website. Use the words in bold above and the key phrases to help.

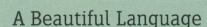
enroll • enrol

V SUCCESS

1 A Underline the correct alternative to complete the quotes. Which quotes do you think could be important for you? Why?

1 "When you are not *believing/practicing*, remember someone else is *believing/practicing*, and, when you meet him, he will win."

2 "I was seldom able to see *an opportunity/a talent* until it had ceased to be one."

3 "Focus *on/in* where you want to go, not on what you fear."

4 "Some people dream of success, while other people wake up and work hard *on/at* it!"

B Work in pairs and discuss.

1 Do you know anyone who is a high achiever? What have they done?

2 What are you focusing on at the moment in your work/studies?

3 How do you think you can get better at speaking English?

G PRESENT PERFECT CONTINUOUS

2 A Complete the sentences with the present perfect continuous form of the verbs in parentheses.

1 I _____ (practice) my lines. Rehearsals start next week.

2 I _____ (visit) patients in their homes.

3 I _____ (grade) homework for hours.

4 I _____ (try) some new ideas for a recipe.

5 I _____ (research) a news story.

B Think of a job to go with each sentence above. Write two or three sentences that this person could say at the end of a busy day. Use the present perfect continuous.

I've been reading all day. I've been saying my lines out loud.

C Work in pairs. Take turns saying your sentences. Can your partner guess the job?

V ABILITY

3 Complete the text with the words in the box.

~~hopeless~~	gifted	skillful
useless	expert	ability	have

As a child, I was [1] *hopeless* in school. I was [2]_____ at math, English, science, everything, because I just didn't [3]_____ an aptitude for schoolwork. One day, we were playing football, and the ball got stuck in a tree. I climbed the tree to get it, and one of my teachers, John Marston, looking out of the window, noticed that I was a talented climber. He was an [4]_____ in climbing—he'd been in the Alps and up Mount Kilimanjaro—and he invited me to try it one weekend. I really enjoyed it. After a month, he told me I was a very [5]_____ climber for my age. I left school three years later with no degree, but I kept climbing regularly until I became very [6]_____ at it. In my early twenties, I became a professional climber. I'll always remember Mr. Marston because he showed me I had an [7]_____ that no one else, including me, knew about.

G PRESENT AND PAST ABILITY

4 A Underline the correct alternative.

1 I *can to/am can/can* type fast.

2 When I first heard English, I *not able/not could/couldn't* understand anything.

3 Even when I'm stressed, I'm usually *able to/can/able* sleep.

4 I recently had a problem, but I *can able to/was able to/not managed* solve it.

5 I *'m not able/was able not/wasn't able* to do the job of my dreams (not yet, anyway).

6 Last weekend, I *managed to/managed/am managed to* relax.

B Check (✔) the sentences that are true for you. Compare your answers with other students.

I can type fast because I don't have to look at the letters when I type.

F CLARIFYING OPINIONS

5 A Read opinions 1—4. Find two mistakes in each.

1 In the my opinion, if you want to be a successful parent, you need to be very patient. The reason for I say this is that parenting is a long process.

2 By my view, if you want to be a world-class athlete, it isn't enough to rely on natural talent. For the one thing, other people will be as gifted as you. For another, you need to focus on your weaknesses.

3 I'm do think some people have an aptitude for learning. Let me give you example: my cousin doesn't work hard, but he gets A's in every subject. He's just a gifted student.

4 I must to say, learning an instrument is good for children. For the example, my friend's daughter has been learning the violin since she was three, and she has amazing discipline and focus.

B Work with a partner. Give your opinions on two of the topics below. Include examples of what you mean.

> Being a Successful Parent
> Becoming Good at a Sport
> Being a Successful Student
> Learning an Instrument

grade / mark

8))) communities

NEIGHBORS p92

MY PLACE IN CYBERSPACE p95

What makes a
good neighbor?

INTERVIEWS

MAKE YOURSELF AT HOME p98

TRIBE p100

G articles and quantifiers
P stress patterns: compound nouns
V getting along; compound nouns

VOCABULARY
GETTING ALONG

1 Work in pairs and discuss.

1 Do you know your neighbors? How well do you know them?

2 Do you have a good relationship with them? Why?

2 A Work in pairs. Match sentences 1—5 with the opposite meanings a)—e).

1 I **get along well with** my neighbor. We always say hello and chat.

2 I prefer to **mind my own business,** so I don't ask the neighbors personal questions.

3 I sometimes **invite** my neighbor **over** for coffee.

4 My neighbor's dog is **a nuisance**; he's always barking early in the morning.

5 We didn't **get to know** our neighbors for years.

a) My neighbor has pets, but they never **disturb** me.

b) My neighbor **gets on my nerves**; he's always complaining.

c) We **made friends with** our neighbors immediately.

d) I like to **keep to myself**, so my neighbor hasn't been in my house.

e) I can be quite **nosy**, so I often ask my neighbors about their lives.

B Which sentences are true for you? Tell other students.

▶ page 155 VOCABULARY**BANK**

GRAMMAR
ARTICLES

3 A Read the paragraph about neighbors. Are you surprised by any of the information? Why?/Why not?

(a) A study says that 24 percent of Americans know most of their neighbors' names. (b) The study was conducted by a group called Pew Research, and (c) a reporter called Aaron Smith wrote a well-known report on the study. It turns out that (d) parents are more likely to speak to neighbors than non-parents and (e) the most common way to interact with neighbors is face-to-face. The results of the study are very different from the figures in (f) England.

B Look at the underlined words and match a)—f) with rules 1—3.

RULES

1 Use *a/an*:

• the first time something is mentioned (new information). *a*

• with jobs. ____

2 Use *the*:

• when we know which one we are talking about. ____

• with superlatives. ____

3 Use no article:

• to talk generally about people or things. ____

• with most names of places. ____

4 Complete the sentences below with *a/an, the* or - (no article).

1 My neighbor has _____ cat that climbs through my window and terrorizes my goldfish.

2 My neighbor is _____ writer. He writes a gossip column, but he keeps to himself.

3 I have _____ nicest neighbor in the world. She invites me over for cake and coffee!

4 _____ People are funny! My neighbor ignored me for years. Now he'll chat all day.

5 My neighbor is _____ old lady who made friends with us as soon as we moved in.

6 My neighbor plays the drums. He's a nice man, but I hate all _____ noise.

7 My neighbor is from _____ Mexico, and she cooks amazing Mexican food.

8 My best friend lives next door. She's _____ plumber.

▶ page 142 LANGUAGE**BANK**

neighbor / keep to myself / terrorize   neighbour / keep myself to myself / terrorise

NEIGHBORS: THE GOOD, THE BAD AND THE BIZARRE

Some people just get lucky. There were the neighborhood friends in the U.S. who turned out to be a long-lost brother and sister. There was the man whose house caught fire and who was saved by his neighbor, who scaled a wall, climbed through a window and beat off smoke to reach the victim. And there are all those tales of people who rescue their neighbor's cat, fight off burglars, or do the shopping for their elderly neighbors.

But there are plenty of bad neighbors, too: people who refuse to repair broken fences, let their cigarette smoke drift into your kitchen, or knock on your door to tell you there's a strange car parked outside (probably your guest's) or to remind you to mow the lawn.

In life's lottery, you can only hope you get the good guys moving in next door. Here are a few of your stories: the good, the bad and the strange neighbors you've had.

My neighbor keeps his yard full of action figures. He has so many that they cover the lawn. He's in his fifties, so I find it very odd, but he's always cheerful and happy, so we have no complaints. **Mary Perlmutter**

I was expecting a problem with my neighbor because I have a tree with branches that hang over their fence. One day they knocked on the door and gave me a huge apple pie that they'd baked. Then they said, "This is made from the apples on your tree! We hope you enjoy it." We've been friends ever since. **Max24**

My neighbor has a steam engine in his garden. I think he was a historian or something like that. He keeps it in excellent condition and lets the local kids play on it. **RGH**

My upstairs neighbors hang their laundry from the windows of their apartment. The clothes drip down onto our laundry because we live below them. So one day the mother came down and suggested that we do our laundry on Mondays and Thursdays and she do hers on Wednesdays and Saturdays. We tried it and it worked perfectly! **Paulina**

My downstairs neighbors have lots of parties on the weekends. I'm half-deaf, but even I can hear the noise. I complained once, so they invited me in. I refused. I'm eighty-three. At my age, I can't dance like I used to. **Vince**

READING

5 A Discuss with other students.

1 What types of things do good neighbors do?

2 What types of things do bad neighbors do?

B Read the text. Are any of your ideas in it?

C Work with a partner. Which of the five stories from the public describe good neighbors? Which describe bad or bizarre neighbors? Which could be more than one?

6 What do you think the following words/expressions mean?

a) long-lost (paragraph 1)
b) scaled a wall (paragraph 1)
c) drift (paragraph 2)
d) mow (paragraph 2)
e) action figures (paragraph 4)
f) steam engine (paragraph 6)

GRAMMAR
QUANTIFIERS

7 A Read sentences a)—f) from the text. Circle the words that describe quantity.

a) My downstairs neighbors have (lots of) parties.

b) But there are plenty of bad neighbors, too.

c) Here are a few of your stories.

d) We have no complaints.

e) There are all those tales of people who rescue their neighbor's cat.

f) He has so many that they cover the lawn.

B Of the words you circled in Exercise 7A, which of them …

1 … mean *a large number/amount*?

2 … mean *a small number/amount*?

3 … means *none*?

4 … can only be used with countable nouns (things we can count)?

▶ page 142 **LANGUAGE**BANK

8 A Circle the correct alternatives.

> **How to Be a Good Neighbor**
>
> If someone moves in next door, introduce yourself. If they're new to the area, they'll probably have [1]*a little/a lot of* questions, e.g., how [2]*much/many* times per week the garbage is collected. Get to know them and give them [3]*a bit/plenty* of information about yourself. If you do [4]*all of/a lot of* gardening or if your kids sometimes make too [5]*much/many* noise, let them know. Some families have [6]*several/plenty* pets. Dogs can be noisy, and cats sometimes wander into neighbors' yards or homes. If it happens only [7]*a few/little* times, that's OK, but if it happens [8]*a lot/much*, it's a problem. People who say they never have [9]*much/many* trouble with their neighbors are usually good communicators. It's easy: tell them about community news and events. Tell them beforehand about your parties. Or, better still, invite them!
> If they're partying with you, will they complain about the noise? [10]*None!/No!*

B Do you agree with the advice? What else makes a good neighbor?

> You might rent an apartment in the U.S. or let a flat in the U.K. or pick a duplex or rowhouse in Philadelphia, but a semi-detached or terraced house in Manchester.

yard / apartment / garbage garden / flat / rubbish

SPEAKING

9 A Work in pairs. What features where you live do you like/dislike? Use the photos below to help you. Make notes about the following:

• things you like

a beautiful city center with lots of trees and parks

• things that are nice but not essential

a good local supermarket

• things you hate

graffiti on the buildings

B Think about your neighborhood. What would make it:

• more beautiful?
• better for your health?
• more interesting?
• safer?
• more of a community?

I'd really like to see a good shopping mall where people can meet.

My neighborhood would be healthier if there were less traffic congestion in the mornings.

C Compare your ideas in groups.

VOCABULARY *PLUS*
COMPOUND NOUNS

10 A Read sentences 1—4 about local features. Find and underline a compound noun in each sentence.

1 I live next to the <u>main road</u>, so it's a bit noisy.
2 There's a wonderful bookstore near where I live.
3 There's a nice public swimming pool by my house, and it's free for children.
4 Where I live is good for window shopping, but too expensive to buy anything!

B Match the compound nouns in Exercise 10A with patterns a)—d) below.

a) noun + noun   **c)** verb + noun

b) adjective + noun   **d)** noun + verb

> **American Speak out TIP**
> Compound nouns combine two related words. The first word gives us more information about the second, e.g., *shoe store, history teacher, paper bag*. What other words make compound nouns with *store, teacher* and *bag*? Compound nouns can be written as one word, two words or with a hyphen. Use a dictionary to check.

11 A Which words complete these compound nouns?

1 _____ ⎡ jam
        ⎣ lights

2 _____ ⎡ accident
        ⎣ rental

3 _____ ⎡ center
        ⎣ mall

4 super ⎤
  outdoor ⎦ _____

5 elementary ⎤
  language ⎦ _____

6 sports ⎤ _____
  city ⎦

7 main ⎡ _____
  one-way ⎣

8 dream ⎡ _____
  brick ⎣

9 business ⎤ _____
  industrial ⎦

10 duty-free ⎤ _____
  gift ⎦

B STRESS PATTERNS: COMPOUND NOUNS Listen to check your answers. Then think about the stress patterns. Which word is usually stressed: the first or the second? Listen again to check.

C Discuss. Think about the place where you are studying now. Which of the compound nouns does it have nearby?

▶ page 155 **VOCABULARY**BANK

city center, downtown / bookstore /
shoe store / main street

city centre / bookshop
shoe shop / high street

8.2)) MY PLACE IN CYBERSPACE

G relative clauses
P pausing for effect
V the internet

VOCABULARY

THE INTERNET

1 **A** Work in groups. Look at the picture. Which type of website would you use to:

1 find out what is happening in the world?

2 plan a vacation?

3 contact friends?

4 show your vacation pictures?

5 meet the partner of your dreams?

6 show your wedding video?

7 find out whether a new movie or book is good?

8 find out about a big company?

9 share facts about yourself?

10 read and write opinions about anything and everything?

11 read or write factual information about a topic?

12 find information quickly?

B Rank these types of websites in order of importance for you. Which are the five most important? Which are the two least important? Compare your lists with other students.

LISTENING

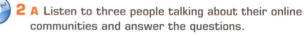

2 **A** Listen to three people talking about their online communities and answer the questions.

1 What does Speaker 1 use her website for?

2 What does she put on the website during "a gig" (a concert)?

3 What does Speaker 2 write for his blog?

4 Why does he use Instagram?

5 What does Speaker 3 say is "probably one of the best uses" of Facebook?

6 What does he like most about Facebook?

B Work in pairs. Listen to each speaker again. When the speaker finishes, take turns using the words and phrases below to explain what the speakers say.

Speaker 1: band promote newsletters photos share reach thousands

Speaker 2: food blog review restaurants photos Instagram different dishes 2,000

Speaker 3: work from home stay in touch parties blanket invitation phone calls family photographs

3 Discuss the questions.

1 Do you think websites are real communities?

2 What are the benefits of online communities?

3 Are there any dangers or problems in spending a lot of time in online communities?

GRAMMAR
RELATIVE CLAUSES

4 Do you know how YouTube started? Read about its origins. Why did it become successful?

The Rise and Rise of YouTube

In 2005, three friends, Chad Hurley, Steve Chen and Jawed Karim, who were also colleagues, were having problems trying to email a video clip. Within two hours, they came up with an idea that would solve the problem and change Internet history. They created YouTube. It's a familiar story for anyone who follows the development of the Internet: technology-minded entrepreneurs under thirty, a garage or bedroom where dreams become reality, little money and a big need. The site was an instant success. The key was a number of features: links to the videos, which made them easy to email; tell-a-friend functions; a feature that allowed YouTube videos to be played on social networking sites; and another feature that let users comment. This helped to develop a community: YouTube was a place where you posted videos but also chatted about them. Two years after the launch, Google Inc. bought YouTube for $1.65 billion.

5 A Look at the underlined clauses in the sentences below. Which contains essential information? Which contains extra, non-essential information?

a) Chad Hurley, Steve Chen and Jawed Karim, <u>who were colleagues</u>, were having problems trying to email a video clip.

b) YouTube was a place <u>where you posted videos</u>.

B Read rules 1 and 2 to check your answers. Then complete rule 3 with *which*, *who*, *where* and *that*.

<table>
<tr><td rowspan="1">**RULES**</td><td>

1 Defining (essential) relative clauses tell us exactly which thing, person or place we are talking about.

2 Non-defining (non-essential) relative clauses add extra information to a sentence. They tell us what a thing, person or place is or does. The sentence is still grammatically possible without the extra information.

3 _____ is used to talk about places.

_____ is used to talk about people.

_____ is used to talk about things.

_____ can be used to talk about places, people or things (in defining relative clauses only).

</td></tr>
</table>

C Read the text in Exercise 4A again. Find and underline eight relative clauses. What type of relative clauses are they: defining (D) or non-defining (ND)?

▶ page 142 LANGUAGE**BANK**

---

6 A Circle the correct alternatives to complete the text.

For people who liked to send and receive very short messages, Twitter.com was a dream come true. This social networking site, [1]*that/which was/who was* the fastest growing site in 2009, became amazingly popular in a short space of time. So how does it work? You write your message, [2]*of which must be/what must be/which must be* no longer than 140 characters, onto your profile via a web, SMS or phone application. Then the message, [3]*what is called/this is called/which is called* a "tweet," is sent automatically to your subscribers or "followers." The people [4]*use/that use/who use* Twitter say it's fantastic. Jerry Jones, [5]*who works for/who works where/which works for* an Internet company, describes it as "a mini-revolution." He says that when Twitter arrived it was the moment [6]*which online/for online/when online* communication changed. No more boring blogs, [7]*what go/where people go/who people go* on and on about nothing. "Me and my friends, [8]*who all use/all use/we use* Twitter, have a saying: Keep your tweet short and sweet!"

B Discuss the questions.

1 Do you or does anyone you know use Twitter?
2 What social networking websites do you know?
3 Which are the most popular now?

 7 A PAUSING FOR EFFECT Listen for the pauses where there are commas. Check (✔) the sentence you hear.

1 a) The travel site that we developed is really popular.
   b) The travel site, which we developed, is really popular.

2 a) Those children who spend too much time on the Internet don't communicate well.
   b) Those children, who spend too much time on the Internet, don't communicate well.

3 a) Video sharing sites that are free are a great resource for students.
   b) Video sharing sites, which are free, are a great resource for students.

4 a) On that dating site where I met my wife there are hundreds of single people.
   b) On that dating site, where I met my wife, there are hundreds of single people.

B Work in pairs. Take turns choosing a sentence from Exercise 7A and read it aloud. Your partner says which sentence you read, a) or b).

Go

http://www

a) Say the purpose of the website. _____

b) Say whom you'd recommend the website to. _____

c) Introduce the name of the website. _____

d) Say what special features the website has. _____

C Find and underline three phrases we use to recommend something.

10 A Compare the pairs of sentences. Which sounds more fluent: a) or b)?

1 a) It's a website. You can use it to find magazine articles. The articles are on lots of different topics.

   b) It's a website that you can use to find magazine articles on lots of different topics.

2 a) I know several journalists. They use magportal. com. They use it for research.

   b) I know several journalists who use magportal. com for research.

American Speak out TIP

Think about using complex sentences. Simple sentences can be effective, but when we use many simple sentences together, it sounds childish: *I swim every day. I love the water. It's good exercise.* We can make sentences more complex by using conjunctions (*and, because, but,* etc.) and relative clauses: *I swim every day **because** I love the feel of the water, **and** it's **also** good exercise.* How have the b) sentences in Exercise 10A been made more complex?

SPEAKING

8 Look at the activities in the box below. Do you prefer doing them online or in the real world? What are the advantages/disadvantages of doing them online? Discuss your opinions with other students.

I prefer to do my shopping online because it's convenient and easy.

do my shopping	meet new people	find out the news
learn a language	reserve flights/hotels	
watch movies/programs	speak to friends	
look up information	explore new places	

WRITING

A WEBSITE REVIEW; LEARN TO USE COMPLEX SENTENCES

9 A Read the website review and answer the questions.

1 What type of website is it?

2 Why does the writer recommend it?

3 Who uses the website? Why?

Archive ▼

Website of the Month for January is **magportal.com**. It's a website that you can use to find magazine articles on lots of different topics. One reason I'd recommend it is the range of subjects, which include health, finance, entertainment, science and technology, sports and even pets and animals.

The best thing about magportal.com is that the design is very simple, which makes it really easy to use. There's a menu of categories and a search engine if you want something specific. Another excellent feature is that you can get articles by typing the date—the most recent ones are shown first—or the name of a specific magazine.

I know several journalists who use magportal.com for research. I suggest that readers try it out; there's something for everyone.

B Rewrite sentences 1—4 to make them sound more fluent.

1 The website is well-designed. The good design makes it user-friendly.

2 The site has too much animation. This makes it very slow. It takes a long time to upload.

3 The website's content comes from its users. Users send in their photos.

4 The site feels friendly. It has user profile areas. Here, users can say who they are.

C Work in pairs and compare your answers.

11 A What is your "Website of the Month"? Choose a website and think about the questions below.

1 What type of website is it (photo sharing, social networking, etc.)?

2 Why do you like it?

3 How often do you visit it?

4 Is there a community of users?

5 Whom would you recommend it to?

B Write your review (120—150 words). Show it to other students. Which websites sound interesting to you?

8.3)) MAKE YOURSELF AT HOME

F being a good guest
P linking words
V welcoming

VOCABULARY
WELCOMING

1 A Read situations a)–f). What expressions might we use in these situations?

a) You are apologizing for how your home (or office) looks.

I'm sorry about all the mess!

b) You know someone is tired and you want them to relax.

c) You are inviting someone to sit down, maybe at work.

d) You want someone to feel relaxed in your house.

e) You give permission for someone to use something that is yours.

f) You are offering someone food.

B Match phrases 1–6 to situations a)–f).

1 Make yourself at home.

2 Excuse the mess.

3 Be my guest.

4 Help yourself.

5 Have a seat.

6 Put your feet up.

 C LINKING WORDS Listen to the phrases and notice how words ending in a consonant sound (e.g., /f/) link together with words beginning with a vowel sound (e.g., /æ/ or /ə/), so there is no pause between them. Then listen and repeat.

Make yourself_at home.

*yoursel **f**at home*

 D Listen to the conversations. Listen again and repeat the final line.

FUNCTION
BEING A GOOD GUEST

2 A Work in pairs. Discuss the questions.

1 When was the last time you were a guest? What was the situation?

2 When was the last time you had a guest? Was he or she a good guest? Why?/Why not?

3 What types of things do good and bad guests do in your country?

 B Listen to six situations. Which speakers did something wrong? Which speakers are asking for advice?

C Listen again and complete the notes below.

1 She says her family doesn't …

2 He wants to know if he should bring …

3 He should come back in …

4 She forgot to take …

5 In the restaurant you have to …

6 It's Thanksgiving, but her family doesn't eat …

3 Look at the phrases in the table and check (✔) the ones you heard in the conversations in Exercise 2. Read audio script S8.6 on page 172 to check.

Asking for Advice	
Question	**Answer**
Is it OK if I (do this)?	Yes, of course./No, you'd better not. It's considered a bit rude.
What should we do (in this situation)?	If I were you, I'd …
Do I need to (take a dish)?	Yes, you should./No, it's not necessary.
Did I do something wrong?	No, of course not./It's OK. We can sort it out./Don't worry about it.
Is this a bad time? I can come back later.	Can you come back in ten minutes?/Not at all. It's fine.
Apologizing	
Sorry about that. I didn't know …	
My apologies. I didn't know …	

▶ page 142 **LANGUAGE**BANK

LEARN TO
ACCEPT APOLOGIES

 4 A Listen to the extracts from the six situations. Number the phrases a)–f) in the order you hear them.

a) It's no problem.

b) Not at all.

c) That's all right. *1*

d) You really don't have to …

e) It's fine.

f) It's nothing.

B Work in pairs. Read situations 1–4 below and take turns apologizing and accepting the apology.

1 You agreed to meet your partner for dinner. You are thirty minutes late.

2 You accidentally wake up your partner by singing loudly. You didn't know he/she was asleep.

3 You borrowed your partner's book. You accidentally tore one of the pages.

4 You are buying something in a store. You accidentally walk in front of your partner because you didn't realize there was a line.

SPEAKING

5 A Read the situations. Have you experienced any of these? Work in pairs and discuss what you would do/say.

Situation 1

A friend of a friend is visiting your town and staying with you for a week. You don't know her, and she is from a different culture. You want to give her a warm welcome, but you are not sure how to greet her, what food and drinks to offer, or what activities to recommend while she is visiting. You phone your friend to ask for advice.

Situation 2

You are staying with a host family abroad. The family seemed nice at first, but now there are some problems and they don't talk to you much. You want to study, but the family is very noisy. They smoke inside even though you asked for a non-smoking house. In the morning, there is never any hot water left for your shower. You decide to talk to the mother of the family.

Situation 3

You are a vegetarian. You were invited to a barbecue at your boss's house. When you get there, your boss gives you a large plate of meat to eat. You do not want to offend your boss and her family by not eating their food. A close friend/colleague is at the barbecue, and you decide to ask for his advice.

B Choose one of the situations. Use the flow chart below to plan and role-play your own situation.

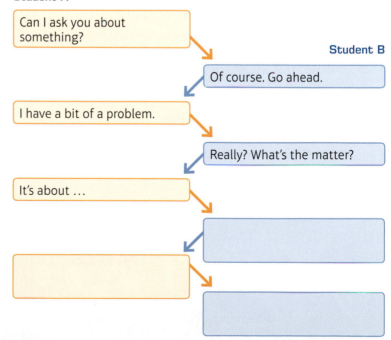

Student A

Can I ask you about something?

Student B

Of course. Go ahead.

I have a bit of a problem.

Really? What's the matter?

It's about …

C Now choose a second situation from Exercise 5A and role-play that situation.

DVD PREVIEW

1 A Work in groups. Look at the photos. Where do you think this is? What do you think life is like for people on an island like this? Do you think their lives are changing in today's modern world?

B Read the program information. What does Bruce Perry hope to learn from visiting the tribe?

▶ Tribe: Anuta

Tribe is a TV program in which host Bruce Parry goes to some of the world's most isolated places. In this episode, he goes to the Pacific island of Anuta, one of the most remote communities on Earth. There, he learns about its traditions and discovers how the community survives. There are just twenty-four families on Anuta. Bruce meets them all and experiences how their customs help to bind the people together.

2 What do you think the words in the box mean? Match them with definitions 1–6.

> tribe   isolated   remote   customs   survive
> bind (people together)

1 form a strong connection between people
2 continue to live normally even when there are great problems
3 something that people in a particular society do because it is traditional
4 a group of people with the same race, language and customs who live together in the same area
5 far away from other places (can also describe a person who is lonely and can't meet other people)
6 far away from other places (usually used to describe places)

DVD VIEW

3 Watch the DVD and number the scenes in the correct order.

a) Bruce meets the children.
b) Bruce meets the community leaders.
c) Bruce catches a fish.
d) Bruce helps to repair a wall in the water.
e) Bruce arrives on the island.   *1*
f) Bruce says "I'm in Paradise."

4 A Circle the correct answer, a) or b).

1 When visitors arrive in Anuta, what must they do?
   a) Shake everyone's hand.
   b) Bring gifts to the community leaders.
2 What do the community leaders tell Bruce?
   a) Their island is like Paradise, and he is welcome.
   b) He can stay on Anuta.
3 What happens during a "community fish drive"?
   a) The men catch fish, and the women cook.
   b) Everyone in the community helps to catch fish.
4 What do they do with the fish?
   a) They put them in a pile together.
   b) Everyone takes home only the fish they caught.

B Watch the DVD again to check.

5 Discuss the questions.

1 Do you think it is good that Bruce visited Anuta? Why/Why not?
2 Would you like to visit this place? Why?/Why not?
3 Can the modern world learn anything from places like Anuta?

American Speakout design a community

6 A Read the paragraph from a news report. What is going to happen? Why?

> Mohamed Nasheed, the new President of the Maldives, has a very difficult task: to find a place for the population to live. Most of the two hundred inhabited islands of the Maldives are about three feet above sea level. Scientists have explained that, in the future, the Maldives will be underwater because of global warming. No one will be able to live there, and nothing will remain.

B What would you do if you had to start a new community? Think about the questions below.

1 Where would it be?
2 Who would live there? Would it be a large or small community?
3 What laws would there be?
4 What type of government would the community have?
5 What special customs would there be? How would these bind the community together?

7 A Listen to two people discussing the first three questions above. What do they decide for each question?

B Listen again. Check (✔) the key phrases that you hear.

> **KEYPHRASES**
>
> I'd probably choose …
>
> I'd go for a place that …
>
> It'd need to be somewhere …
>
> They'd need to be able to …
>
> The most important thing would be …
>
> Ideally, there would be …

8 Work in pairs and plan your community. Present your ideas to another pair.

writeback a web ad

9 A Read about a project that was the subject of a documentary. What type of community is it?

> Tribewanted is a community tourism project on Vorovoro Island, Fiji. The members of Tribewanted work with the local people to build a village community. This community combines Fijian traditions with international ideas for environmentally-friendly living. Visitors can stay between one and twelve weeks. While there, visitors work on projects, look after the gardens on the island, feed the pigs and chickens, help with the construction of buildings and write for the Tribewanted blog. They can also learn Fijian songs, relax in a hammock, and enjoy the incredible sunsets and ocean. It is the adventure of a lifetime.

B You are recruiting people for the Tribewanted project. Write a web ad for people to apply. Use the key phrases and the prompts below.

- Amazing opportunity for adventurers!
- We are looking for …
- We need people who …
- We also want people who are able to …
- Your responsibilities on the island will include …
- The community is special because …
- The community will …
- By the end of your stay, you will …
- Please send …
- Interviews will be …
- Other information …

V GETTING ALONG

1 A Use words to make phrases connected with "getting along." You can use the words more than once in any order.

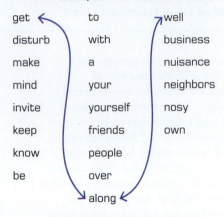

get	to	well
disturb	with	business
make	a	nuisance
mind	your	neighbors
invite	yourself	nosy
keep	friends	own
know	people	
be	over	
	along	

B Use the phrases to write four questions to ask other students.

Do you get along well with your boss?

G ARTICLES AND QUANTIFIERS

2 A Choose the correct option, a), b) or c), to complete the text.

For sixteen weeks, the only thing we saw was [1]_____ ocean. One night, fifty miles from [2]_____ Solomon Islands, [3]_____ storm hit us, and [4]_____ ship swayed like a drunk soldier. [5]_____ of the sailors were washed into the ocean, and [6]_____ of us were exhausted. The next day, we found a hundred fish on the deck, a [7]_____ of them still alive, mouths open. We ate them with a [8]_____ bread and salt. A week later, we were attacked by pirates. They didn't kill anyone, but they stole [9]_____ our food. The captain said there was [10]_____ for one week, and we were two weeks away from land.

1 a) a   b) the   c) —
2 a) a   b) the   c) —
3 a) a   b) the   c) —
4 a) a   b) the   c) —
5 a) Little   b) Few   c) Some
6 a) little   b) much   c) all
7 a) plenty   b) few   c) all
8 a) little   b) lot   c) few
9 a) a lot of   b) many   c) lots
10 a) plenty of   b) too   c) enough

B Re-read the story. What do you think happens next? Tell other students.

V THE INTERNET

3 A Complete the questions with the words in the box.

sites	blog	search	travel
video	networking		

1 Have you ever planned a vacation using a _____ site? Was it a success?

2 Do you ever use _____ sharing sites, like YouTube? Do you have a favorite clip?

3 What _____ engine do you usually use? Do you know others, apart from Google?

4 Do you like social _____ sites? Do you ever get bored with them?

5 Have you ever contributed to a _____ ? What was the topic, and what did you write?

6 What do you think of dating _____ ? Do you know anyone who uses them?

B Work in pairs. Ask and answer the questions.

G RELATIVE CLAUSES

4 A Underline the correct alternative.

1 _____ is *which/when/that* four wolves and a lamb vote on what to have for lunch.

2 _____ is a place *that/how/ where* animals study humans.

3 _____ is a ship *who/what/that* is big enough for two people in good weather but only one person in bad weather.

4 _____ is the hour *where/which/ when* the traffic stops.

5 _____ is a man *whose/where/ who* has stopped thinking.

6 _____ is a person *who/whose/ which* job is to lend you an umbrella when the sun is shining and take it back when it rains.

B What or whom do sentences 1–6 describe? Complete the sentences with the words in the box.

rush hour	an expert
a banker	friendship
a zoo	democracy

5 Work in pairs. Look at the list below and take turns defining things. Your partner guesses what/who you defined.

- a person in the room
- an object in your bag
- a room in the building
- a famous book or movie
- a famous singer
- an object on the table
- a town or city
- a person in the news

He's the singer who …

F BEING A GOOD GUEST

6 A Match comments/questions 1–5 with responses a)–e).

1 Did I do something wrong?

2 Sorry about that. I didn't know that was the boss's chair.

3 My apologies. I didn't realize I had to shake everybody's hand.

4 Is this a bad time? I can come back another time.

5 Do I need to bring gifts?

a) No, it's not necessary. We don't expect them in our country.

b) Don't worry about it. She didn't mind at all.

c) No problem. You said hello to everybody, so that's OK.

d) Can you come back tomorrow? I'm busy for the rest of the day.

e) Yes, you did. No one talks during the national anthem, but don't worry. We can sort it out.

B Work in pairs. Cover responses a)–e). Take turns reading the comments/questions in 1–5 and replying with the correct response or one of your own.

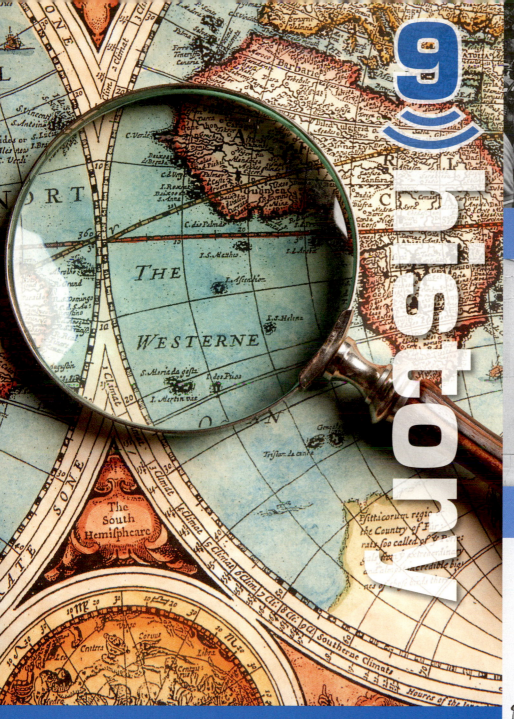

9 History

GIANT LEAPS

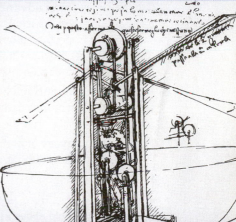

IN OUR TIME

I HAVE NO IDEA!

Do you think life is better now than in the past?

INTERVIEWS

MICHELANGELO

9.1)) GIANT LEAPS

G hypothetical conditional: past
P word stress: contractions
V history

VOCABULARY
HISTORY

1 A Work in pairs. What do you think are the three most important events in history? Which important developments are shown in the photos?

B Read the comments below. Are any of your ideas mentioned?

> 66 A lot of **revolutions** have been important. For example, the Industrial Revolution was a great **turning point** in history. 99

> 66 The **development** of the Internet. The **spread** of the net has been so fast. 99

> 66 For me, the greatest **advances** in history have been about social justice. There have been some really important **movements**, such as the Civil Rights Movement. These have made the world a better place. 99

> 66 I'd choose the **invention** of the wheel. It's the **foundation** of most transportation and machines. 99

> 66 Maybe the **discovery** of fire? I think it was the most important thing in human beings' **progress**. 99

C Put the words in bold above in the definitions below.

1 A moment of great change: *revolution* _____
2 When someone makes or finds something new: *development* _____ _____
3 Something getting better: *advance* _____
4 When a group of people work to achieve an aim, e.g., human rights: _____
5 The basic idea behind something: _____
6 When something increases and affects more people: _____

D WORD STRESS Listen to the answers to exercise 1C. Circle the stressed syllable in each word. Listen again and repeat.

E Complete sentences 1–5 in any way you choose. Compare with other students.

1 The biggest turning point in my country's history was ...
2 A discovery that changed my life is ...
3 My favorite invention is ...
4 One thing I hope won't spread is ...
5 My country has made progress in ...

▶ page 156 VOCABULARYBANK

READING

2 A Read the introduction to an article from *BBC History Magazine*. What "alternative moments" do you think the historians will choose?

> *Giant Leaps for Mankind* looks at why we should be celebrating the moon landing of July 1969 and asks twelve historians to nominate alternative moments in the past that they consider to be giant leaps for mankind.

B Student A: read the texts on page 105, and make notes using the prompts below. Student B: turn to page 162.

• What was the development?
• Where did it take place?
• When did it happen?
• Why was it important?

3 A Work in pairs. Cover your texts. Look at the notes you made in Exercise 2B. Take turns telling each other what you read. As you listen, make more notes.

B Work in pairs and answer the questions.

1 Which two books helped the spread of new developments?
2 Which advances help us to study things?
3 Which developments happened mainly because of one person? Which happened because of many people?

C Which of the four big moments did you know about? Which do you think are the two most important?

Galileo Explores the Heavens

When Galileo became the first person to look at the sky through a telescope, it changed our view of the universe. His discoveries about the sun, moon and other planets disagreed with older theories because he claimed that Earth revolved around the sun and was not the center of the universe. He then wrote a book, *Two World Systems*, published in Italy in 1630, which led to his problems with the Roman Catholic Church, which insisted on the older theory. At his trial, Galileo was found guilty of heresy (anti-religious beliefs). It was only in the twentieth century that the Vatican finally agreed with him. If Galileo hadn't defended his theories, he would have been a free man, but we wouldn't have understood the science of our universe.

The Steam Engine

For most of human history we were not very different from other animals that also communicate, act as a group and have organizational systems. But the steam engine gave us the ability to do things faster and to do things that other animals couldn't. This development, which took place in Britain in the 18th century, was not one invention, but many. Different people were involved at different stages: Thomas Newcomen, James Watt and George Stephenson. The steam engine allowed us to transform the way we use energy. It changed so many things, including transportation, manufacturing and communication. Life would have been totally different if we hadn't invented it.

GRAMMAR
HYPOTHETICAL CONDITIONAL: PAST

4 A Read the sentences below. Do they describe an imaginary situation in the past or an imaginary situation in the present?

1 If he hadn't written *Doctrinale*, education would have remained the same.

2 If Galileo hadn't defended his theories, he would have been a free man.

B Look at the sentence patterns and find one other example in the texts.

If + subject	had(n't) + past participle		would(n't) + have + past participle	
If we	had invented	the wheel earlier, life	would have been	easier.
	hadn't discovered	fire, man's progress		slower.

C Read two more sentences from the article. How is the grammatical structure different from the sentences in Exercise 4A?

1 We wouldn't have become the most imaginative of the animals if we had continued eating only plants.

2 Life would have been different if we hadn't invented the steam engine.

▶ page 144 LANGUAGE**BANK**

5 A Complete the sentences with the correct form of the verbs in parentheses.

1 Machu Picchu _____ (remain) unknown if Hiram Bingham _____ (not explore) the Andes in Peru.

2 If the "I love you" virus _____ (be) found earlier, forty-five million computers _____ (not crash) in 2000.

3 The development of modern medicine _____ (be) different if Alexander Fleming _____ (not discover) penicillin.

4 If John Lennon _____ (not meet) Paul McCartney, they _____ (not form) the Beatles.

5 The invention of the cell phone _____ (not be) possible if Alexander Graham Bell _____ (not invent) the telephone.

6 If the Nestor Film Company _____ (not open) a film studio there in 1911, Hollywood _____ (remain) a quiet town.

B Listen and check your answers.

C WORD STRESS: contractions Listen again and repeat. How are *had, hadn't, would* and *wouldn't have* pronounced in fast speech?

6 Work in pairs. Make a note of three things that have happened to you in the last year. Show your partner. Write sentences about how your partner's life would have been different if these things hadn't happened.

I got a new job.

If Marcela hadn't gotten a new job, she wouldn't have bought her house.

SPEAKING

7 A Work in pairs. You are going to describe a big moment in history. Choose an important historical event. If you need help, Student A: turn to page 163. Student B: turn to page 162.

hadn't gotten   hadn't got

WRITING

A SHORT ESSAY; LEARN TO STRUCTURE PARAGRAPHS

8 Read the short essay below and answer the question. What does the writer think would have happened if China had reached the Americas before the Europeans?

WHAT IF ... Chinese explorers had landed in the Americas first?

At one time, China led the world in technology. Centuries before Europe, the Chinese had printing and gunpowder. They also had the compass, which meant they could navigate without relying on the position of the moon. Furthermore, they were brilliant shipbuilders. This ability to build large, strong ships went hand in hand with their other talent: exploration.

In 1405, a Chinese explorer named Zheng He went on a journey. The idea was to create new trade routes for China. On his first trip, he took 28,000 men in 62 ships. Zheng He landed in India and brought home many things that were new to the Chinese: plants, animals, even people.

Zheng He made seven westward journeys. If he had continued to explore, he would probably have reached the Americas before Columbus and the Europeans. However, for political reasons, China stopped exploring. Its leaders believed that China didn't need to trade with other nations, so the country became isolated.

Now, let's imagine Zheng He had reached the Americas first. What would have happened? He would have seen the incredible size of the country and the riches in the ground. He probably would have returned with more men and maybe gone to war with Native Americans in order to steal their land. If the Chinese had won, they would have become rich. The new Chinese colony would have grown and grown, and perhaps they would have later spread to other lands.

Would China have created the next great empire if Chinese explorers had landed in the Americas first? We will never know.

9 Work in pairs. Put the six stages of essay writing in order.

a) Write a second, final draft. _____

b) Proofread before you submit your work. Look for errors in grammar, spelling and punctuation. _____

c) Look carefully at the task/title you are given. What do you need to do: analyze, compare, argue? _____

d) Check that the sections of the first draft are well organized. Think about how you can reorganize any unclear parts. _____

e) Brainstorm ideas. Write down lots of thoughts quickly, and don't worry if they are not all good ideas. _____

f) Write a first draft quickly—it doesn't have to be perfect. _____

10 A Read the paragraph below. Then read the key.

Chinese ships were extremely advanced compared to ships in other parts of the world. First, they were larger; the biggest was 400 feet long and weighed 1,500 tons. They were also better designed; unlike European ships at the time, they had rooms that were "watertight"—water could not get inside them. What's more, Chinese ships had better equipment: they all had compasses, which meant the sailors would never get lost.

Key:

◯ = linking words

▬ = topic sentence

▬ = supporting sentence 1

▬ = supporting sentence 2

▬ = supporting sentence 3

B Complete statements 1–3 using the labels from the key.

1 Each paragraph should have a _____ _____ that explains the main idea. Often this is the first sentence.

2 Each paragraph needs several _____ _____ to provide examples that illustrate the main idea.

3 The examples should connect well, using _____ _____.

C Look at the essay in Exercise 8 again. Use the labels in **10A** (*linking words, topic sentence,* etc.) to label the first paragraph of the essay.

11 A Read instructions 1–4 for a *What if ... ?* essay.

1 Choose an important development in history: an invention, a discovery or an event.

2 Think about the world without this development. How would life be different? How would people's ideas or actions be different? Brainstorm ideas.

3 Plan and write your essay.

4 When you finish, follow the instructions in the Speakout Tip.

> **American Speakout TIP**
> **1** Check the "big" things first: did you answer the question in the title? Are the paragraphs in the right order? Is there anything missing?
> **2** Check the "little" things second: grammar, spelling, punctuation, missing words.

B Exchange your essay with another student and check each other's work.

9.2)) IN OUR TIME

GRAMMAR
ACTIVE VERSUS PASSIVE

1 Look at the picture. When do you think it was taken? What do you think life was like for these people compared to the way young people live now?

Maybe the picture is from the 1960s. They probably had more fun than young people now.

2 A Read the paragraph and choose the best title.

1 The Best Time to Live
2 How the Young Found Their Voice
3 New Generations, New Names

After World War II, a generation was born that has come to be known as Baby Boomers. They are thought to be healthier, wealthier and more optimistic than any previous generation. They were followed by Generation X, a name that was invented by photographer Robert Capa. Generation X includes people born between the mid-60s and the early 80s. This generation is sometimes called the MTV Generation because it supposedly grew up watching music videos. Generation X is known for entrepreneurship and open-mindedness in regard to race, gender, class, and religion. Following Generation X is Generation Y or Millennials, who were born between the early 1980s and 2000. They are known for being confident, informal and desperate to share their lives with others via social networking. They arrived at a time of great technological change and are perhaps the first generation that is being educated for jobs that may not exist at the moment.

B Read the extracts from the text and do questions 1–3.

a) They are thought to be healthier ... than any previous generation.

b) This generation ... grew up watching music videos.

c) [This] generation has come to be known as Baby Boomers.

d) They arrived at a time of great technological change.

e) The first generation that is being educated ...

1 Underline the verbs in each sentence.

2 Three of the sentences don't say who "did" the action (because we don't know or it's not important). Which three?

3 Which sentences use active verbs? Which use the passive?

C Look at the sentences again. Complete the rule.

> **RULES**
>
> We form the passive with: subject + the verb _____ (in the present, past or other tense) + past participle.

D Find other examples of the passive in the text.

▶ page 144 LANGUAGE BANK

3 A Rewrite the sentences below using the passive.

1 Douglas Coupland made the name Generation X famous through his novel *Generation X: Tales for an Accelerated Culture*.

The name Generation X was made famous by Coupland's novel.

2 Sometimes the media invent names for different generations.

3 *Newsweek* magazine used the term Generation 9/11 in 2001.

4 Someone gave the people growing up after the war the name "Baby Boomers."

5 In the future, people will know today's babies as Generation Z.

6 William Strauss and Neil Howe wrote a book about Millennials (*Millennials Rising: The Next Great Generation*).

7 Sometimes people call the generation born from 1910 to 1920 "The Greatest Generation."

8 Older people have always criticized younger people for their bad behavior!

B WEAK FORMS: *are, has been, was* and *were*
Listen and check your answers.

C Listen again and notice the pronunciation of *are* /ɑr/, *has been* /həzbɪn/, *was* /wʌz/ and *were* /wɜr/. Then listen and repeat.

D Discuss with other students. What do you think of the idea of different generations? Are there real differences between them? Give examples.

criticize • criticise

LISTENING

4 A Listen to three people speaking about different decades. Which decades did they grow up in? Generally, do they feel positive or negative about those decades?

> **American Speak TIP** Before listening, read the task. What are the most important words? Listen for those words and for their synonyms, or words with a similar meaning. For example: *Americans* = people from the United States; *films* = movies; *environmental problems* = pollution and the hole in the ozone layer; *fashion* = clothes/hairstyles. Read the task in Exercise 4B and listen for the key words and synonyms.

B Listen again and answer the questions.

1 What "two important aspects" of his life does Speaker 1 mention?

2 What "celebrations" do you think Speaker 1 is talking about?

3 Where is Speaker 2 from?

4 Which musician was "an icon" for Speaker 2?

5 What two things did Speaker 3 think he didn't like during the '80s (he later changed his mind)?

6 What trend did Madonna start in the mid-eighties?

5 A Read the underlined sentences in audio script S9.4 on pages 173 and answer the questions.

1 Which decade do you think was good for movies and music?

2 What was "one of the most memorable moments" of the decade in which you grew up?

3 Were things "developing and getting better" for your generation?

4 What part of your past do you like "in retrospect"?

B Discuss your answers with other students.

VOCABULARY
PERIODS OF TIME

6 A Put the words and phrases in order from the shortest to the longest periods. Use a dictionary to help you.

> a decade   a millennium   an era   a century
> a quarter-century   an age
> the nineteen-seventies/eighties (1970s, 1980s)
> the seventies/eighties ('70s/'80s)   a generation

B Complete sentences 1–8 with your own words.

1 The best thing about this decade so far has been …

2 The worst thing about this decade so far has been …

3 One thing I know/remember about the nineteen-nineties is …

4 My generation is sometimes criticized for our …

5 One thing that represents my parents' era is …

6 This era is represented by …

7 This is the first century in which …

8 One big change in the next quarter century might be …

C Compare your sentences with other students. Are there any that you agree on?

SPEAKING

7 A Choose a period when you were a child, a teenager or in your twenties. What did people listen to/do/watch/wear? How did it change as you got older? Make some notes about the following:

- music
- fashion
- technology
- sport
- TV and/or movies
- issues in the news

B Work with other students and talk about your chosen period of time.

When I was young, only a few programs were shown on TV. Now there are hundreds.

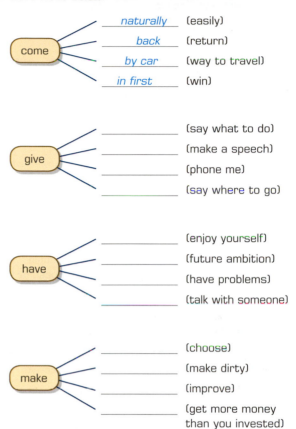

VOCABULARY PLUS
COLLOCATIONS

8 A Read the text and answer the questions.

1 According to the writer, what do "normal people" think of time travel?

2 Why is time travel probably boring?

3 Why is it probably not the solution to man's problems?

B Read the text again. Find and underline eight phrases with *come*, *give*, *have* and *make*. Two have been done for you.

Time Travel

All theoretical physicists have the same dream. They want to travel in time. Normal people like you and me have trouble believing that time travel is possible. The idea is outside our imagination, and such thoughts just don't <u>come naturally</u> to us. We can't imagine seeing our parents as little children taking their first steps or our grandparents' youthful faces as smooth and unlined as glass. We can't imagine watching Stone Age men dragging dead animals to their caves or watching Alexander the Great conquering half the world or seeing Mozart at his piano. And the truth is, even if we could travel in time, unless we could also choose an exact moment in an exact place, it would probably be very boring. When we read history books, the past always sounds exciting. But humanity makes progress slowly. And Stone Age man didn't own TVs for entertainment.

If time travel is ever possible in the future, time travelers are probably with us now, today. And if they exist, they have <u>come back</u> from a time in the future and are watching while we make a mess of the world. Why don't they give us directions on how to save the planet? Why don't they give instructions about the environment or how to stop war? Here's a sad thought: maybe they don't know the answers either.

C Look at the underlined phrases and add them to the word webs below.

come
- _naturally_ (easily)
- _back_ (return)
- _by car_ (way to travel)
- _in first_ (win)

give
- _____ (say what to do)
- _____ (make a speech)
- _____ (phone me)
- _____ (say where to go)

have
- _____ (enjoy yourself)
- _____ (future ambition)
- _____ (have problems)
- _____ (talk with someone)

make
- _____ (choose)
- _____ (make dirty)
- _____ (improve)
- _____ (get more money than you invested)

D Look at the words in the box and add them to the word webs above. Then add any other phrases with *come*, *give*, *have* and *make* you can think of.

> ~~by car~~   ~~first~~   a talk   a conversation   a profit
> a good time   a decision   (someone) a call

▶ page 156 VOCABULARY**BANK**

9 A Think of a time when you …

1 … made really good progress in something.

2 … gave instructions on how to do something.

3 … had trouble with a machine or a person.

4 … had a good time.

5 … had an interesting conversation.

6 … gave a talk to an audience.

7 … came in first at something.

8 … made an excellent decision.

9 … made a mess of something.

10 … had an interesting dream.

B Choose two or three of your experiences and tell other students what happened.

> Collocations can vary. For instance, you "take a break" in the U.S., but "have a break" in the U.K. Likewise, if you live in the U.S., you take a vacation, but if you live in the U.K., you have a holiday.

F expressing uncertainty
P intonation: showing interest
V describing people

SPEAKING

1 Work in pairs and discuss.

1 What are the most famous quiz shows in your country? Do you like them?

2 What type of questions do they ask (history, general knowledge, culture, etc.)?

3 If you had to answer quiz questions on one subject, which subject would you choose?

4 If you had to answer questions on one famous person in history, whom would you choose?

I'd choose Walt Disney because I loved his movies when I was young and I read his biography.

VOCABULARY
DESCRIBING PEOPLE

2 Work in pairs. Take the quiz about famous people in history. If you don't know the answers, guess or look at the photos to help.

3 A Work in pairs and look at the quiz again. What do the words in bold mean? Use a dictionary to help you.

B Choose three or four of the adjectives in Exercise 2 and think of a famous person for each adjective. Compare your ideas with other students.

Diego Maradona—He is probably the most influential athlete in the history of Argentina.

1 What **charismatic** religious leader, who spoke out against racism in South Africa, first worked as an English teacher?
a) Mother Teresa **b)** Desmond Tutu **c)** Pope John Paul II

2 What **influential** politician was killed by her own bodyguards?
a) Margaret Thatcher **b)** Eva Peron **c)** Indira Gandhi

3 What **innovative** anthropologist fed bananas to wild chimpanzees to gain their trust?
a) Jane Goodall **b)** Louis Leakey **c)** Margaret Mead

4 What **inspirational** scientist spent his free time playing the violin when he wasn't changing the world?
a) Galileo **b)** Albert Einstein **c)** Isaac Newton

5 What **brave** and **exemplary** activist refused to give up a bus seat and helped start the civil rights movement?
a) Che Guevara **b)** Nelson Mandela **c)** Rosa Parks

6 What amazingly **original** and **creative** writer was banned from entering the United States for years?
a) Isabel Allende **b)** Charles Dickens
c) Gabriel Garciá Márquez

FUNCTION
EXPRESSING UNCERTAINTY

4 A Listen to someone taking the quiz. Which questions does he get right?

B Look at the phrases in the box. Match them to the groups of phrases below.

> I don't know   I know it isn't/wasn't …
> I'm not sure, but I think …   I used to know

1 _____, I have no idea, I don't have a clue

2 _____, I'm not a hundred percent certain, but it might be …, I'm fairly sure it's …

3 _____, It's definitely not, I'm sure it isn't

4 _____, I can't remember, I've forgotten

C Listen again and check (✔) the phrases you hear.

▶ page 144 LANGUAGEBANK

5 A Complete speaker B's responses in the conversations by adding the groups of words in the box.

> ~~have no~~   fairly sure   percent certain   sure it
> don't have a   I've forgotten   I can't   it's definitely

1 A: Which sculptor is famous for the statue of David? Was it Leonardo da Vinci or Michelangelo?

  have no

  B: I idea. I don't know anything about art.

2 A: What's the name of that American politician who made a movie about the environment?

  B: Oh, um, remember. Was it Rumsfeld? No, um, Bush?

3 A: Who was the white South African leader who freed Mandela?

  B: I'm it was Botha, wasn't it?

4 A: Who's that Mexican actor who was in *Amores Perros*?

  B: Oh, his name, but I know who you mean. He's quite small and good-looking.

5 A: Which company invented the CD-ROM?

  B: I'm not a hundred, but it might be Sony.

6 A: Do you know who wrote *The Lord of the Rings*? Wasn't it William Golding?

  B: I don't know, but not Golding.

7 A: Who won the last World Cup?

  B: I'm wasn't England.

8 A: What was the name of that Steven Spielberg movie about dinosaurs?

  B: I clue. I don't watch Hollywood movies.

B Work in pairs and answer the questions. Try to use some of the phrases for expressing uncertainty in exercises 4A and 5A. Then turn to page 159 to check your ideas.

LEARN TO
REACT TO INFORMATION

6 A INTONATION: showing interest Read the extracts from audio script S9.5. Then listen and notice the intonation patterns speaker B uses.

1 A: It was B, Desmond Tutu.

  B: Oh, really?

2 A: Yes.

  B: Oh, no, I didn't know that.

3 A: It leaves you with A. Very good. It was Jane Goodall.

  B: Yes, that's right!

4 A: So the last one.

  B: That's interesting.

5 A: It was C!

  B: Excellent, excellent!

B Answer the questions.

1 Which information did speaker B know already?

2 Which information was new?

SPEAKING

7 A Work in pairs. Student A: you are going to ask Student B the questions below. First, add two more questions of your own. The answers can be found on page 159. Student B: turn to page 162.

Geography

1 What's the capital of Australia? Is it Sydney, Melbourne or Canberra?

2 Which country has the second biggest population? Is it China, India or Russia?

3 Which one of these countries is not next to the ocean: Venezuela, Ecuador or Paraguay?

4 _____

5 _____

B Discuss with other students. Do you think it's important for people to know facts about the past? Why?/Why not? What do you think we can learn from history? Think of some examples.

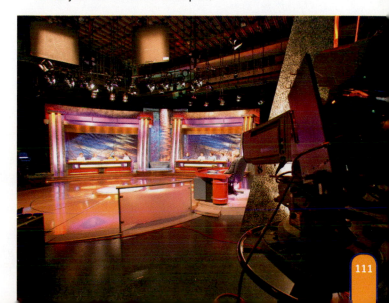

DVD PREVIEW

1 Discuss. What do you know about the painting below and the artist who created it?

2 Read the sentences about Michelangelo. What do you think the words in bold mean? Which two pairs of words have opposite meanings?

1 His work is **unique**—no one has ever done anything similar.

2 Some said his work was **divine** because only God could create such beauty.

3 His fame is **eternal**. He will never be forgotten.

4 The sculptures are **extraordinary**. They are incredibly beautiful and realistic.

5 Although he was **mortal**, his work will never die.

6 His art is **awe-inspiring**. We feel small when we look at it.

7 His painting on the ceiling of the Sistine Chapel is an incredible **feat**.

8 In those days, many normal men worked with stone, but he was far from **ordinary**.

9 Even as a child, he had **aspirations** to be a great artist.

10 As a young man in Florence, he began his **quest** for fame.

3 Read about the TV program, *The Divine Michelangelo*. What is the contrast between Michelangelo's life and his art?

▶ The Divine Michelangelo

This documentary examines the life and work of Michelangelo Buonarroti, one of the greatest artists in history. It looks at his background as a child in Florence and how he went on to produce works such as the statue of David, the awe-inspiring ceiling of the Sistine Chapel and the dome of St. Peter's Cathedral, described here as "the jewel in the crown on the Roman skyline." The program also reveals Michelangelo's tempestuous life, his fights with rivals and with his own demons, showing that an imperfect life can produce perfect art.

DVD VIEW

4 A Which of these sentences do you think are true?

1 Michelangelo was a sculptor, painter and architect.

2 He said he was divinely inspired (inspired by God).

3 He lived and worked three hundred years ago.

4 His mother died when he was a child.

5 He was from a rich family.

6 His father always wanted him to be an artist.

B Watch the DVD to check.

5 A Read the notes. Which words do you think are missing?

Who was Michelangelo?

… a tempestuous genius … he wanted eternal fame and [1] _riches_

… an outsider who created works so big and so [2]_____ that nobody believed they were produced by a mortal

… NOT an ordinary laborer or honest, [3]_____ stonecutter

Background

… had an [4]_____ childhood, father, Ludovico, was a lowly-paid local official

What did he do?

… persevered and produced works which showed an extraordinary [5]_____

… created a unique vision of heaven on [6]_____

B Watch the DVD again and complete the notes.

C Work in groups and discuss. What do you think of Michelangelo's work? Have you ever seen any of his work? How do you think his work has influenced other artists?

St. / laborer / that   St / labourer / which

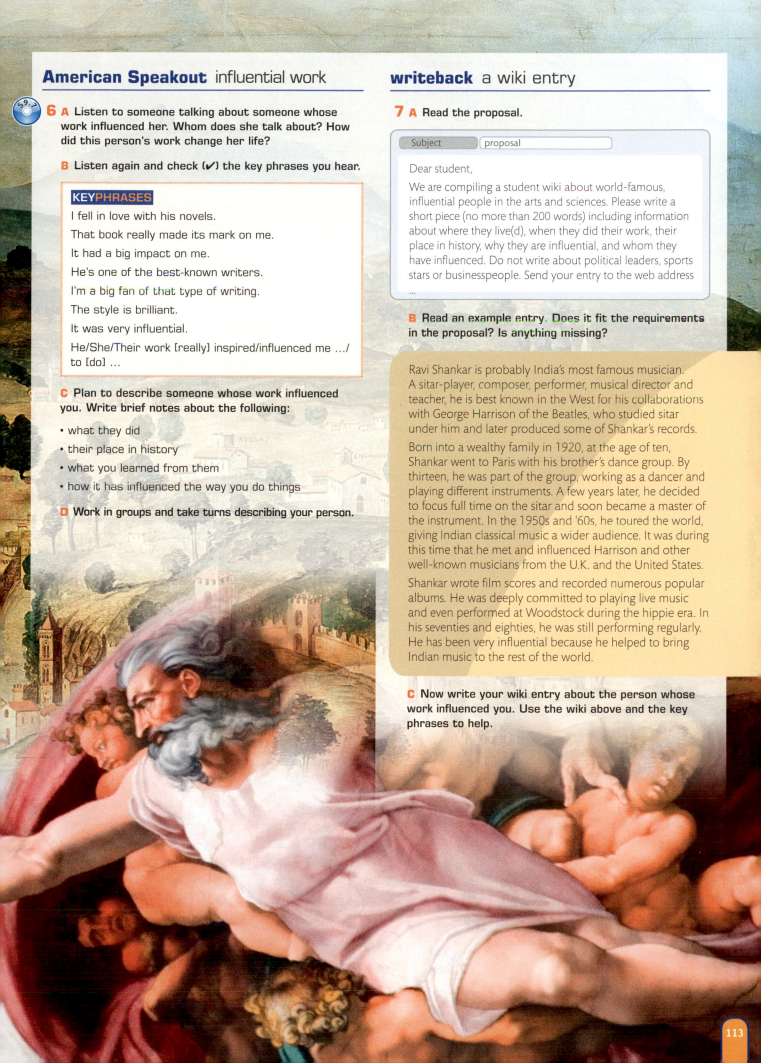

American Speakout influential work

6 A Listen to someone talking about someone whose work influenced her. Whom does she talk about? How did this person's work change her life?

B Listen again and check (✔) the key phrases you hear.

> **KEYPHRASES**
>
> I fell in love with his novels.
>
> That book really made its mark on me.
>
> It had a big impact on me.
>
> He's one of the best-known writers.
>
> I'm a big fan of that type of writing.
>
> The style is brilliant.
>
> It was very influential.
>
> He/She/Their work [really] inspired/influenced me …/ to [do] …

C Plan to describe someone whose work influenced you. Write brief notes about the following:

• what they did

• their place in history

• what you learned from them

• how it has influenced the way you do things

D Work in groups and take turns describing your person.

writeback a wiki entry

7 A Read the proposal.

Subject	proposal

Dear student,

We are compiling a student wiki about world-famous, influential people in the arts and sciences. Please write a short piece (no more than 200 words) including information about where they live(d), when they did their work, their place in history, why they are influential, and whom they have influenced. Do not write about political leaders, sports stars or businesspeople. Send your entry to the web address …

B Read an example entry. Does it fit the requirements in the proposal? Is anything missing?

Ravi Shankar is probably India's most famous musician. A sitar-player, composer, performer, musical director and teacher, he is best known in the West for his collaborations with George Harrison of the Beatles, who studied sitar under him and later produced some of Shankar's records.

Born into a wealthy family in 1920, at the age of ten, Shankar went to Paris with his brother's dance group. By thirteen, he was part of the group, working as a dancer and playing different instruments. A few years later, he decided to focus full time on the sitar and soon became a master of the instrument. In the 1950s and '60s, he toured the world, giving Indian classical music a wider audience. It was during this time that he met and influenced Harrison and other well-known musicians from the U.K. and the United States.

Shankar wrote film scores and recorded numerous popular albums. He was deeply committed to playing live music and even performed at Woodstock during the hippie era. In his seventies and eighties, he was still performing regularly. He has been very influential because he helped to bring Indian music to the rest of the world.

C Now write your wiki entry about the person whose work influenced you. Use the wiki above and the key phrases to help.

V HISTORY

1 A Work in teams. Use the words in the box to make ten true sentences. Use one word in each sentence.

> revolution   turning point   development
> movement   spread   advance   invention
> foundation   discovery   progress

B Write down three of your sentences and read them to the class. Are any of your sentences similar? Which group has the most original sentences?

G HYPOTHETICAL CONDITIONAL: PAST

2 A Read headings 1–6. Write a sentence about your past for each heading.

1 School

I loved school and did well in my final exams.

2 Hobbies and How You Began

3 Work: Choices or Hopes

4 Family and Relationships

5 Influences in Life

6 Opportunities to Do Interesting Things

B Exchange sentences with a partner. Choose three of your partner's sentences. Write about your partner's life using hypothetical conditionals in the past.

If David hadn't liked school, he probably wouldn't have done so well on his exams.

V PERIODS OF TIME

3 A Complete the sentences with words for periods of time.

1 In which d_ _ _ _ _ were you born?

2 What can you remember about the n _ _ _ _ _ _ _-n _ _ _ _ _ _?

3 How did you celebrate the new m _ _ _ _ _ _ _ _ _?

4 What's your favorite e_ _ in history?

5 If you could go back in time, where and what c_ _ _ _ _ _ would you choose?

6 What do you think your g _ _ _ _ _ _ _ _ _ will be famous for?

B Work in pairs. Take turns asking and answering the questions.

G THE PASSIVE

4 A Complete the sentences with the correct passive or active form of the verbs in the box.

> ~~discover~~   assassinate   become   build   climb
> declare   destroy   elect   release   identify

1 The tomb of Tutankhamun *was discovered* in the Valley of the Kings, Egypt.

2 U.S. and French scientists _____ the AIDS virus.

3 A wall _____ between East and West Germany.

4 Edmund Hillary and Tenzing Norgay _____ Mount Everest.

5 The Titanic _____ after hitting an iceberg in the North Atlantic.

6 Nelson Mandela _____ from prison.

7 Mahatma Gandhi _____ by a terrorist.

8 Margaret Thatcher, the U.K.'s first female prime minister,_____.

9 The U.K. and France _____ war on Germany.

10 Two-year-old Pu Yi _____ Emperor of China.

B Match the events above with the dates in the box.

> ~~1922~~   1908   1912   1939   1948   1953
> 1961   1979   1984   1990

1922: The tomb of Tutankhamun was discovered.

C Work in groups. Compare your answers and correct each other's work if necessary.

F EXPRESSING UNCERTAINTY

5 A Put B's words in the correct order to complete the conversations.

1 **A:** What is the name of that restaurant again?
   B: forgotten / sorry, / I've

2 **A:** Is there anywhere you can smoke in this building?
   B: allowed / it's / definitely / no, / here / not

3 **A:** What time does this school open in the morning?
   B: at / fairly / opens / sure / I'm / it / 7 a.m.

4 **A:** What was your last teacher's name?
   B: remember / can't / I

5 **A:** Do you know where the nearest restaurant is?
   B: clue / sorry, / have / I / a / don't

6 **A:** What's the school director's name?
   B: it / not / a / might / I'm / percent / but / certain, / be / hundred / Timothy

7 **A:** How far away is the nearest supermarket?
   B: isn't / it / sure / far / I'm

8 **A:** Where's the nearest bank?
   B: no / I / idea / have / sorry,

B Work in pairs. How many of your partner's questions can you answer?

10 World

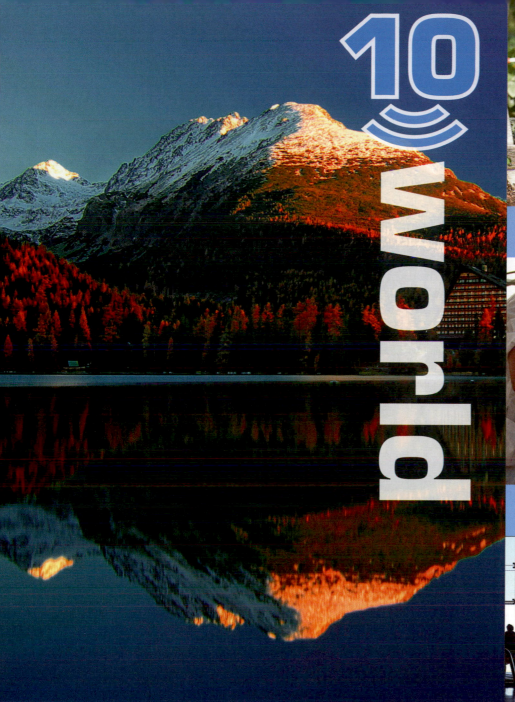

SPEAKING
10.1 Discuss ideas for reducing plastic waste
10.2 Recommend a city for food
10.3 Ask for/Give travel advice
10.4 Talk about an endangered place

LISTENING
10.2 Listen to descriptions of the world's best food cities
10.3 Listen to people giving advice/warnings
10.4 Watch a documentary about the Arctic's melting ice caps

READING
10.1 Read about a man who tried to live ethically for a year
10.3 Read advice about what not to do in an airport

WRITING
10.2 Write a restaurant review
10.4 Write an email campaigning for action

What are the biggest problems facing the world today?

INTERVIEWS

10.1)) ETHICAL MAN

G reported speech
P weak forms: auxiliary verbs
V the environment; word building: prefixes

VOCABULARY
THE ENVIRONMENT

1 A Work in pairs and discuss. How important is "green living" to you?

B Look at the sentences below and try to explain the meaning of the words/phrases in bold. Then use a dictionary to check.

1 How much of the food you buy is **pre-prepared** or **processed**? How much is **organic**?
2 How much of the food you eat is produced in the country you live in?
3 How is your home heated? Do you use **energy-saving light bulbs**?
4 Is your house **insulated** and/or **double-paned**?
5 Do you turn lights/machines off or leave them **on standby**?
6 When you're buying a product, do you consider how to recycle the **packaging**?
7 How often do you buy, sell or give away **secondhand items**?
8 How much of your **garbage** is **recycled**?
9 How many hours a year, on average, do you spend flying?
10 How often do you use a car?

C Answer questions 1–10 above.

D Work in pairs and compare your answers.

▶ page 157 VOCABULARYBANK

READING

2 A Justin Rowlatt, a British journalist, decided to try living a greener lifestyle for a year. What changes do you think he made?

B Read the article to find out.

C Work in pairs and answer the questions below.

1 Why did Justin decide to try living ethically for a year?
2 Did he and his family enjoy the experience?
3 What kinds of things did they try to change?
4 Why is Justin traveling to America?
5 How does he plan to travel?
6 What sorts of solutions is he looking for?

D Discuss. Do you think the "Ethical Man" experiment is a good idea? Why?/Why not? How do you think society could reduce carbon emissions?

3 Read the article again. Underline words/phrases in the text that match meanings 1–6.

1 the amount of damage we do (by our actions) to the air, water and land on Earth (paragraph 2)
2 threw away or destroyed (paragraph 2)
3 terrible, like a bad dream (paragraph 2)
4 period of very hot weather (paragraph 2)
5 the effects of trying very hard (paragraph 3)
6 to follow something or someone (paragraph 6)

ETHICAL MAN

1 My name's Juston Rowlatt, and I'm the Ethical Man.

2 My family and I spent a year doing everything we could to try to reduce our impact on the environment. We changed the light bulbs in our house to energy-saving bulbs. We changed the way we heat and power our home. We stopped flying, and we got rid of the car. Instead, we walked, used bicycles, or took public transportation. We did our grocery shopping online, ate organic vegetables, and I even stopped eating meat (for a month). My heavily pregnant wife, Bee, walked two miles to the hospital, in the middle of the night, to give birth to our third daughter, Elsa. When we went on vacation to France, instead of choosing a two-hour flight, we went on a nightmarish twelve-hour journey on the train, in a heatwave.

3 I had hoped our efforts would demonstrate how normal families could help to reduce their impact on the environment. But, despite our best efforts, we only reduced our greenhouse gas emissions by 20 percent. Clearly the efforts of ethical men and women acting alone are not the answer. So what is?

double-paned / garbage / grocery shopping   double-glazed / rubbish / supermarket shopping

in the USA

4 I had a new idea. And now I'm traveling across America in search of some solutions. Each American is responsible for 20 tons of CO_2 emissions, more than twice that of the average European.

5 The idea of the trip is simple. I think if we can solve it here, we can solve it anywhere. But, as Ethical Man, I have to keep my environmental impact to a minimum. Of course, I'm going to fly from Britain, but, after that, my challenge is to get around in the most low carbon way possible. I'll be traveling 6,500 miles, so it's not going to be easy. But, I will use public transportation wherever possible. During my trip, I'll talk to ordinary people, businessmen and politicians to hear their views on climate change and discuss ways in which we can try to reduce carbon emissions. And I'll drive an electric car.

6 You can track my progress on the map and watch our video reports along the way. Please give me advice; I want your thoughts on what we need to do as societies to make the cuts in emissions that are needed. Do you have an idea for a solution to climate change? Are you inventing the solution in your garage? If you are, please let me know.

GRAMMAR
REPORTED SPEECH

4 A Complete the table to show how tenses change in reported speech.

Direct Speech	Reported Speech
"I' ¹_____ across America …"	He said he **was traveling** across America …
"I ²_____ use public transportation wherever possible."	He said he **would** use public transportation wherever possible.
"My heavily pregnant wife, Bee, ³___ two miles to hospital."	He said that his wife **had walked** to the hospital.
"I **think** if we can solve it here, …"	He said he ⁴_____ if **they could** solve it **there**, …'
"I ⁵_____ a new idea."	He said he**'d had** a new idea.
"I ⁶_____ hoped our efforts would demonstrate … "	He said he **had hoped** their efforts would demonstrate …
"Do you **have** an idea … ?"	He asked if anyone ⁷_____ an idea …
"Each American ⁸_____ responsible for 20 tons of CO_2 emissions."	He said each American **is** responsible for 20 tons of CO_2 emissions.

B Check your answers using the article in Exercise 2B.

C Look at the table again. Match each sentence to one of the rules.

> **RULES**
>
> **1** When we report speech, we often move the tenses back (backshift), e.g., present simple → past simple, present continuous → past continuous, present perfect → past perfect, *will* → *would*.
>
> **2** If what the person says is still true, we can keep the tenses the same, e.g., "It's the 16th." → She said it's the 16th.
>
> **3** We may also need to change pronouns and time references, e.g., "I'll see you <u>tomorrow</u>." → He said he would see her <u>the next day</u>.
>
> **4** In reported questions, the word order is the same as that for statements.

▶ page 146 **LANGUAGEBANK**

5 A Complete the sentences by adding one word.
1 We changed the light bulbs in our house. (Justin)
   He said they had changed the light bulbs in __*their*__ house.
2 I have a new idea. (Justin to his wife)
   He said he _____ a new idea.
3 We're going to live a more ethical lifestyle. (Justin to Bee)
   They said that _____ were going to live a more ethical lifestyle.
4 I'm going to take a taxi to the hospital. (Bee to Justin)
   She said she _____ going to take a taxi to the hospital.
5 We're hot. (children to parents)
   The children said _____ were hot.
6 We've achieved a lot. (Justin and Bee)
   They said they _____ achieved a lot.
7 I didn't eat meat for a month. (Justin)
   Justin said he _____ eaten meat for a month.

 B WEAK FORMS: auxiliary verbs Listen to check your answers. Notice how *have/had/was/were* are weak forms or contractions. Listen again and shadow the sentences.

SPEAKING

6 A Work in groups. Group A: look at the photo and read the fact file below. Discuss the questions and make notes about your discussion. Group B: look at the photo and read the fact file on page 163.

THE PLASTIC PROBLEM

Did you know ...?

- The world uses 1 million plastic bags per minute.
- Over the last ten years, we have produced more plastic than during the whole of the last century.
- 50 percent of the plastic we use, we use just once and throw away.
- The "Pacific Ocean Garbage Patch" is an area in the Pacific Ocean filled with plastic waste. The area may be as big as 5 million square kilometers (more than twice the size of the U.S.A.). Millions of marine animals die when they eat the plastic, become caught in it or feed it to their young.
- Enough plastic is thrown away each year to circle Earth four times.

1 Why does the problem exist?
2 What should be done about it?
3 What laws/schemes would you introduce to deal with the problem?

B Look at your notes and prepare to tell another student about your discussion. Use reported speech.

We talked about ... Juan said that ...
Caterina thought that ... Akiyo asked if ...

C Work in pairs with a student from the other group. Tell them about the discussions you had in your group and any ideas you had.

VOCABULARY *PLUS*
WORD BUILDING: PREFIXES

7 A Look at the example sentences 1–10 and underline the prefixes.

un-
1 It's very unusual to have snow in April.
2 The whole situation was completely unreal.

re-
3 Most glass bottles and aluminum cans can be recycled.
4 Don't throw away the bottles. They are reusable.

dis-
5 I disagree with using the car for short trips.
6 She would never disobey her parents.

mis-
7 Don't misunderstand me. I want to help.
8 I always mispronounce his name.

over-/under-
9 She hardly eats anything, and she's very underweight.
10 I think I've overcooked the pasta.

B Match the prefixes above with meanings 1–5.

1 not: *un-* and _____   3 too much: _____   5 wrong: _____
2 again: _____   4 too little: _____

8 Add prefixes to the words in parentheses to complete the sentences.

1 He's lying. His story about how he cycled across Africa was completely _____ (believable).
2 It's easy to _____ (judge) somebody's character by looking at the clothes they wear.
3 Much of the snow in the Arctic has completely _____ (appeared).
4 These potatoes are delicious. Don't _____ (cook) them!
5 Jessica decided not to accept the job because the company's policies were _____ (ethical).
6 I did this all wrong. I probably _____ (understood) the instructions.
7 My desk is always _____ (organized). I don't have enough time to clean it up.
8 She walks to work every day, despite her _____ (ability).

▶ page 157 **VOCABULARY**BANK

> **American Speak TIP** Use prefixes to guess the meaning of words you don't know. Look at the words in bold below. Can you use the prefix to guess their meaning?

9 Work in pairs and take turns. Ask and answer the questions.

1 What professions in your country do people often **mistrust**?
2 Who in your country is very famous now, but was **unknown** last year?
3 What kinds of documents do you sometimes need to **renew**?
4 Do you believe scientists have **overestimated** or **underestimated** the problem of climate change?
5 Do you **disapprove** of people who drive their cars everywhere? Why?/Why not?

aluminum   aluminium

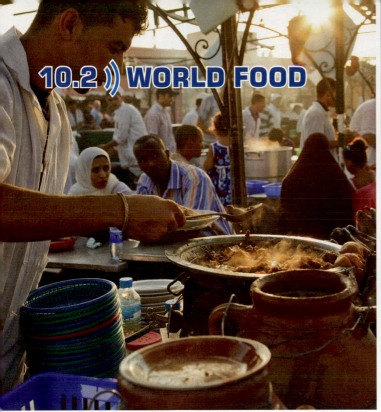

10.2)) WORLD FOOD

G verb patterns
P weak forms: *to, for, that*
V reporting verbs

LISTENING

1 **Work in pairs and discuss.**

1 What's the best street food you've ever eaten?

2 Is there anything you would never eat?

2 **A** **Listen to two people talking about their favorite food city. According to the speakers, which city, Hiroshima (H) or Madrid (M), has the following:**

1 a small, cheap restaurant that serves wonderful seafood?

2 informal restaurants where you order lots of dishes that everyone shares and eats from the middle of the table?

3 something to eat that is like a cross between a pancake and a pizza?

4 people getting together at lunchtime on Sunday to have a few bites to eat?

5 a restaurant that specializes in grilled chicken?

B **Listen again and complete the extracts below. Then check your answers in the audio script on page 175.**

1 They have the very famous sushi that everyone thinks about when they think of Japanese food, but they have so much else to _____.

2 Hiroshima is really _____ for its *okonomiyaki*.

3 *Tempura* is shrimp and _____ deep fried in a really light, fluffy batter.

4 I lived in Madrid, in Spain, for around _____ years on and off.

5 The quality of the food is _____.

6 *Tarta de Santiago* is a great pastry _____.

7 I once tried pig's ear, which I have to say was possibly the _____ thing I've ever tasted.

SPEAKING

3 **A** **Do you know any cities that are good for food? What types of food are they best known for? Which areas have good restaurants? Plan to talk about your favorite food city. Use these phrases from the listening to make some notes.**

> My favorite food city is …
>
> They have all sorts of …
>
> XXX is really famous for its …
>
> It's a kind of …
>
> It's really good (for) …
>
> I think my favorite restaurant in … is …
>
> One of my favorite restaurants is a place called …, which specializes in …
>
> It's a cheap/basic/fine/expensive …
>
> You can get …
>
> I'd love to take you to XXX; you'd love it!
>
> I know a really good … that I should take you to.

B **Work in groups and take turns talking about your favorite food city. Have you been to any of these cities? Do you agree with the other students? Which city would you like to visit?**

specialize   specialise

VOCABULARY
REPORTING VERBS

4 A Match the verbs with the statements.

1 offer
2 warn
3 refuse

a) I can't eat anything else, thank you.
b) Would you like a coffee?
c) Be careful. It's hot.

B Look at the statements/questions below. Rewrite each statement in reported speech using a verb from the box.

> warned   explained   refused   promised   invited
> suggested   offered

1 "You have to be careful not to eat too much."

She _____ us not to eat too much.

2 "Come to Palermo, and I'll take you to my favorite restaurant?"

He _____ us to Palermo, and he _____ to take us to his favorite restaurant.

3 "It will definitely be a good deal. I'm sure of it."

She _____ that it would be a good deal.

4 "I think Lima could be one of the greatest food cities."

She _____ that Lima could be one of the greatest food cities.

5 "The restaurant specializes in grilled chicken."

He _____ that the restaurant specializes in grilled chicken.

6 "I don't believe that there is any better food than in Singapore."

He _____ to believe that there was any better food than in Singapore.

GRAMMAR
VERB PATTERNS

5 A Look at the verb patterns in bold in sentences a)–e). Then complete the table below with the sentences.

a) We **explained that** it was our first trip to the area.

b) He **agreed to show** us around Palermo.

c) She **suggested trying** some of the local dishes.

d) They **promised to cook** for us.

e) He **warned us not to eat** the chili peppers.

verb + infinitive with *to*	verb + *-ing*
She offered to show us around. 1 _____ 2 _____	They recommended taking the bus. 3 _____
verb + object + infinitive with *to*	**verb + *that***
They invited us to stay. 4 _____	She decided that she would stay. 5 _____

B WEAK FORMS: *to, for, that* Listen to the sentences above and underline the stressed words.

C Listen again and check your answers. Pay attention to the weak forms of to /tə/, for /fər/ and that /ðət/. Then listen and repeat.

D Some verbs use more than one pattern. Find two in Exercise 4B that can use different patterns.

*Agree: She **agreed to** show us around. They **agreed that** it was a good idea.*

▶ page 146 LANGUAGE**BANK**

6 Complete the second sentence so that it means the same as the first. Use the correct form of the verbs in bold.

1 "During the festival, street vendors sell nothing but chocolate." **explain**

She _____, during the festival, street vendors only sell chocolate.

2 "People should come to the Tomatina festival in Spain." **suggest/visit**

Beatrix _____ Spain during the Tomatina festival.

3 Don't eat anything before the cheese festival. There are more than 1,000 cheeses to try." **warn/eat**

He _____ us not _____ anything before going to the cheese festival.

4 "We'll definitely go to the Mango festival in India in July." **promise/take**

He _____ me to the Mango festival.

5 "Would you like me to show you around the Eurochocolate festival?" **offer/show**

The tour guide _____ us around the Eurochocolate festival.

SPEAKING

7 A Read the comments about food below. Do any of the people have similar ideas to you?

> 66 I love good food, but I never cook it myself. I would rather go to a restaurant. 99

> 66 Food isn't at all important to me. I just eat when I'm hungry. 99

> 66 Food is like a passion for me. I love cooking for lots of people. 99

> 66 People who eat in restaurants are lazy. It's such a waste of money. 99

> 66 Fast food is the best treat. I love nothing more than a hamburger and fries. 99

B In pairs, talk about food and cooking. What kinds of food do you like/dislike? Try to give examples. Take notes.

C Tell another student about your last partner and decide on a meal that would be good for them.

D Tell the class about your ideas.

"Davide suggested having pasta because you said you loved it. He promised to make a special seafood sauce for you."

🍴 DEATH BY BURRITO
PIONEER SQUARE

Situated below a live music venue, this is a great place to eat contemporary Mexican street food and maybe even enjoy a cocktail. The restaurant has a great atmosphere if you're young and like to enjoy a party. The food is reasonably priced. It's served on plastic plates with plastic cutlery, but the burritos and tacos are delicious. Beware if you're on a diet though. Even the smaller dishes of nachos, guacamole, black beans and tortilla chips will keep you dancing for a while to burn off those calories.

🍴 SUPER TUSCAN WINE BAR AND KITCHEN
BROOKLYN

This is a small and friendly wine bar tucked down a side street near the grocery store. The décor is Mediterranean, as is the menu. There's a selection of typically Tuscan dishes, like lentil or bean soup and bruschetta with porcini mushrooms, as well as all the usual pizza and pasta dishes. The food is cooked simply and tastes great, and in an authentic Italian atmosphere. This is a good place to meet friends and enjoy a glass of wine and an antipasto, although you'll probably find quite a few city bankers doing that, too.

🍴 BACK IN 5 MINUTES
SILVERLAKE

You wouldn't find this restaurant unless you were looking. It's hidden behind a clothes store. Walk through the store and open a curtain at the back. It will take you down some stairs and into the 1970s-style dining room. Open from Wednesdays to Saturdays only, you can choose from a selection of three starters, three main courses and three desserts. While the food is seasonal and elegant, it isn't cheap. However, the atmosphere is so cozy and welcoming that you could easily forget you're in a restaurant at all. You feel as if you've been invited into someone's house for dinner.

WRITING
A RESTAURANT REVIEW; LEARN TO LINK IDEAS

8 A Match headings a)–e) with questions 1–5 to complete the guide to writing a restaurant review.

a) Information about the Price

b) Information about the Menu

c) Details of the Restaurant

d) Information about the Sevice

e) Information about the Atmosphere

1 _____ : Where is it? How can you contact them? How do you get there? What are the opening hours?

2 _____ : What's the décor like? Is it child-friendly? Is it noisy? Is it romantic?

3 _____ : What kind of food does it serve? Are there any specialities? Do they serve vegetarian food? Are there any particular dishes you recommend?

4 _____ : Is the staff friendly? Do you have to wait a long time?

5 _____ : Is it a good deal? How much does it cost per person? Are there any special offers?

B Read the reviews above. Which restaurant would you like to visit and why?

C Try to answer the questions in Exercise 8A for each restaurant.

9 A Look at the examples and answer questions 1–3.

*The food was **so** delicious **that** I didn't mind spending more than usual.*

*It was **such** an enjoyable meal **that** I would recommend this restaurant to anybody.*

*It was so expensive that I wouldn't go back there **unless** I wanted to impress a client.*

***Although** it's a five-star restaurant, the service was appalling.*

***While** the staff is friendly and the atmosphere is fun, the food isn't anything special.*

1 Which linking words do we use to connect ideas that contrast with each other?

2 Which do we use to talk about the consequences of a situation?

3 Which do we use to suggest a condition?

B Underline the linking words in Exercise 8B.

C Write sentences to connect the five pairs of ideas below. Use the words in parentheses to help.

1 Starbucks has been very successful. Now they want to open new stores in China. (so)

2 The restaurant has had very bad reviews. Nobody wants to go there. (such)

3 The food was very bad. I will only go back there again if they get a new chef. (unless)

4 The food was delicious. The service was poor. (although)

5 The restaurant had a good atmosphere. The food was disappointing. (while)

10 Choose or invent a restaurant in your town/city. Write a short review (80–100 words). Use the guide in Exercise 8A to help you. Use the linking words in Exercise 9B to connect your ideas.

10.3)) WHEN YOU TRAVEL, …

F giving advice/warnings
P individual sounds: vowels
V airports

VOCABULARY
AIRPORTS

1 A Discuss the questions.

1 Do you ever travel by plane?

2 Do you enjoy it?

3 What do you like/dislike about air travel?

4 Which part of the airport can you see in the picture?

B Complete the questions/statements you might hear in an airport with the words in the box.

proceed   aisle   boarding pass   passport   priority
X-ray   carry-on   gate   check   boards

1 Can I see your _____ ?

2 Your _____ number is 42.

3 In a few minutes, we will be calling all passengers with _____ boarding.

4 Would you like an _____ seat or a window seat?

5 Your flight _____ at 9:30.

6 Please have your _____ ready.

7 How many bags do you have to _____ in?

8 Do you have any _____ luggage?

9 Please _____ to gate number 30.

10 Put your carry-on luggage through the _____ machine.

C **INDIVIDUAL SOUNDS: vowels** Put the words in Exercise 1B next to the matching vowel sound. Listen again and check your answers.

/i/ (l<u>ea</u>ve)   /ɛr/ (f<u>a</u>re)   /ɔr/ (d<u>oo</u>r)   /ɑ/ (n<u>o</u>t)

/aɪ/ (dr<u>i</u>ve)   /eɪ/ (pl<u>a</u>ne)   /ɛ/ (<u>e</u>xit)   /æ/ (b<u>a</u>g)

D Put the phrases in the order you might hear them in an airport. Where would you hear each phrase?

2 A Work in pairs. Write a list of three things you must and must not do in an airport.

B Read the article below. Does it mention your ideas?

C Discuss in pairs. Do you agree with the advice? Have you ever experienced any of these problems?

D Can you find any words in the text to add to each phoneme group in Exercise 1C?

Seven Things You Should NEVER Do in an Airport

1 Take too much luggage: If the airline says only take one bag of carry-on luggage, that's what it means. No extra shopping bags allowed.

2 Go to the wrong terminal: Don't wait until your taxi has left you and driven away before checking which airport terminal your flight leaves from.

3 Make jokes about bombs or drugs: The security personnel might not have a very good sense of humor, and you might be arrested.

4 Take too many liquids: You're only allowed 100ml, so don't take extra bottles of shampoo and suncream.

5 Waste people's time: Get ready for the X-ray machine. Make sure you take your laptop out of your bag, find your phone, and take off your belt so you don't keep everybody waiting.

6 Forget things in the trays: Don't wait until you board the airplane before realizing you left your keys, wallet and passport in the tray.

7 Sleep: Flying is exhausting, but don't close your eyes. If you're traveling alone, you might wake up to find you missed your flight.

boarding pass / carry-on luggage   boarding card / hand luggage

FUNCTION
GIVING ADVICE/WARNINGS

3 A Listen and match conversations 1–4 with situations a)–d).

a) crime in a city

b) the journey to J.F.K. airport

c) traveling in the jungle

d) arriving at the airport

B Listen again. What problems do they talk about in each conversation?

4 A Match 1–10 with a)–j) to complete the warnings/advice.

1 Watch out for

2 Make sure

3 Don't ... (or else)

4 You'd better

5 If I were you,

6 Be careful

7 Don't forget to

8 Whatever you do,

9 You need to

10 The most important thing is

a) when you take trips into the jungle.

b) you find out how much the trip is supposed to cost.

c) watch out for groups of young children on the streets.

d) the taxi drivers who tend to hang around outside the airport.

e) I'd allow about an hour and a half.

f) don't drink the water.

g) leave plenty of time.

h) get in until you've agreed on the price with the driver, or else you could ...

i) to remember to hold on to your purse.

j) take your malaria pills.

B Listen and check. Then listen and repeat the phrases. Which words are stressed?

▶ page 146 LANGUAGEBANK

5 Find and correct the mistake in each sentence.

1 The most important thing is not going out alone.

2 If I were you, I'll bring waterproof clothes.

3 Make sure if you wear a helmet and protective clothing when you ride a bike.

4 Be carefully when you're on the main roads.

5 Don't forgetting to keep your luggage with you.

6 Whatever you are do, don't buy food from the street vendors. It's terrible.

7 Watch out for people try to sell you fake watches.

8 You'll better leave your valuables in the hotel.

LEARN TO
MAKE GENERALIZATIONS

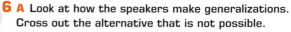

6 A Look at how the speakers make generalizations. Cross out the alternative that is not possible.

1 Watch out for the taxi drivers who *tend to/are tend to/have a tendency to* hang around outside the airport.

2 You'd better leave plenty of time, because *often/never/usually* there are delays on the subway.

3 Be careful when you take trips into the jungle. *Sometimes/Generally/Always* there are a lot of mosquitoes there, so remember to take mosquito nets and insect repellent.

4 *On the whole/It doesn't often happen/It's not very common*, but don't walk around the city obviously carrying money in a big money belt or anything.

5 There isn't really much crime. *On the whole/For the whole/Generally*, it's a pretty safe city.

B Listen and underline the words or phrases the speakers use.

7 Look at the sentences below. Then make generalizations using the prompts in parentheses.

1 I usually travel by train. (tend)

I tend to travel by train.

2 I hate sitting around in airports. (whole)

3 The beaches are clean and safe. (generally)

4 The trains to the airport are sometimes delayed. (not common)

5 Criminals target tourists. (tendency)

6 English people complain about the weather. (often)

SPEAKING

8 A Work in pairs and role-play the situation. Student A: read the instructions below. Student B: turn to page 163.

Student A: you are a tourist. You want to go on a tour in the Australian Outback. Ask the tourist office for advice, e.g., Are there any dangerous animals? What special clothes/equipment do you need?

I'd like some information about going into the Outback. First of all, what dangerous animals are there? ...

B Change roles and role-play the following situation. Student B turn to page 163.

Student A: you work in a diving center. A customer would like to go snorkeling on the reef. Give him/her some advice using the phrases in Exercise 4A and the prompts below:

1 Wear a T-shirt so you don't get a sunburn. Sunscreen washes off in the ocean.

2 Don't touch the coral. You might break pieces off.

3 Stingrays can give you a nasty sting.

4 There are strong currents. You need to be able to swim to the shore or the boat.

5 Take an underwater camera for photos.

street vendors /subway
bug, insect repellent / snorkeling

street sellers / tube
insect cream / snorkelling

123

DVD PREVIEW

1 Read about the TV documentary. Why do you think life gets difficult for the polar bears?

▶ **Nature's Great Events: The Great Melt**

This nature documentary shows how life changes when the Arctic ice melts in the summer. This is the greatest seasonal change on the planet. During the long winter, the sun never rises, and temperatures plummet to minus 40 degrees. When the ice melts in the summer, the landscape changes completely, and life gets difficult for the polar bears.

DVD VIEW

2 Watch the program and answer the questions.

1 Why is the melting ice a problem for the polar bears?

2 Is the problem worse than it was in the past?

3 A Complete the sentences using the words in the box below.

ice flicker rises drown summer sea islands

1 The northern lights _____ across the sky.

2 Polar bears are busy, hunting for seals on the frozen _____.

3 In February, the sun _____ for the first time in four months.

4 At the height of _____, even the permanent ice caps are touched by the power of the sun.

5 Over 7 million square kilometers of ice has melted away, creating thousands of _____, surrounded by open ocean.

6 A mother bear and her cub rest on a small piece of sea _____.

7 If future ice melts are as extreme as this one, bears like these may starve or _____, lost at sea.

B Watch the program again to check your answers.

4 Work in groups and discuss.

1 Do you think humans can do anything to improve the situation? What?

2 Do you think television programs like this help to change the situation? How?

American Speakout an endangered place

5 A You are going to give short presentations about places to see before they disappear. First, listen to someone else's presentation. Which question below does he not answer?

1 What is the place?
2 Why is it in danger?
3 Why should you go there/see it?
4 How much does it cost to go there?
5 What can be done to change the situation?

B Listen again and Check (✔) the key phrases you hear.

KEY PHRASES

One of the most beautiful places ... (is under threat)

One of the most endangered places is/has ...

One of the biggest problems ...

Something that everyone should have the chance to see is ...

The problem is that ...

Fortunately/Unfortunately, ...

Interestingly/Hopefully, ...

Many/Much of the ... have/has been

We have an opportunity to ...

In the past, ... but now ...

... before it's too late.

6 A Work on your own and plan a three-minute presentation. Do some research if necessary. Use the prompts below and the key phrases to help.

• What is the place?
• Why should you go there/see it?
• Why is it in danger?
• What can be done to change the situation?

B Work in pairs and take turns.

Student A: practice your presentation. Use your notes, but try not to read all the information. Try to look up when you're talking.

Student B: help your partner improve his/her presentation. Time the presentation. Was it long enough? Give him/her feedback about his/her style and language.

Then change roles and practice your presentations again.

C Give your presentation to the whole class. Watch the other students' presentations. Which places would you like to visit?

writeback email for action

7 A Read the email and answer the questions. Where is Little Green Street? What is the problem?

Little Green Street is an old cobbled street just outside the center of London. It is only 2.5 meters wide, and the houses here were built more than 225 years ago. The street, with its pretty, painted houses and cobblestones, survived World War II. But now it is under threat from a developer who plans to build a parking lot and houses on the land near it. The houses on Little Green St. are protected by law (nobody can get permission to demolish them), but the street itself is not. In order to build his parking lot, the developer plans to send heavy work trucks and machinery up and down this little old street. We are in no doubt that the trucks would destroy the street and possibly the houses along with it. If you would like to join us in our protest against these plans, please sign your name at the bottom of the email. Thank you.

B Write an email calling for action to protect one of the places presented in Exercise 6. Use the email above and the key phrases to help.

parking lot / St. / trucks   car park / St / lorries

V THE ENVIRONMENT

1 A Complete the words/phrases in bold with the missing letters.

1 I only eat **o_ _ _ _ _ c** food because it's grown without using chemicals.

2 I buy **p_ _-_ r_ _ _ _ _ d** food because I don't have time for cooking.

3 I don't use **e _ _ _ g_ -s_ _ _ _ g** light bulbs because they're expensive.

4 My house isn't **in_ _ l _ _ _d** very well, so it's always cold in the winter.

5 I try to **r_ _ y_ _ _** glass, plastic and paper, but nothing else.

6 I'm careful to turn the computer and TV off at night and not leave them **o_ s_ _ _d_ _**.

7 I buy a lot of **s_ _ _ _dh_ _ _** clothes. I like them, and they're cheap.

8 I think **p_ _ _ _ ss_ _** food is great because you can always make a quick meal at home.

B Write two statements that are true for you using the words/phrases in bold. Compare your sentences with a partner.

G REPORTED SPEECH

2 Rewrite the reported conversation using direct speech.

> Samantha introduced me (Franco) to Tom who said he was pleased to meet me. I replied that it was a pleasure to meet him, too, and that I hoped Tom was enjoying his stay in Milan. He said he thought Milan was a beautiful city, and he had very much enjoyed his stay there. He said that he had met lots of wonderful people and eaten some delicious food. I asked Tom if he had had the chance to do any sightseeing. Tom told me that, unfortunately, he hadn't had very much time at all, but that he had enjoyed seeing the cathedral. I asked Tom if he planned to visit Italy again soon. He replied that he would love to, but that Italy was a long way from Queensland. I said that was true and then invited Tom to come and join us for a coffee before he had to leave for the airport. Tom accepted.

Samantha: Franco, this is Tom.

Tom: Pleased to meet you, Franco.

Franco: It's ...

3 A Work in pairs. Take turns asking and answering questions 1–5. Make a note of your partner's answers.

1 What are your plans for your next vacation?

2 Where did you grow up? Is it different there now?

3 What do you usually do on Saturday afternoons?

4 What are you going to do later?

5 What two promises can you make concerning your English studies?

B Work with another student. Tell them what you learned about your partner using reported speech.

V REPORTING VERBS

4 Student A: choose a word. Don't say the word, but say something in the manner of the word. Student B: listen and guess which word your partner is describing.

> explain   refuse   promise   warn   invite   suggest   offer

A: If you do that again, I'm leaving.
B: warn?

G VERB PATTERNS

5 A Circle the correct alternative.

1 He promised *to give/giving* me back the money.

2 I refused *to answer/answering*.

3 She invited us *to stay/for staying*.

4 He offered *pay/to pay*.

5 I agreed *it to be/that it was* the best thing to do.

6 They explained *wanting/that they wanted* our address.

B Work in pairs and discuss. When was the last time:

• you promised to do something?

• you agreed with someone's idea?

• someone explained something to you?

• you refused to do something?

• someone offered to do something for you?

F GIVING ADVICE/WARNINGS

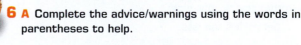

6 A Complete the advice/warnings using the words in parentheses to help.

1 _____, don't tell the teacher. (whatever)

2 _____ buy a phrase book. (forget)

3 _____ you get in shape before you do it. (make)

4 _____ wear that old shirt, ___ you'll never get the job. (else)

5 If _____, I'd buy her some flowers. (were)

6 _____ you don't oversleep and miss the plane. (careful)

7 You _____ look for a hotel on the Internet (better)

8 _____ ask your manager who can approve it. (need)

B Match the advice/warnings above with a)–h).

a) I haven't done my homework.

b) I forgot my mother's birthday.

c) I arrive in New York late at night. I don't know where I'm going to stay.

d) My plane leaves at 6 a.m., but I don't have an alarm.

e) I'd like to take a vacation, but I'm not sure whom I have to get permission from.

f) I'm planning to run a marathon, but I haven't done any training.

g) I can't speak the language.

h) I have a job interview, but I don't have any clean clothes to wear.

C Work in pairs. Give each other advice using a–h above.

take a vacation   have a holiday

)) IRREGULAR VERBS

Verb	Past Simple	Past Participle
be	was/were	been
beat	beat	beaten
become	became	become
begin	began	begun
bend	bent	bent
bet	bet	bet
bite	bit	bitten
bleed	bled	bled
blow	blew	blown
break	broke	broken
bring	brought	brought
broadcast	broadcast	broadcast
build	built	built
burn	burned/burnt	burned/burnt
burst	burst	burst
buy	bought	bought
catch	caught	caught
choose	chose	chosen
come	came	come
cost	cost	cost
cut	cut	cut
deal	dealt	dealt
dig	dug	dug
do	did	done
draw	drew	drawn
dream	dreamed/dreamt	dreamed/dreamt
drink	drank	drunk
drive	drove	driven
eat	ate	eaten
fall	fell	fallen
feel	felt	felt
feed	fed	fed
fight	fought	fought
find	found	found
fly	flew	flown
forbid	forbade	forbidden
forget	forgot	forgotten
forgive	forgave	forgiven
freeze	froze	frozen
get	got	got/gotten
give	gave	given
go	went	gone
grow	grew	grown
hang	hung	hung
have	had	had
hear	heard	heard
hide	hid	hidden
hit	hit	hit
hold	held	held
hurt	hurt	hurt
keep	kept	kept
know	knew	known
lay	laid	laid
lead	led	led
leap	leaped/leapt	leaped/leapt

Verb	Past Simple	Past Participle
learn	learned/learnt	learned/learnt
leave	left	left
lend	lent	lent
let	let	let
lie	lay	lain
light	lit	lit
lose	lost	lost
make	made	made
mean	meant	meant
meet	met	met
mistake	mistook	mistaken
pay	paid	paid
put	put	put
read /ri:d/	read /red/	read /red/
ride	rode	ridden
ring	rang	rung
rise	rose	risen
run	ran	run
say	said	said
see	saw	seen
sell	sold	sold
send	sent	sent
set	set	set
shake	shook	shaken
shine	shone	shone
shoot	shot	shot
show	showed	shown
shrink	shrank	shrunk
shut	shut	shut
sing	sang	sung
sink	sank	sunk
sit	sat	sat
sleep	slept	slept
slide	slid	slid
speak	spoke	spoken
spend	spent	spent
spill	spilled/spilt	spilled/spilt
split	split	split
spread	spread	spread
stand	stood	stood
steal	stole	stolen
stick	stuck	stuck
sting	stung	stung
swim	swam	swum
take	took	taken
teach	taught	taught
tear	tore	torn
tell	told	told
think	thought	thought
throw	threw	thrown
understand	understood	understood
wake	woke	woken
wear	wore	worn
win	won	won
write	wrote	written

GRAMMAR

1.1 Question Forms

Object Questions
Object questions use the word order: question word + auxiliary verb + subject + infinitive.

Question Word	Auxiliary Verb	Subject	Verb
Where	do	you	work?
What	did	she	say?
When	are	they	coming?

Yes/No Questions
Yes/No questions don't use a question word. The answer to the question is Yes or No.

Auxiliary Verb	Subject	Verb
Does	he	smoke?
Did	we	win?
Have	they	arrived?

Subject Questions
When the wh- question word is the subject of the question:
- we don't use an auxiliary verb (do, did, etc.).
- we use the same word order as in an affirmative sentence.

Question Word	Verb	Object
Who	wants	ice cream?
What	happened?	
Who	ate	the cheese?

Questions with Prepositions
When we use a verb + preposition expression (but not multi-word verbs), such as *look for, depend on, write about,* etc., we usually keep the verb and preposition together:

*What did you **talk about**?   Whom are you **looking for**?*

In very formal English, we sometimes move the preposition to the front of the sentence. Compare:

*What does it **depend on**?   **On** what does it **depend**?*

1.2 Review of Verb Tenses

Simple Present

+	He **looks** happy.
–	He **doesn't look** happy.
?	**Does** he **look** happy?

Use the simple present to talk about something that is always or generally true, habits, routines, with *be* and other state verbs (see below).

Present Continuous

+	We're **staying** here.
–	We **aren't staying** here.
?	**Are** we **staying** here?

Use the simple continuous to talk about an activity happening at the time of speaking or a temporary activity happening around now. It may be happening at the moment, but may not be.

Simple Past

+	They **worked** hard.
–	They **didn't work** hard.
?	**Did** they **work** hard?

Use the simple past to talk about finished actions, events or situations in the past.

Past Continuous

+	I **was living** there during the '90s.
–	I **wasn't living** there during the '90s.
?	**Were** you **living** there?

Use the past continuous to talk about an action or situation in progress at a particular time in the past. This action was not finished at that time.

State Verbs and Dynamic Verbs
State verbs are not usually used in the continuous form. The most common state verbs are:

- **attitude verbs:** *love, hate, like, want, prefer*
- **thinking verbs:** *believe, know, remember, understand, mean, imagine*
- **sense verbs:** *see, hear, sound, appear, seem*
- **belonging verbs:** *own, possess, belong to, have, contain, include*

Some state verbs can be used in the continuous form when they describe actions, e.g., *see, have, think*:

*I'm **seeing** Phil tonight.* (see = meet)
*We're **having** a party.* (have = organize)
*I'm **thinking** of going to college.* (think = consider)

1.3 Talking about Yourself

Introducing a Question
Could I ask a question?
There are a couple of things I'd like to ask about.
Can I ask you about that?
I have a question.

Introducing an Opinion
For me, (the most important thing is) …
I'd have to say …
In my opinion, …
One thing I'd like to say is that …

PRACTICE

1.1

A Write questions for the answers in italics.

1 Where _____?
  I live *in Madrid*.

2 Who _____?
  Nick won the game.

3 Does _____?
  No, he doesn't eat meat.

4 What _____?
  They are *sleeping*.

5 What _____?
  I'm writing about *my first holiday*.

6 When _____?
  We arrived *yesterday*.

7 Who _____?
  We ate the chocolate.

8 Did _____?
  Yes, we liked the movie.

B Put the words in parentheses in the correct places to make questions.

1 the President? (killed, who)
  _____

2 were you thinking? (what, about)
  _____

3 to the old theater? (happened, what)
  _____

4 Where your great-grandparents come? (from, did)
  _____

5 your ancestors from here? (come, did)
  _____

6 she here for a long time? (worked, has)
  _____

7 is all that noise? (who, making)
  _____

8 house you looking for? (are, which)
  _____

1.2

A Underline the correct alternatives.

"Like most translators, I ¹*'m speaking/speak* several languages. At the moment, I ²*'m attending/attend* a conference. I ³*was doing/did* some work for an Internet company when I ⁴*was hearing/heard* about this conference. I ⁵*was arriving/arrived* three days ago, and I'm going to stay until Monday, when it ends."

My best friend is called Gina. We ⁶*aren't speaking/don't speak* to each other every day, but we're very close. I ⁷*was meeting/met* her on my first morning at college. I ⁸*was looking/looked* for the library when she came up to me and asked, "Excuse me, ⁹*do you know/are you knowing* where the library is?" We ¹⁰*were finding/found* it together!

B Put the verbs in parentheses into the correct tense.

1 Sit down and watch the game! We _____ (win) 2–1. Ronaldo scored two minutes ago.

2 John wasn't here last summer. He _____ (travel) around Africa.

3 Fifty years ago, my favorite writer _____ (die).

4 I didn't do the homework because I _____ (not listen) when the teacher told us what to do.

5 DVDs _____ (not work) very well on my laptop, so I use the TV and DVD player.

6 What's that smell? Can you turn off the oven? I think the food _____ (burn).

7 _____ (see) that movie last night? What did you think?

8 Everyone knows that smoking _____ (cause) cancer.

1.3

A Find and correct the mistakes in the conversation below. There are six mistakes.

A: There are a couple of things I'd like ask about.

B: Go ahead.

A: First, which of your movies do you think is the best?

B: I'd having to say *Millennium Dreamer*. For me, it's my best movie, and it was my first comedy.

A: Can I ask you around that? You've never done comedy before. Why not?

B: I don't know. I suppose people think I'm a serious actor.

A: Could I ask question about your image? Is it accurate? Are you really the strong silent type in real life?

B: No. One of thing I'd like to say is that these images are invented by the media. By my opinion, good actors are never just one thing. That's why they're actors.

GRAMMAR

2.1 ### Present Perfect and Simple Past

Present perfect simple: *have/has* + past participle (*lived, worked, seen* etc.)

+	I've **been** to Poland a few times.
–	He **hasn't worked** here before.
?	**Have** you **bought** a new car?

For irregular past participles, see the list of irregular verbs on page 127.

Time Up to Now

Use the present perfect for actions that have happened in your life before now. These are often general experiences. It isn't important exactly when these things happened. Conversations that begin like this in the present perfect usually continue in the simple past as the speaker adds details:

I've been to Colombia. Really? Where did you go?
He's played in indie bands. What were they called?

We often use the adverbs *ever* and *never* with the present perfect:

We've never been to China.   Have you ever been to the Opera?

Recent Events

Use the present perfect to talk about events which happened a short time ago. We often use the adverbs *just*, *yet* and *already*:

I've just finished his book. It was brilliant.
We've already eaten.
Have you done your homework yet?
We've seen a lot of Jude recently.

Present Perfect or Simple Past?

Use the past simple to talk about a specific event that happened at a specific time:

I've been to Sweden.
(At some time in my life up to now. We don't know when.)
We went to Stockholm in 2002.
NOT *We've been to Stockholm in 2002.*
(This is a specific occasion and date, so we use the simple past.)

2.2 ### Narrative Tenses

Simple Past

Use the simple past for states and actions in the past. We often specify the time when they happened:

I left college in 1996.   He didn't know the way to Sal's house.

Past Continuous

Use the past continuous to talk about the background information for a story. Use the simple past to talk about the main events.

BACKGROUND INFORMATION Past Continuous		MAIN EVENT Simple Past
I was walking through the park … *The sun was shining …* *The birds were singing …*	WHEN	*… I heard a noise*

As I was walking through the park, the sun was shining, and the birds were singing. Suddenly, I heard a loud noise.

Often the past continuous action is interrupted by another action (in the simple past):

I was taking a bath when the phone rang.

We can use conjunctions like *as* and *while* to talk about two actions that were happening at the same time:

While I was reading the paper, I watched the women buying vegetables in the market.

For more information on state and dynamic verbs, see section 1.2, page 128.

Past Perfect

+	I **had finished** my work.
–	They **hadn't had** time.
?	**Had** they **been** there before?

Use the past perfect to make it clear that one action happened before the other.

past perfect	simple past	present

I lost my wallet. I didn't have any money.
past ├————————┼————————┤ now

I didn't have any money because I had lost my wallet.

When *before* or *after* is used in the sentence, it's already clear which action comes before the other, so we can use the simple past instead of the past perfect:

She had lived in London for five years before she moved to New York.
She lived in London for five years before she moved to New York.

We often use the past perfect with "thinking" verbs like *remember*, *realize*, *think*, *discover*, *find out*, etc.:

When I got to the school, I realized I'd left my books at home.

2.3 ### Telling a Story

Beginning the Story	This happened when … In the beginning, …	Questions to Keep a Story Going	So, what happened? What did you do? What happened next? Really?
Describing What Happened	Well, … Anyway, … Before long, … So, … And, then, all of a sudden, … The next thing I knew, …	Responses to Show Interest	I don't believe it! Oh, no. / Oh, dear. How embarrassing! That's really funny. You must be joking. Yes, I know.
Ending the Story	In the end, … Finally, …		

PRACTICE

2.1

A Check (✓) the correct sentences, a) or b).

1 a) I've been to India last year.
   b) I went to India last year.
2 a) I finished my studies in 2005.
   b) I've finished my studies in 2005.
3 a) Did you have lunch yet?
   b) Have you had lunch yet?
4 a) Did you ever see *Metallica* play live?
   b) Have you ever seen *Metallica* play live?
5 a) Is this the first time you've tried judo?
   b) Is this the first time you tried judo?
6 a) It's the most beautiful place I've ever been to.
   b) It's the most beautiful place I ever went to.

B Use the prompts to make short conversations.

1 A: you / be / here / before? (ever)
   B: no / not
2 A: you / see / the film *The Reader*?
   B: no / not / see (yet)
3 A: he / be / to Budapest?
   B: yes / go / last summer
4 A: you / finish / that book? (yet)
   B: yes / start / the next one (already)
5 A: you / see / Maria?
   B: yes, she / leave / a message for you
6 A: he / decide / what job / want to do? (yet)
   B: no / have / not

2.2

A Underline the correct alternatives to complete the story.

I remember when Marvin Gaye ¹*died/had died*. I ²*had been/was going* to one of his concerts a few months before. In fact, he ³*hadn't played/wasn't playing* very well, and I was disappointed. I also remember when J. F. K. was shot. I ⁴*had lived/was living* with my parents in New York, and I ⁵*studied/was studying* at the time. I remember the cleaning lady ⁶*came/was coming* into the room and said to me, "Hey, President Lincoln has been shot." I ⁷*replied/was replying*, "I know that." "No," she said. "President Lincoln has been shot!" So I said, "What do you mean?" And she said, "Oh, no. I mean … President, you know, what's his name, the one now. President Kennedy's been shot." So then I ⁸*was turning/turned* on the radio.

B Find and correct the mistakes. One sentence is correct.

1 I was leaving the room when I had heard someone shouting.
2 I couldn't open the door because I left my keys at home.
3 We drove through the tunnel when the car broke down.
4 As soon as the movie started, I realized I seen it before.
5 I never been to Egypt before, so I was really excited to see the pyramids.
6 By the time we arrived at the party, everybody else is leaving.
7 We had waited for nearly an hour before the waiter took our order.
8 I looked through some old photographs when I found this one of you.

2.3

A Complete the conversation with the words and phrases in the box.

In the end | don't believe it | The next thing I knew | this happened when | So, what happened
Well | really funny | Anyway | You must be joking | So

A: Well, ¹_____ I was working in a photographic store.
B: ²_____?
A: ³_____, one day a woman came in and asked if we could fix the problem she had with a photograph. ⁴_____ I asked her what the problem was.
B: OK.
A: ⁵_____, she had taken this old photo out of her bag. It showed an old man sitting behind a cow, milking it. ⁶_____, when I asked her what she wanted us to do to the photo, she said, "Can you move the cow?" "Move the cow?" I asked. "Yes," she replied. "I want to see what my grandfather looked like." She pointed to the feet sticking out from under the cow.

B: Oh, no. ⁷_____.
A: No, seriously. She wanted us to move the cow, so that she could see her grandfather's face.
B: I ⁸_____! So, what happened next?
A: ⁹_____, when I told her we couldn't do it, she got quite angry and left the shop saying, "Then I'll have to take it to someone else."
B: That's ¹⁰_____.

GRAMMAR

3.1 The Future (Plans)

Be Going To

+	I'm **going to** start college next year.
–	He **isn't going to** get a job this year.
?	Where **are** you **going to** stay?

When using *be going to,* use the word order: subject + *am/are/is* + *going to* + infinitive without *to*. Use *be going to* to talk about future plans or intentions. When the verb is *go* or *come*, we often use the present continuous:

We're going to (go to) Spain. We're going to Spain.
I'm going to come and see you later. I'm coming to see you later.

Present Continuous

+	I'm start**ing** my course in September.
–	We**'re** not go**ing** away for very long.
?	What time **are** you leav**ing** in the morning?

The present continuous is formed: subject + *am/are/is* (*not*) + verb + *-ing*. Use the present continuous to talk about future plans, when arrangements have already been made. We usually specify a future time, such as *next week*, *on Friday*, etc., unless it is already clear that we are talking about the future:

We're flying to Greece on Friday. (We've already bought the tickets.)
She's staying in a hotel near the airport. (The hotel is already reserved.)

In some cases, it doesn't matter if it's the present continuous or *be going to*:

I'm playing football on Saturday.
I'm going to play football on Saturday.

Will

+	We**'ll meet** you at the station.
–	I **won't see** you tomorrow.
?	**Will** you **want** a taxi?

When there is no plan or arrangement (when we make a decision at the time of speaking), we often use *will*: *I'm tired. I think I'll go to bed.* (subject + *will* + infinitive)
For use of *be going to* and *will* for prediction, see section 3.2 below.

Might

+	I **might go** out later.
–	We **might not be able** to finish all this work tomorrow.

Use *might* + infinitive without *to* to talk about plans, when we are unsure what the plan is:

I might stay at home and watch a DVD.
(But I'm not sure. I might go out.)

Spoken Grammar

We do not usually use *might* + infinitive without *to* in the question form. It seems old-fashioned and formal:

Do you think you might see Evelyn?
NOT *Might you see Evelyn?*

3.2 The Future (Predictions)

Will

Use *will* to make predictions:

Smartphones will organize our lives. She's so talented that I'm sure she'll become famous.

We often use *I think* and *I hope* with *will*:

I think John will become a doctor. She hopes she will work in the theater.

Be Going To

Use *be going to* to make predictions when there is present evidence:

We only have two cars. It's going to be difficult to take eleven people tomorrow.

We use *probably* to make the prediction less certain. *Probably* usually comes after *will*:

The dollar will probably get stronger this year.

Probably comes after *to be* when we use it with *be going to*:

E-readers are probably going to become cheaper.

May and Might

Use *may* or *might* to make predictions that are less certain. The negative forms are *may not* and *might not*:

Some of our workers may lose their jobs because of the restructuring. We might not go away this year because we don't have any money.

Could

Use *could* to make predictions that are less certain:

Global warming could destroy large parts of Asia in the next thirty years.

Be Likely To

Use *be likely to* to make predictions when something is probable. The negative is *be unlikely to* or *not be likely to*:

Karie is likely to be late because she works until seven.
We're unlikely to reach Portland before lunch because of all the traffic.
Are you likely to be hungry later?

Likely/Unlikely are adjectives:

Will we start at 5:00? It's unlikely.

Spoken Grammar

Might is more common than *may* in spoken English.
May is a little bit more formal.

3.3 Dealing with Misunderstandings

Saying You Didn't Hear Something	I didn't catch any of that.
Saying You Don't Understand Someone's Opinion	You've lost me. I don't get what you're saying.
Asking Someone to Explain Something More Clearly	What exactly do you mean? Do you mean to say …?
Asking Someone to Repeat Something	Can you say that again? Could you repeat the last part/name/thing you said?

PRACTICE

3.1

A Complete the conversation. Use the prompts in parentheses where necessary.

A: Where ¹_____ you going?

B: I'm ²_____ to Paul's house. We' ³_____ going to watch the football game.

A: OK. Who ⁴_____? (play)

B: The Denver Broncos and the Seattle Seahawks.

A: I see. And what time are you ⁵_____ home? (come)

B: I don't know.

A: How ⁶_____ getting home?

B: I'm not sure. I ⁷_____ his dad to drive me home, or I ⁸_____ catch the bus. (ask/might)

B Find and correct the mistakes. There is one mistake in each sentence.

1 Will you going out this weekend?

2 I'm sorry I can't come. I playing tennis after work.

3 I don't feel very well. I think I stay at home.

4 What you going to do?

5 We go for a picnic, so I hope it doesn't rain.

6 Is that the phone? Don't worry—I'm going to get it.

7 They might going to a concert.

8 I'm sorry we can't come, but we going to visit my mother this weekend.

3.2

A Rewrite the sentences below using the words in parentheses.

1 We probably won't win the cup this year. (might)
We _____

2 I may be late. (likely)
I'm _____

3 That company will close in July. (going)
That company _____

4 He probably won't call after 10:00. (unlikely)
It _____

5 I'm not going to give up exercise. (won't)
I _____

6 We might have a problem with the flight. (may)
There _____

7 She'll get angry when she sees this. (going)
She _____

8 Are you going to visit us? (will)
_____

9 I would love it if he came to the party. (hope)
_____

10 It is thought that prices will rise if they complete the development. (could)
Prices _____

B Put each pair of words in the box into the correct place to complete the sentences.

| will be | aren't going | won't know | might not |
| likely to | may arrive | is going | not likely |

1 Jenny be able to meet us tonight because she has to work late.

2 Several of our workers are lose their jobs this year because of the economic recession.

3 In twenty years' time, cars able to fly.

4 The predicted storm at any moment.

5 The children to stay with me because I'm busy.

6 I my test results until August.

7 It's that we'll arrive before 6:00 because there are train delays.

8 Watch out! That painting to fall off the wall!

3.3

A Match 1—7 with a)—g) to make sentences and questions.

1 I didn't catch	a) you're saying.
2 You've lost	b) you mean?
3 I don't get what	c) that again?
4 What exactly do	d) to say …?
5 Could you repeat the	e) any of that.
6 Do you mean	f) last name?
7 Can you say	g) me.

You're where? Don't shush me!

SUSHI BAR

GRAMMAR

4.1 Must, Have to, Should (Obligation)
Must, Have to

+	I **must** get up at 5 tomorrow. They **have to** start work early. We **must** start on time. She **has to** get there early.
–	You **must not** do that! We **don't have to** worry. They **must not** be late. He **doesn't have to** bring anything.
?	Do I/we/you **have to** bring …? (**Must** you go so early?)* **Does** he/she/it **have to** go?

*Question forms with *must* are not very common, and sound quite formal. We usually use *Do you have to …?* instead.

Use *must* and *have to* to talk about obligations. These things are necessary or important. *Must* is often used for a personal obligation (something we have decided for ourselves that we need to do):

*I **must** give up eating chocolate.*

Must is also used in written rules:

All applicants must provide proof of identity.

Have to is used for external obligation:
*We **have to** wear a uniform.* (It's a company rule.)
Often you can use *must* or *have to* with the same meaning, but in spoken English *have to* is more common.
Don't have to and *must not* have different meanings.
Must is not used that often in American English as obligation or prohibition:

Must not means "it is not allowed." *Don't/Doesn't have to* means it is not necessary, but you can do it if you want:

*You **must not** smoke cigarettes anywhere in the building.* (It is not permitted, and it's dangerous.)
*You **don't have to** work after 6.* (It's not necessary.)

Must can only be used to talk about present or future obligation. To talk about a past obligation, use *had to*:

*We **had to** get up early to catch the plane.*

Spoken Grammar
Have/Has got to means the same as *have/has to* in the context of obligation and is used a lot in spoken English:

*I've **got to** get some money from the bank.*
*She's **got to** get another job.*

Should/Shouldn't

+	I/You/He/She/	**should** see this movie.
–	It/We/They	**shouldn't** smoke in the house.
?	Do you think we **should** …?*	

Use *should* to talk about weak obligations (not as strong as *must* or *have to*). Often it is used for things that you think are a good idea (advice):

*You **should** come to work in nice clothes.*

Use *shouldn't* to talk about things that are not a good idea:

*You **shouldn't** go to bed so late.*

Ought to has the same meaning as *should* but is not usually used in the negative or questions:

*You **ought to** call her.* = You should call her.

4.2 Used To, Would
Used To

+	I/You/He/She/	**used to** live in France.
–	It/We/They	**didn't use** to see my parents.
?	Did they **use to** visit?	

Use *used to* to talk about past habits/states that have often changed or are not true now. You can also use the past simple.

*As a child, I **used to** love eating candy.*
*As a child, I **ate** a lot of candy.*

We can also use *would* to talk about past habits, but not to talk about past states.

*I **would** go to the candy store every day.* (habit)
*As a child, I **was** very happy.*
*As a child, I **used to be** very happy.* (state)
NOT *As a child, I would be very happy.* (state)

Do not use *used to* to talk about things that happened only once or for a specific number of times/length of time. Use the past simple for this:

*My family **moved** to the U.S. last year.*
NOT *My family used to move to the U.S. last year.*

*We **went** to Italy twice on vacation.*
NOT *We used to go to Italy twice on vacation.*

*I **studied** at college for three years.*
NOT *I used to study at college for three years.*

Spoken Grammar
Never used to is more common in spoken English than *didn't use to*.

*We **never used to** see them, except for in August.*

In short answers in spoken English, we often leave out the verb or phrase after *used to*.

*Do you smoke? No, I **used to**, but I don't any more.*

4.3 Reaching Agreement

Giving Opinions

I (really) feel that …
The way I see things, …
The way I see it, …

Suggestions

What about …?
I suggest we focus on …
I think we should think about …
I suggest we think about …
How about if / Why don't we (call it)…?

Commenting on Others' Opinions

That's a good idea.
That's a good point.
That's fine by me.
That's OK by me.
Exactly!
I (don't) see what you mean.
I'm not sure that I agree, actually.
I'm not sure that … is a good idea.

PRACTICE

4.1

A Underline the correct alternative to complete the text.

The worst jobs in the world?

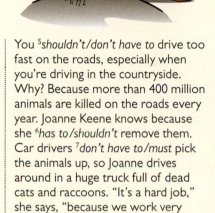

If you like traveling to exotic places, perhaps you ¹*should/ shouldn't* try this job. Helge Zieler is a mosquito researcher. In order to study the biting habits of the mosquito that spreads malaria in Brazil, Helge ²*has to/doesn't have to* sit inside a mosquito net while hundreds of mosquitoes bite him. Every time he sees a mosquito land on his body, he ³*must/have to* suck it into a tube in his mouth and then blow it into a container. On a good evening, Helge can catch 500 mosquitoes in three hours. But to do this, he receives 3,000 bites (an average of seventeen bites per minute for 180 minutes). He ⁴*must not/must* forget his anti-malaria pills. Once he caught malaria, and it took him two years to recover.

You ⁵*shouldn't/don't have to* drive too fast on the roads, especially when you're driving in the countryside. Why? Because more than 400 million animals are killed on the roads every year. Joanne Keene knows because she ⁶*has to/shouldn't* remove them. Car drivers ⁷*don't have to/must* pick the animals up, so Joanne drives around in a huge truck full of dead cats and raccoons. "It's a hard job," she says, "because we work very long hours. We ⁸*must not/must* be on call 24 hours a day."

B Match 1–8 with a)–h) to make sentences.

1 It's a good job, but we
2 I love Saturday mornings because I don't have to
3 I think you should
4 The doctor told me that I
5 You must not
6 You don't have to
7 Francois is very lucky. His father is very rich, so he
8 I really must

a) have to work hard.
b) should do more exercise.
c) come to work dressed in jeans. You have to look neat.
d) doesn't have to work at all.
e) give up smoking. It's not good for my health.
f) get up for work. I can stay in bed until 10 a.m.
g) send the forms in until September, but it's a good idea to send them early.
h) think about whether you really want to apply for the job.

4.2

A Cross out the alternative that is not possible.

1 I *used to play/played/play* a lot of tennis when I was younger.
2 After school, I *would take/used to take/take* the bus home.
3 He *never used to play/would play/ played* the guitar, but he doesn't play any more.
4 I *didn't use to enjoy/didn't enjoy/ wouldn't enjoy* school, but I worked hard anyway.
5 Tim *used to have/would have/had* long hair.
6 I *studied/used to study/did use to study* French.

B Make sentences with *used to* or *would* using the words in parentheses. Sometimes both may be possible.

1 In Ancient Greece, people _____ (think) the world was flat, but Aristotle thought it was round.
2 In the olden days, people _____ (not have) cars, so they rode horses.
3 _____ people really _____ (enjoy) watching gladiator fights in Ancient Rome?
4 In the sixteenth century, ladies _____ (put) a white powder containing lead on their faces. It was poisonous.
5 Two hundred years ago, they _____ (not use) anaesthetics to perform operations.
6 Before iron was invented, soldiers _____ (fight) using bronze swords, but they weren't very strong and often changed shape in battle.
7 The Romans _____ (make) themselves sick so that they could eat more during their huge banquets.
8 Why _____ people _____ (eat) garlic in Ancient Egypt? It was to cure toothaches.

4.3

A Using the words in italics, rewrite the second sentence so it has the same meaning as the first.

1 Let's begin.
   I think we _____*should begin*_____ .
2 I suggest we look at the emails first.
   Why _____?
3 I don't understand.
   I _____ you mean.
4 I agree with that idea.
   That's _____ me.
5 From my point of view, it works very well.
   The way _____ things, it works very well.
6 I agree with what you have just said.
   That's _____ point.

GRAMMAR

5.1 Comparatives and Superlatives

One-syllable Adjectives and Two-syllable Adjectives Ending in -y

Adjective	Comparative	Superlative	Notes
cheap fast	cheaper faster	the cheapest the fastest	+ -er / the + -est
easy friendly	easier friendlier	the easiest the friendliest	-y changes to -i + -er / the + -est
big	bigger	the biggest	adjective ending in *CVC double final consonant
large	larger	the largest	adjective ending in -e, add -r / the + -st

*CVC—consonant, vowel, consonant

Two-syllable and Longer Adjectives

Adjective	Comparative	Superlative	Notes
important	more/less important than	the most/least important	+ more/less ... than, or the most/the least ... (in the ...)

Irregular Adjectives

Adjective	Comparative	Superlative
good	better	the best
bad	worse	the worst
far	farther/further	the farthest/furthest

Ways of Comparing

Here are some common expressions used for making comparisons: *It's exactly/about the same as ...*, *It's very similar to ...*, *It's not as ... as*:

*It's **exactly the same as** the one we had.*
*It's **very similar** to somewhere I stayed.*
*He's **not as tall as** I expected.*

It's a lot/much/far more + adjective:

*It's **far more beautiful** than I imagined.*

It's a little/a little bit/slightly:

*It's **slightly smaller** than the last apartment I lived in.*

Using Superlatives

Here are some common expressions used with superlatives: *by far the most ...*, *one of the most ...*, *the second (third/fourth) most ...*

*It's **by far the most** delicious meal I've ever eaten.*
*It's **one of the most** beautiful places in the world.*

We often use superlatives with a phrase beginning with *in the ...*:

*She's by far the best student **in the class**.*
*It's one of the tallest buildings **in the world**.*

5.2 Question Tags

To make question tags, add auxiliary verb + pronoun at the end of the question. For a positive sentence, use a negative tag: *You **play** tennis, **don't you**?* For a negative sentence use a positive tag: *They **weren't** here, **were they**?*
Use contractions in the tag, not the full verb: *He's nice, isn't he?* NOT *He's nice, is not he?* N.B. Use a comma before the question tag and a question mark after it.

	Positive Verb + Negative Tag	Negative Verb + Positive Tag
Present	You're twenty, aren't you?	She doesn't swim, does she?
Past	They came back, didn't they?	You didn't see Tim, did you?
Present Perfect	You've lost it, haven't you?	He hasn't seen us, has he?
Future	I'll be back by 10:00, won't I?	We won't lose, will we?

Use question tags to check information that you think is true. Also use question tags to sound less direct (a way to sound polite).
If we are sure of the information, the intonation falls on the question tag:

You're coming tomorrow, aren't you?
(Presumes a positive answer.)
If we are really not sure, the intonation rises on the question tag:

She's from Europe, isn't she?
(Is less certain about the answer.)

5.3 Polite Requests

Request	Responses
Could you carry this bag **for me**? **Could you** bring your laptop with you?	Yes, of course. I'm afraid I can't/ I'm sorry, I can't.
Could you tell me the way to the hotel? **Could you tell me** what time it is?	Yes, I can. It's ... Let me have a look.
Do you know what time the stores open? **Do you know** how to get there?	I'm not sure.
Would you mind coming a little bit earlier? **Would you mind** reserving us a table?	Of course not. OK./Sure.

Watch out!

Could you tell me ...? and *Do you know ...?* are not direct questions; the word order is the same as for statements:
Could you tell me what time it is?
NOT *Could you tell me what time is it?*

Do you know what time the stores open?
NOT *Do you know what time do the stores open?*

Would you mind ... + -ing:
Would you mind watering my plants when I go away?
NOT *Would you mind to water ...?*

Would you mind ...? is followed by a negative response:
Would you mind helping me? No, of course not.
(I'm happy to help you.) NOT *Yes, of course.*
(I would mind helping you—I'm not happy to help you.)

PRACTICE

 5.1

A Complete the sentences with the comparative or superlative form of the adjectives in parentheses.

1 We usually fly to Boston instead of going in the car, because it's _____. (quick)

2 They had to travel _____ than they wanted to find a hotel. (far)

3 When I was a teenager, I was much _____ than I am now. (not confident)

4 He's one of _____ children in the class. (naughty)

5 Tests are much _____ now than they were when I was in school. (easy)

6 Canada is _____ than the U.S. (big)

7 K2 is the second _____ mountain in the world. (high)

8 This book is slightly _____ to understand than his last book. The plot is very complicated. (difficult)

9 He used to be a teacher, but he's decided to become a firefighter. It's a much _____ job. (dangerous)

10 It's by far _____ movie I've ever seen. (good)

B Rewrite the sentences using the words in bold so that they have the same meaning.

1 My brother is slightly taller than I am. **bit**

_____

2 The trip to the coast took much longer than we had expected. **far**

_____

3 It's easily the most expensive restaurant I've ever been to. **by**

_____

4 Your shoes and my shoes are almost the same. **similar**

_____

5 People here are much healthier now that they have clean water. **lot**

_____

 5.2

A Match 1—8 with a)—h) to make tag questions.

1 Clint was an engineer,
2 You're from Ethiopia,
3 Shania isn't an actress,
4 They haven't been here before,
5 He'll be home soon,
6 You work here,
7 She hasn't met you,
8 They won't finish on time,

a) have they?
b) won't he?
c) has she?
d) aren't you?
e) is she?
f) will they?
g) wasn't he?
h) don't you?

B Find and correct the mistakes in each question.

1 You weren't happy, weren't you?
2 It'll probably rain, doesn't it?
3 She researched her roots, didn't her?
4 They always ask tricky questions, they don't?
5 I take after my dad, doesn't he?
6 You've met Kevin's fiancée, have not you?
7 I put my foot in my mouth yesterday, haven't I?
8 My mentor will give me a hand, he won't?
9 You had a lot on your mind, doesn't you?
10 Phil and Luke are on vacation, are not they?

5.3

A Find the mistakes and correct them. There is an extra word or two in each line.

1 **A:** Excuse me, could you is hold the door for me?
  B: Yes, I do of course.

2 **A:** Do you know when the next train does to leaves?
  B: I'm not OK sure.

3 **A:** Would you to mind staying behind after the meeting?
  B: It's sure. That's fine.

4 **A:** Could is possible you tell me what Tim's phone number is?
  B: Let me have a to look.

5 **A:** Would you mind to looking after my bag while I go to the bathroom?
  B: No, of course not mind.

6 **A:** Could you tell for me the way to the station?
  B: Yes, so I can.

GRAMMAR

6.1 Real Conditionals

When we talk about situations that are always true or events that are possible or probable in the future using *if/when*, we can call these "real conditionals". They are also often referred to as "zero (0) conditionals" (always true) and first (1) conditionals (possible or probable in the future).

Real Conditional (Zero)

If/When +	Simple Present +	Simple Present
If/When	you* **heat** water to 100 °C,	it **boils**.

* Here *you* is a general subject meaning "anyone" or "people in general."

Use the real conditional (zero) to talk about a general situation or something that is always true (a fact):

*If plants **don't have** water, they **die**.   Ice **melts** if you **heat** it.*
(*You* here refers to "anyone," or people generally, not "you" specifically.)
If/When can come at the beginning or in the middle of the sentence:

If I'm not in the office by 8 a.m., my boss gets angry.
My boss gets angry if I'm not in the office by 8 a.m.

If and *when* have the same meaning in zero conditional sentences. In this case, *if* means "when this happens" or "every time this happens":

When I'm feeling stressed, I eat chocolate.
If I'm feeling stressed, I eat chocolate.

Real Conditional (First)

If/When +	Simple Present +	Will/Could/Might + Verb
If	you **give** me your phone number,	I'll **call** you when we're ready.
When	you **go** into the kitchen,	you'll **see** the keys on the table.

Use the real conditional (first) to talk about possible situations in the future and their consequences. If you are sure about the result, use *will/won't*. If you're not sure, use *could/might*. We can change the order of the sentence, but *if/when* is always followed by the present simple:

*If my train **arrives** on time, I'll meet you at 10 o'clock. OR I'll meet you at 10 o'clock if my train arrives on time. NOT if my train will arrive on time.*

In first conditional sentences, *if* and *when* have different meanings. Use *if* when you are not sure if the situation will happen:

If I pass my exams, I'll be very happy.

Use *when* for a situation which you know will happen: *When I pass my exams, I'll have a party.*

Unless has the meaning of "if not" or "except in this situation":

I'll go straight to the restaurant unless you call me first. (I will go straight to the restaurant if you don't call me first.)

Note the difference between zero and first conditional in the sentences below:

*If you sit in the sun, you **get** a sunburn.*
(Zero conditional for a general situation/fact. "You" means anyone or people in general.)

*If you sit in the sun, you'll **get** a sunburn.*
(First conditional for a specific situation. I'm talking to you (personally) about what will happen today.)

6.2 Hypothetical Conditional: Present/Future

If +	Subjunctive +	Would Clause
If	I **worked** longer hours, he **were** the President, we **bought** the house,	I **would** make more money. he'**d make** a lot of changes. we'**d need** to sell our car.

Use the hypothetical conditional to talk about an unreal or imaginary situation and its consequences. In conditional sentences, the subjunctive is used to indicate that something is hypothetical or imaginary. **The subjunctive is usually the same as the simple past, except for *be*.**

*Was is a variant that is becoming more common.
In spoken English, *would* is contracted in the positive and negative form:

I'd be there if I had time.   If she had enough food, she'd feed us all.

Would is not usually contracted in the question form:
*If you passed your exam, **would** you go to college?*
***Would** you help me if I paid you?*

Use *If I were you ...* to give advice:
If I were you, I'd change teams.

Instead of *would*, we can use *could* or *should*:
*If you got in shape, you **could** probably play again.*

It is common to use other expressions in the *would* clause: *would be able to*, *would need to* and *would have to*:

*If I lost my job, I'd **need to** find another one.*
*We **would have to** cancel the game if it rained.*
*If you bought a larger quantity, we'**d be able to** offer you a better deal.*

6.3 Giving News

Good News	I've got some good news (for you). I'm really pleased to tell you ... You'll never guess what.
Bad News	Bad news, I'm afraid. I'm sorry to have to tell you, but ... I'm afraid/Unfortunately, ... I'm afraid I've got some bad news ... There's something I've got to tell you.
Good or Bad News	You know ...? Well, ... I've/We've got something to tell you.
Responding to Good News	Wow! That's fantastic/great news. Congratulations! You're joking! You lucky thing! Well done. Have you?/Did you?
Responding to Bad News	That's a shame. That's terrible/awful. That's really annoying. I'm really sorry to hear that.

PRACTICE

6.1

A Complete the sentences with the correct form of the verbs in parentheses.

1 If I _____ (pass) my exams, my teacher _____ (be) very surprised.

2 When we _____ (visit) my mother, she usually _____ (look after) the children.

3 When Gaby _____ (leave) her job in the summer, she _____ (worry) about what to do next.

4 If I _____ (not find) any cheap tickets, we _____ (not go) to Malta.

5 If you _____ (not water) plants, they _____ (die).

6 I _____ (be) surprised if Martha _____ (come) to the party. She said she wasn't feeling well.

7 If you _____ (get) lost, do you usually _____ (ask) someone for directions?

8 They _____ (not come) unless you _____ (invite) them.

B Underline the correct alternative.

1 You can't come to the conference *unless/if/when* you're invited.

2 I'm not talking to you *unless/if/when* you calm down first.

3 They'll arrive as soon as dinner *is/will be/won't be* ready.

4 They'll cancel the flight *if/unless/when* the weather is bad.

5 If you eat all of that chocolate mousse, you *'ll feel/feel/won't feel* sick.

6 We'll organize a taxi when we *know/will know/might know* what time the concert starts.

7 When I see a spider, I always *scream/might scream/will scream*.

8 I'll get some money as soon as the bank *will open/opens/might open*.

6.2

A Complete the sentences with the correct form of the verbs in parentheses. Use contractions where possible.

1 If I _____ (sell) my house now, it _____ (not/be) worth very much.

2 _____ (your parents/come) if I _____ (organize) a party?

3 He _____ (not/be) able to study here if _____ (not/pass) that test.

4 If you _____ (lose) your passport, _____ (need) visit the embassy.

5 They _____ (be) healthier if _____ (not/eat) so much junk food.

6 If you _____ (write) a novel, what _____ (call) it?

7 If the students _____ (not/have) Internet access, _____ (find) it difficult.

8 We _____ (not/work) there if the boss _____ (not/give) us a lot of freedom.

9 Where _____ (she/live) if _____ (have) to move to a different country?

10 If he _____ (can) study on Tuesdays, _____ (not/need) to come on Wednesday.

B Write answers to the questions using the prompts. Use contractions.

1 A: Can we walk to the game?
   B: No. (be/late)
   If we _____ *walked to the game, we'd be late* _____.

2 A: Why doesn't the team enter the competition?
   B: (it/lose)
   If the team _____.

3 A: Can I borrow his car?
   B: No. (get/angry)
   If you _____.

4 A: Why don't we call her now?
   B: No. (we/wake her up)
   If we _____.

5 A: Why can't we start the project again?
   B: (waste/money)
   If we _____.

6 A: Can we extend our vacation?
   B: No. (miss/school)
   If we _____.

6.3

A Complete the conversations.

1 A: You'll never g_*uess*_ what.
   B: What?
   A: I'm moving to Australia.
   B: You're j_____!
   A: No, I'm leaving in March.
   B: You l_____ dog.

2 A: I passed my test!
   B: D_____ you? Congratulations!
   A: Yes, I got the results this morning.

3 A: There's s_____ I've got to tell you.
   B: What is it?
   A: I've decided to leave my job at the university.
   B: I'm s_____ to hear that. What's the problem?

4 A: I'm a_____ we're going to be late.
   B: Why? What happened?
   A: The flight's been delayed.
   B: Oh, that's a s_____. That's really a_____.

GRAMMAR

7.1 Present Perfect Simple versus Continuous
Present Perfect Continuous

+	I She	've/have 's/has	been	reading a book. playing the piano.
–	You	haven't		listening to me.
?	Have	you		going there for a long time?

Use the present perfect simple or continuous for actions/activities that started in the past and continue until now:

I've studied German for six years.
I've been studying German for six years.

Often, there is little change in meaning between the two tenses (especially for verbs such as *live, work, teach, study*):

I've lived here for years.
I've been living here for years.

Use the present perfect continuous to emphasize the length or duration of an activity:

I've been doing yoga for years. (but I'm still not very good at it)
He's been playing football since he was three.

As with other continuous forms, do not use the present perfect continuous with state verbs (e.g. *love, hate, enjoy, know*, etc.). With these verbs, use the present perfect simple:

I've known him for ages.
NOT *I've been knowing him for ages.*

We often use *for, since* and *How long have you ...?* with the present perfect simple and continuous:

How long have you been waiting for?
She's been working here since 2010.

7.2 Present and Past Ability
Modal Verbs to Talk about Ability

	Present	Past
+	I **can** cook.	I **could** run fast.
–	I **can't** drive.	He **couldn't** do math.
?	**Can** you **speak** Spanish?	**Could** you **cook** when you were younger?

We can also use *be able to* to talk about ability.

	Present	Past
+	She's **able to** write well.	By age three, I **was able to** read.
–	He's **not able to** drive.	At age two, he **wasn't able to** walk.
?	**Is** he **able to** speak French?	**Were** you **able to** get a job?

Expressions to Talk about Ability at a Particular Moment

We can use *be able to* to talk about one particular situation:

We are able to offer you a special discount on the fridge today.

She didn't answer her phone, so I wasn't able to speak to her.

Use *manage to* to show that an action is/was difficult.

	Present	Past
+	I usually manage to finish my work on time.	We managed to reserve a great hotel.
–	I don't always manage to speak to my parents every week.	She didn't manage to pass the exam.
?	Do you manage to see the grandchildren regularly?	Did you manage to finish washing the dishes?

7.3 Clarifying Opinions

Giving Opinions

The reason I say this **is that** he didn't ask our permission.
For me, there are two options here.
In my view, we should stop selling the product.
I do think we should talk to them first.
I have to say I agree with Robert.

Giving Examples

For example, she forgot her keys yesterday.
Let me give you an example: there was a festival last week.
For one thing, I don't like caviar.

PRACTICE

7.1

A Complete the sentences with the present perfect simple or continuous form of the verbs in the box. Where both forms are possible, choose the present perfect continuous.

> do   sit   (not) listen   hate   (not) watch   study
> teach   (not) know   read   live   wait

1 I'm tired. I _____ in boring meetings all day.
2 They _____ for their exams since 5 o'clock this morning.
3 I'm glad you're here. We _____ for you all day.
4 I can't listen to jazz. I _____ always _____ it.
5 He _____ karate for nearly twenty years.
6 You _____ to me. You haven't heard what I said.
7 She's got a new job. She _____ economics in college since June.
8 How long _____ you _____ in the U.S.? When did you move here?
9 I _____ TV. I _____ my book.
10 We _____ each other for very long.

B Underline the correct alternative to complete the sentences.

1 Hi, Tariq. I haven't *seen/been seeing* you for ages!
2 I have *been knowing/known* Justin since we were at school.
3 Yes, we've *met/been meeting* each other before.
4 I *'ve been playing/did played* the guitar for as long as I can remember.
5 My brother *has been traveling/ has been traveled* around the world for the last two years.
6 He has always *been enjoying/enjoyed* traveling.
7 Excuse me. I *'ve been waiting/have wait* for this phone call all morning.
8 I *have studying/have been studying* Mandarin for more than ten years, and I still find it difficult.

7.2

A Find and correct the mistakes. There are five mistakes in the text.

> Johnny isn't able make full sentences, but he can to say several words, such as Mama and Dada, which he couldn't a month ago. He able to understand various commands like "No!" and "Come here," and he recognizes his name. He's becoming more mobile; yesterday he managed crawl from the living room to the kitchen. He's also getting better with his hands. He can hold a pen, and he sometimes manages to drawing simple pictures.

B Rewrite the sentences using the words in parentheses. Write three words (contractions are one word).

1 She knows how to ride a motorcycle.
   _____ a motorcycle. (can)
2 I'm not able to play any instruments.
   _____ any instruments. (can't)
3 Seyi and Denia couldn't come last night.
   They _____ come last night. (able)
4 Were you able to take any photos?
   _____ to take any photos? (manage)
5 Can you make pizza?
   _____ to make pizza? (able)
6 I can usually sleep for eight hours, even on a plane.
   Usually I _____ for eight hours, even on a plane. (manage)
7 Were you a fast runner when you were a child?
   _____ fast when you were a child? (could)
8 I haven't finished my homework.
   I _____ finish my homework. (managed)

7.3

A Underline the correct alternative.

1 Jackie has been so nice. *For example,/For me,* she took us to the movies.
2 You all think that new restaurant is great, but, *for one thing,/in my view,* the food isn't that good.
3 Ibrahim said the concert was disappointing, and *I have to say/the reason I say* I agree.
4 Shakespeare borrowed most of his stories. *Let me give you an example:/I must say* the plot of *King Lear* is taken from a much older story.
5 I like that laptop. *For one thing/I do think* it's a bit heavy, though.
6 People love the Rolling Stones, but, *for me,/ the reason I say this is* Led Zeppelin is the greatest rock band.
7 Dogs are the best pets. *For another/The reason I say this is* that they are so faithful.
8 You should buy that cell phone. For one thing, it looks fantastic. *For another,/For example,* it's cheap.

GRAMMAR

8.1 Articles

We use articles in front of nouns for various purposes:

Use *a/an* (indefinite article):

- the first time something is mentioned.
- before singular nouns. *She's watching a movie.*
- with jobs. *I'm a doctor.   He's an artist.*

Use *the* (definite article):

- when there is only one of something.
- when something has been mentioned before.
- with seas, oceans, rivers and country names that are plural or use extra words like States, e.g., *the United States*
- before the names of some areas, e.g., *the south of France, the coast of Italy*
- with superlatives. *Ali was the greatest boxer.*
- with some defining expressions, e.g., *the first, the only*
- in some phrases with prepositions, e.g., *in the morning, in the end, by the next day*
- with dates in spoken English, e.g., *the 5th of May.*

Use *no article* (zero article):

- to talk generally about things or people.
- with most names of towns, cities and countries.
- before plural nouns. *I bought six books.*
- in some phrases with prepositions, e.g., *on Monday, at work, for lunch, on foot*
- with sports. *I like tennis.   He plays football.*

Quantifiers

Use *some* when talking about "a limited amount/number" (not a large or small amount/number). We often use *some* in positive sentences. In this instance *several* can also be used:

I have some close friends.   I have several close friends.

We also use *some* in questions, especially in requests and offers:

Can you give me some sugar?   Do you want some help?

We often use *any* in negatives and questions: *I don't have any children.* We sometimes use *any* in positive sentences when we want to emphasize that there are no limits: *I can come any time.*

Use *much* and *many* in questions and negatives. *Much* is used with large amounts of an uncountable noun: *How much time do we have? Many* is used with large numbers of a countable noun: *I don't have many friends.*

All means "everything/everyone." We can use it with or without *of*. We use *a lot of*, *lots of*, and *plenty of* with large amounts/numbers. We usually use these in positive sentences. *Plenty of* means "more than enough" (so there won't be a problem): *I spend a lot of time in Paris.*

Too and *too much/many* mean "more than necessary." We use *much* with uncountable nouns. We use *many* with countable nouns.

Enough means "as much as we need." We use it in positive and negative sentences and questions:

There isn't enough time.   Do you have enough sugar?   I have enough.

None and *no* can mean "zero." We use *none of* + noun/pronoun. We use *no* + noun (without article or possessive adjective).

A few means "a small number." We use it with countable nouns. We usually use it in positive sentences: *She knew a few actors.*

A little and *a bit of* mean "a small amount." We use them with uncountable nouns. We usually use them in positive sentences.

8.2 Relative Clauses

There are two types of relative clauses: defining and non-defining.

Defining (Restrictive) Relative Clauses

Use relative clauses to talk about what a person, place or thing is or does.

Use relative pronouns to join the main clause and the relative clause:

- *who* for people *He's the man who sold me the coat.*
- *where* for places *This is the town where I was born.*
- *that* for things *It's the hat that he lost.*
- *when* for times *This was the moment when Mr. Moran knew he was in trouble.*
- *whose* for possessions (it means "of which or of whom") *This is Sarah, whose husband you met.*

Using *that* instead of *who* is becoming more common:

Are you the lady who/that I spoke to on the phone?

We can leave out *who*, *which* and *that* when these words are not the subject of the relative clause. Compare: *She's the girl (who) I saw yesterday.* (The subject of the relative clause is I (not *who*). So we can omit *who*.) with: *She's the girl who speaks French.* (The subject of the relative clause is *who*. So we cannot omit *who*.)

Non-defining (Non-restrictive) Relative Clauses

Use non-defining relative clauses to add non-essential information.

- The sentence is grammatically correct without the non-defining relative clause.
- Use a comma before the clause and a comma or period after it.
- We do not omit the relative pronoun (*who*, *which*, etc.):

  I saw Tim, who looked happy.

8.3 Being a Good Guest

Asking for Advice		Apologizing
Is it OK if I (do this)?	Yes, of course./No, you'd better not.	Sorry about that. I didn't know (you were in a meeting). My apologies. I didn't realize (you were busy).
What should I do (in this situation)?	If I were you, I'd …	
Do I need to (take off my shoes)?	Yes, you should./No, it isn't necessary.	
Did I do something wrong?	It's OK. We can sort it out./Don't worry about it.	
Is this a bad time?	No. Come in./Can you come back later?	

PRACTICE

8.1

A Find and correct the mistakes. There is one mistake with articles in each sentence.

1 Are you ready to go? Flight leaves at 6:00 p.m.
2 Bobby's girlfriend is engineer.
3 Thousands of people were at the game, so there was lot of noise.
4 I saw a doctor about my pain. Fortunately, a doctor said it was nothing serious.
5 Laila was hungry, so she ate piece of bread.
6 The women live longer than men.
7 We went to a party, but there weren't the many people there.
8 We looked up and saw an airplane in sky.
9 I work as cleaner in an office building.
10 My wife and I have lived in United States for several years.

B Read the story. Do you get the joke? Complete the story with the words in the box.

much	many	few	little	lot

An old man reaches his 120th birthday. A journalist comes to interview him. "What is the secret of your long life?" he asks. "Well," says the old man, "I don't have ¹_____ problems. I don't drink ²_____ alcohol. I eat a ³_____ of good food, and I spend a ⁴_____ time every day relaxing. But do you want to know my real secret? I never disagree with anyone." "That's ridiculous!" says the journalist. "There must be another secret." A ⁵_____ moments later, the old man says, "OK. You're right."

8.2

A Complete the sentences with *whom, which, where, when* or *whose*.

1 I met a man _____ house had burned down.
2 This was the moment _____ we knew we would win.
3 I spent several months in Rome, _____ is my favorite city.
4 The village, _____ Teresa grew up poor but happy, was very small.
5 The girl _____ sold you the carpet is from Morocco.
6 That blog, _____ he writes every day, is one of the most popular in the country.
7 Jill married a guy _____ she met on a dating site.
8 I don't want to be with someone _____ whole life is spent surfing the net.

B Rewrite the sentences using relative clauses. Use the words in italics and the words in the box.

~~that~~	who (x2)	which (x2)	where	when	whose

1 What's this program? Did you want to watch it?
Is this the program _____*that you wanted to watch*_____?
2 Last year I met a translator. She spoke six languages.
Last year I met a translator _____.
3 It was 6 o'clock on the 5th of August. At that moment, the world changed forever.
It was 6 o'clock on the 5th of August _____.
4 They gave Jodie an apple. She ate it quickly.
They gave Jodie an apple, _____.
5 You see that apartment? Felipe lived there.
That's the apartment _____.
6 She spent a month in Austin. She loved it.
She spent a month in Austin, _____.
7 The boss's office is next to mine. He's always shouting!
The boss, _____.
8 My boyfriend is coming to visit me. He lives in Kansas.
My boyfriend, _____.

8.3

A Put the words in the correct order to make conversations.

1 **A:** Do I need to shake everyone's hand?
   B: no, / necessary / isn't / it
2 **A:** is / if / it / I / into / take / meeting / coffee / OK / the / ?
   B: Yes, of course.
3 **A:** I / to / realize / didn't / I / send / by / the / information / had / email.
   B: It's OK. We can sort it out.
4 **A:** Did I do something wrong?
   B: don't / it / about / worry
5 **A:** What should I do if I'm late?
   B: if / you / I / were, / I'd / an / train / earlier / catch
6 **A:** sorry / that / about. I / you / know / here / were / didn't
   B: No problem.

GRAMMAR

9.1 Hypothetical Conditional: Past

If Clause	Would Clause
if + had + past participle	would have + past participle
If I had seen my friend,	I would have spoken to her.

Use the hypothetical conditional past to talk about hypothetical or imaginary situations in the past.
It describes an unreal or impossible situation, e.g.,
Real situation = I woke up late. Hypothetical situation:

If I had heard my alarm clock, I wouldn't have woken up late.

(I didn't hear my alarm clock. I woke up late.)
We can start sentences and questions with the *if* or *would* clause:

*They **wouldn't have been** late if they had caught the bus.*
*If they **had caught** the bus, they **wouldn't have been** late.*
*What would you **have done** if I hadn't called? If I **hadn't called**, what **would you have** done?*

Note: The past perfect tense (*had* + past participle) is used to show that the action was in the past. Compare this to the hypothetical conditional, present/future in which the simple past tense shows an action is hypothetical.
Note: When the sentence starts with *if*, we use a comma after the *if* clause.
In written and spoken English, we use contractions with hypothetical conditional sentences in the past, except in very formal documents:

*She'd have told us if **she'd** heard anything.*
*We **wouldn't** have left early if **we'd** known you were coming.*
The defendant would not have been caught if he had stayed in his home. (formal)

9.2 Active versus Passive
The Passive

	Active	Passive
Simple Present	The shop **doesn't** accept **credit** cards.	Credit cards **aren't accepted** here.
Present Continuous	**Is** anyone **using** that computer at the moment?	**Is** that computer **being used** at the moment?
Simple Past	Someone **told** us to be here at 8:00.	We **were told** to be here at 8:00.
Present Perfect	No one **has asked** us about the date.	We **haven't been asked** about the date.
Will	Someone **will give** me a car on my next birthday.	I'll **be given** a car on my next birthday.

Use the active voice to talk about the things people do:
Sam ate the chicken.

To make the passive, use subject + *be* + past participle.
Use the passive voice:

- to talk about what happens to things or people.
  Khaled has been given a prize.

- when we don't know the doer (the person or thing that does the action):
  The movie star was murdered.
- when the identity of the doer of the action is not important:
  This cheese is made in Italy.
  (It's not important who actually makes it.)
- if the doer of the action is obvious:
  The thief was arrested.
  (The police are the only people who could arrest the thief.)
If we want to say who does/did the action, we use *by*:

The microwave oven was invented by Percy LeBaron Spencer.

We sometimes use the passive to emphasize a particular part of the sentence. Compare:

Frank Lloyd Wright designed the Guggenheim Museum of Art in New York.

with

The Guggenheim Museum of Art in New York was designed by Frank Lloyd Wright.

In the second sentence, the emphasis is on Frank Lloyd Wright.
The passive is often used in newspaper reports and other formal writing.

9.3 Expressing Uncertainty

Saying You Don't Know
I have no idea.*
I don't have a clue.*
I'm sorry, but I'm really not sure.
I don't know, but I can try to find out.

*These are both informal.

Saying You Know What It Isn't
It's definitely not …
I'm sure it isn't …

Saying You Are Not Sure, but You Have an Idea
I'm not a hundred percent certain,* but it might be …
I'm fairly sure* it's …

Sure and *certain* mean the same thing. We can use either of them in these expressions.

Saying You Used to Know
I can't remember.
I've forgotten.

PRACTICE

9.1

A Match 1—8 with a)—h) to make sentences.

1 If we had arrived earlier,
2 I wouldn't have told her
3 If he hadn't fallen asleep,
4 We would have called you
5 If I'd done all my homework,
6 John would have brought a present
7 If the teacher hadn't helped him,
8 I would have bought that computer

a) he would have failed the exam.
b) if he'd known it was your birthday.
c) he wouldn't have crashed the car.
d) we wouldn't have missed the plane.
e) if it had been on sale.
f) if I'd known it was a secret.
g) I would have passed the class.
h) if we'd had your number.

B Rewrite the sentences using the third conditional.

1 Maya was late for the meeting. Her car broke down.
  If Maya's car hadn't _____.
2 She felt sick, so she didn't come to the concert.
  She would _____.
3 I didn't get the job. I wasn't qualified.
  If I had _____.
4 They didn't buy the house. They didn't have enough money.
  They would _____.
5 We lost the game. Our best player was injured.
  If our best player hadn't _____.
6 You didn't tell me you were coming, so I didn't cook a meal.
  I would _____.

9.2

A Underline the correct alternative.

1 Oh, no! My wallet *has being stolen/has been stolen/has stolen*!
2 Were those documents *be sent/send/sent* by email or by regular mail?
3 Not many houses *are been built/are being built/are being build* at the moment.
4 That piano *isn't been played/hasn't be played/hasn't been played* for years.
5 Cars that are parked illegally *will be removed/being removed/to be removed*.
6 Are those toys *make/be made/made* by hand?
7 We *weren't employed/not were employed/weren't employ* by the government until 1998.
8 We can't use the photocopier because it's *being repaired/repairing/be repaired* right now.

B Complete the sentences with the active or passive form of the verbs in parentheses. Use the verb tense in italics.

1 The magazine _____ (read) mainly by teenagers. It _____ (publish) every month. *simple present*
2 Most of his programs _____ (not film) in Europe; he usually _____ (work) in Asia. *simple present*
3 The book _____ (write) by an ex-soldier. It _____ (describe) the war in Vietnam. *simple present*
4 My last company _____ (make) clothes. It _____ (buy) by a multinational company named Zed. *simple present*
5 The buildings _____ (clean), and the walls _____ (paint). *present perfect*
6 I _____ (give) a new office, but I _____ (not move) my things in there yet. *present perfect*
7 Today this dish _____ (not cook) in the oven. Instead, we _____ (use) the grill. *present continuous*
8 English _____ (not spoken) everywhere in the future. Lots of people _____ (not speak) it. *future (will)*

9.3

A Underline the correct alternative to complete the sentences.

1 What's my PIN number? *I'm forgetting/I forgotten/I've forgotten*.
2 Can you smoke in the restaurant? *I'm sure isn't/I sure it isn't/I'm sure it isn't* legal.
3 What is this drink? It's *definitely am not/definitely not/definite not* orange juice.
4 How old is he? I'm *surely fair/fair sure/fairly sure* he's twenty.
5 What's Maria's second name? I *haven't the clue/have a clue/don't have a clue*.
6 What's the world's biggest building? I *have no idea/have not idea/am no idea*.
7 Where do the Smiths live? I *not remember/can't to remember/can't remember*.
8 When does the game start? I'm not *a hundred percent certain/certain hundred percent/the hundred percent certain*, but it might be at 2:00.

GRAMMAR

10.1 ### Reported Speech
Grammar

Direct Speech (Actual Words)	Reported Speech
"I always **buy** organic food."	He said (that) he always **bought** organic food.
"**I'm going** to see my mother **tomorrow**."	She told me she **was going** to see her mother **the next day**.
"**I've passed** my test."	He said he **had passed his** test.
"We **saw** her at the station."	They said they **had seen** her at the station.
"**I'll** meet you **here**."	He said he **would** meet me **there**.
"I **can't** hear you."	She said she **couldn't** hear me.
"We **might** be late."	They said they **might** be late.
"I **have to** leave at noon."	He said he **had to** leave at noon.

Use reported speech to report what someone said earlier. After a past tense reporting verb, e.g., *said*, *told*, etc., the original verb often moves one tense back. (This is sometimes called "backshifting.")
There may be other changes to pronouns, possessive adjectives and to references of time or place:

"I'll go." → *She said she would go.*   "It's my car." → *He said it was his car.*
"We'll see you tomorrow." → *They said they would see us the next day.*
"I'll be here." → *She said she would be there.*

Could, *would* and *might* also don't change in reported speech:

"We might see you later." → *They said (that) they might see us later.*

Say and *tell* are the most common reporting verbs. Note the different verb patterns:

He told me that he'd be late.   *She said (to me) that she wanted to stay.*

Sometimes there is no need to change the tenses (no backshift). This is the case when the reporting verb is in the present tense:

"I'll meet you at the airport." → *He says he'll meet us at the airport.*

If the information we are reporting is still true in the present, we do not need to change the tenses, but if the reporting verb is in the past, we can:

"It's a great movie." → *She said that it's a great movie.* (This is still true now.) or *She said that it was a great movie.* (Implies she's seen it and thought it was good at the time.)

Reported Questions
Reported questions have the same tense and word changes as reported statements. To report a *yes/no* question, use *if/whether* after the reporting verb:

"Do you live in Peru?" → *She asked me if I lived in Peru.* or *She asked me whether I lived in Peru.*

To report a *Wh-* question, use the question word:

"Where is the restaurant?" → *She asked me where the restaurant was.*

In reported questions, the word order is the same as for statements. We do not use an auxiliary *do/does/did*:

"Do you like eating sushi?" → *She asked me if I liked eating sushi.*

10.2 ### Verb Patterns

Many different structures can follow a verb in English. Some verbs are followed by an *-ing* form, and some are followed by the infinitive:

I can't stand listening to opera.
He learned to speak Mandarin when he moved to China.

verb + infinitive with to: *agree, ask, tell, expect, learn, manage, help, decide, offer, promise, want, refuse, need*:

We managed to get to the theater on time.
They agreed to give us cheap tickets.

verb + -ing: *like, love, hate, can't stand, (be) fond of, look forward to, miss, enjoy, feel like, give up, practice*:

I miss spending time with my friends and family.
We look forward to seeing you.

Reporting verbs use many different verb patterns, so it's important to learn the patterns. Some verbs can use more than one structure, e.g., *suggest*.

He suggested that we meet at 6 p.m.
She suggested having lunch in the cafeteria.

verb + infinitive with to: *offer, promise, refuse, agree*:

They offered to give us a lift to the station.
They promised to phone when they arrive.

verb + object + infinitive with to: *invite, warn, tell, ask*:

They invited us to stay for the weekend.
He warned them not to tell anyone.

verb + -ing: *suggest, recommend*:

They suggested trying another restaurant.
He recommended eating at Café Fish.

verb + that: *explain, warn (someone), promise (someone), suggest*:

She explained that she had to leave the meeting.
He promised that he would take me out tonight.

10.3 ### Giving Advice/ Warnings

Advice	Warnings
Make sure you … / If I were you, I'd … Don't forget to … / You need to … The most important thing is to …	Watch out for … / Be careful to/of … Don't … (or else …) / You'd better … Whatever you do, don't …

PRACTICE

10.1 **A Complete the reported statements using tense changes (backshift).**

1 "We're going to have a baby."
He said (that) _____ _____ going to have a baby.

2 "I've lived here for more than twenty years."
She _____ that she had lived _____ for more than twenty years.

3 "We grew these carrots in our garden."
They told us that they _____ grown the carrots in _____ garden.

4 "I have to go to the dentist tomorrow."
He said (that) he _____ to go to the dentist the _____ day.

5 "I've lost my passport."
She said that _____ had lost _____ passport.

6 "I'm feeling a bit stressed."
She _____ me that she_____ feeling a bit stressed.

7 "We'd never been to the U.S. before."
They said that _____ _____ never been to the U.S. before.

8 "I can't stay long because I have to go to a meeting."
She said that she _____ stay long because she _____ to go to a meeting.

B Read the pairs of sentences. Then correct the mistakes in the reported speech.

1 "I think that La Tasca's is my favourite restaurant."
She said she thought that La Tasca was their favorite restaurant.

2 "I'm going to meet Mr. Susuki this afternoon."
He told me that he met Mr. Susuki that afternoon.

3 "Maja called me yesterday."
He said that Maja has called him the day before.

4 "We'll meet you here tomorrow."
They told us that they will meet us there the next day.

5 "We haven't received your application."
We told her that we hadn't received your application.

6 "I might see you at the party, Matt."
She told Matt that she will see him at the party.

7 "I've already sent you an email explaining the situation."
He said that he already sent an email explaining the situation.

8 "I can't type very fast."
She told her boss that she could type very fast.

10.2 **A Complete the reported statements below with the verbs in the box and any other necessary words**

~~refuse~~   agree   promise   suggest   offer   warn   invite   explain

1 "I'm afraid I'm not going to pay for this meal."
He _____ *refused to pay* _____ for the meal.

2 "You need to show your passport to immigration," she said to him.
She _____ he _____ his passport to immigration.

3 "If you reserve your tickets in advance, you'll get two for the price of one," she told us.
She _____ our tickets in advance.

4 "I'll pick you up on the way to the station."
He _____ pick me up on the way to the station.

5 "Why don't you all come for lunch on Sunday?"
She _____ us _____ for lunch on Sunday.

6 "I'll definitely cook something for dinner."
He _____ something for dinner.

7 "Be careful to hold on to your bags at the station."
She _____ on to our bags at the station.

8 "Yes. It's a good idea to have the meeting on Tuesday."
He _____ the meeting on Tuesday.

B Find and correct the mistakes. There are mistakes in six of the sentences.

1 The company has agreed that pay for the trip.

2 They recommended going to a different hotel.

3 I suggested to that she look for another job.

4 She suggested to call an ambulance.

5 We offered helping, but there was nothing we could do.

6 The manager refused let us leave the hotel before we met his wife.

7 We promised to sending her a postcard.

8 I explained that there had been a delay.

10.3 **A Make sentences giving advice/warnings using the prompts.**

1 forget / set / alarm.

2 you / need / buy / ticket / before / get on the train

3 if I / you / call them / before you leave

4 watch out / speed cameras. There / lots on the road.

5 make sure / apply for a visa

6 whatever / do / don't / leave valuable items / the room

7 important / thing / check / flight times

8 forget / take your cell phone

Lesson 1.2 RELATIONSHIPS

1 A Complete the family tree with the words in the box.

in-laws   sister-in-law   niece   nephew   grandparents on my mother's side   ex-husband   stepfather   stepdaughter

B Tell your partner about one or two people in your family.

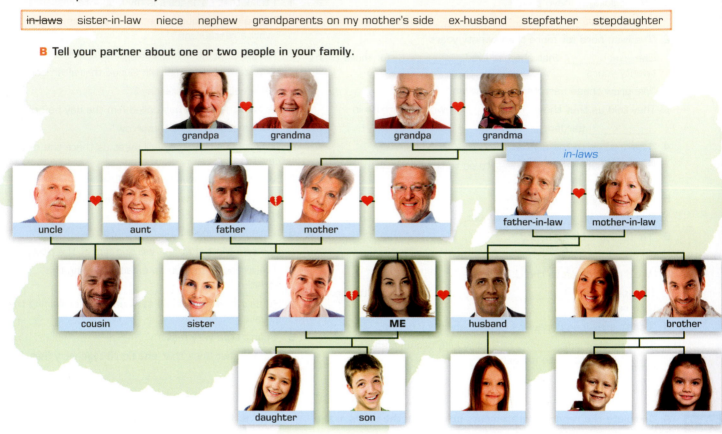

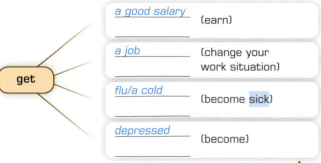

Lesson 1.2 COLLOCATIONS   with *take*, *get*, *do* and *go*

1 Write the words and phrases in italics in the correct places in the word webs below.

1 *your best, someone a favor, nothing for you, the cleaning*

do

- *hobby* _____ (action)
- *well* _____ (good effort)
- *the dishes* _____ (something at home)
- *you good* _____ (be affected)

2 *fired, a prize, excited, food poisoning*

get

- *a good salary* _____ (earn)
- *a job* _____ (change your work situation)
- *flu/a cold* _____ (become sick)
- *depressed* _____ (become)

3 *a look, the blame, a sip, ages*

take

- *medicine* _____ (swallow)
- *ten minutes* _____ (use time)
- *a photo* _____ (action)
- *responsibility* _____ (accepting something)

4 *on vacation, crazy, together, badly*

go

- *blind* _____ (become)
- *well* _____ (happen)
- *by bus* _____ (travel)
- *with* _____ (fit)

dishes / sick   washing up / ill

Lesson 2.1 PREPOSITIONS of place

1 Match descriptions 1—5 with pictures A—E.

1 They drove <u>along</u> the highway, and <u>over</u> the bridge.

2 They went <u>around</u> the city.

3 They drove <u>through</u> the main square, <u>past</u> the post office, and turned left at the station.

4 The hotel is <u>near</u> the city center, <u>between</u> the National Museum and the cathedral.

5 The house is <u>next to</u> the supermarket, <u>across from</u> the movie theater.

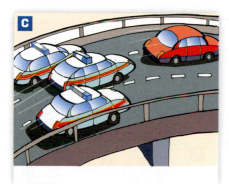

Lesson 2.2 THE NEWS

1 A Read the text and match the words and phrases in bold with definitions 1—10 below.

1 a group of criminals who work together _____

2 thieves carrying weapons _____ _____

3 an attack by criminals on a bank, store, etc., to steal money or valuable things _____

4 (doing something) while threatening to shoot someone _____ _____

5 people whose job it is to protect people or a place or to make sure that a person does not escape _____ _____

6 leave a place or dangerous situation when someone is trying to catch you _____

7 people who saw the crime _____ _____

8 took people who were involved in a crime away (to a police station) _____

9 warn people that something bad is happening _____ _____ _____

10 made someone do this _____

Two **security guards** were kidnapped and held hostage for twelve hours by a **gang** of **armed robbers** who attempted to **raid** a security depot. The robbers held the guards **at gunpoint** and **forced** them to hand over keys and security information. They then proceeded to fill a truck with more than $53 million in bills. Another $150 million was left behind because there was no more room in the getaway vehicle. Luckily, one of the guards managed to **sound the alarm**, and the police arrived and **arrested** the gang before they could **escape**. **Eye witnesses** said that they saw at least eight men being arrested.

B Divide the words and phrases into two groups: people and actions. Which words do not fit in either group?

C Tell your partner about a crime you've heard about. It can be from the news, a movie or your own experience.

highway / bills  motorway / notes

Lesson 3.1 EXPRESSIONS with *get*

1 A Look at the examples for the different uses of *get*.

get + noun = obtain

*Sophie **got a new job** yesterday.*

get + noun = receive

*He **got a letter** from the company.*

get + noun = buy

*Can you remember to **get some milk** on the way home?*

get somewhere

*What time did you **get here**?*

get + adjective

*I'm **getting bored** with this.*

get in phrasal verbs

*I really need to **get on with** my work.*

B Underline the expressions with *get* in sentences 1—6. Match each sentence with the correct use of *get* in Exercise 1A

1 He gets money by selling furniture on the Internet.

2 I don't know when I'll get around to finishing that book.

3 We need to get permission to use the room.

4 I'm getting tired. Should we finish there?

5 Did you manage to get some new pants?

6 What time does the train get to Newark?

Lesson 3.2 IDIOMS

1 A Match pictures A—F with the idioms in the box.

| be of two minds   let your hair down   break the ice   travel light   learn (something) by heart   go window shopping |

A

B

C

D

E

F

B Complete the sentences with the idioms above.

1 Tomorrow there's a test on this poem. I have to _____ it _____ _____.

2 I'm _____ _____ _____. I don't know if I want the black one or the red one.

3 Everyone was nervous, so Jackie told a few jokes to _____ _____ _____.

4 He always _____ _____. He only takes one suitcase even for long trips.

5 I have no money at the moment, but we can go _____ _____ if you want.

6 You've been working non-stop. Why don't you go out and _____ _____ _____ _____?

C What do you think the idioms mean? Use a dictionary to help you.

pants   trousers

VB

Lesson 4.1
PERSONAL QUALITIES

1 A Complete the sentences with the adjectives in the box.

> reliable   sensible   easy-going
> aggressive   bright   honest   eager
> punctual   moody   independent

1 She is very _____. She works well by herself.

2 You never know what to expect. She's very _____. One minute she's happy, and the next minute, she's shouting at you.

3 She's very _____. I'm sure she will know what to do if there's a difficult situation.

4 He's extremely _____. He is never late for appointments.

5 My new manager is very _____. She doesn't mind what time we get to work or what we wear. She never looks stressed.

6 He always tells the truth. He's very _____.

7 She's always looking for extra jobs to do. She's very _____.

8 He's very _____. He learns very quickly.

9 You know that you can trust and depend on him. He's hard-working and very _____.

10 He nearly attacked one of his employees when he arrived late for the meeting. He's very _____.

B Look at the adjectives in the box again. Do they describe positive or negative characteristics? Do you have any of these characteristics?

Lesson 4.1 WORKING LIFE

1 A Match descriptions 1—3 with jobs A—C.

1 I work as a _____ for a large corporation. I usually **work nine-to-five**, but sometimes I have to work late. My job involves checking and responding to emails, **answering phone calls** and **organizing** my boss's calendar.

2 I'm an _____. I tend to **work long hours**. I'm **responsible for** a small team of people. I spend a lot of my time attending meetings and **dealing with problems**. I **advise clients** on their accounts and **write updates and reports** for the website.

3 I'm a _____. Lots of people wouldn't like what I do because it's **an outdoor job** and it's a **physical job**, but I love it. I **work for myself**, so I can be very independent, and I **work flexible hours**, which is good for me. It's a very sociable job, too. I talk to people all day long. I couldn't do **an office job**. I would die of boredom!

Window Cleaner

Personal Assistant

Accountant

B Work in pairs. What do the phrases in bold mean?

Lesson 4.1 CONFUSING WORDS

1 A Choose the correct option from the words in bold to complete the pairs of sentences.

1 actually • currently
a) I expected the first week in my new job to be awful, but _____ it was fine.
b) I am _____ working in Chicago, but before I was working in Los Angeles.

2 career • work
a) There is a convention every year for her _____.
b) Ted spent most of his _____ as a teacher.

3 borrow • lend
a) Do you think you could _____ me a pen?
b) I had to _____ some money from a friend.

4 argument • discussion
a) We had an interesting _____ about the President, and we all agreed he should resign.
b) I had an _____ with my mother. She's always telling me what to do!

5 miss • lose
a) Hurry up, or we'll _____ the bus.
b) Why do I always _____ my car keys?

B Check your answers in a dictionary.

VOCABULARY BANK

Lesson 5.1 TECHNOLOGY

1 Match words and phrases 1—10 with pictures A—J.

1 plug it in
2 press the button
3 get a vaccination
4 have an operation
5 run out of gas
6 break down
7 (not) get a connection
8 restart/reboot the computer
9 do an experiment
10 switch it on/off

A
B
C

D
E
F

G
H
I
J

Lesson 5.2 WORD BUILDING noun (suffixes)

1 A Look at the table in Exercise B. It shows six different suffixes used to form nouns from verbs and adjectives.

B Underline the stressed part of each word in the table. What patterns do you notice about where the stress occurs?

In -ation words, the stress always comes on the a of -ation.

-ation	education relaxation imagination immigration
-ion	pollution instruction depression competition
-ment	entertainment improvement employment agreement
-ing	running smoking laughing eating
-ness	weakness loneliness happiness kindness
-ity	creativity stupidity sensitivity responsibility

C Cover the table and complete sentences 1—10 with the correct form of the verbs and adjectives in parentheses.

1 I think a little _____ (compete) in schools is a good thing.
2 There has been a great _____ (improve) in his work recently.
3 Dealing with problem clients is not my _____ (responsible).
4 _____ (lonely) is one of the worst aspects of getting old.
5 He suffers from _____ (depress).
6 Try to use your _____ (imagine).
7 I couldn't believe my own _____ (stupid)!
8 There is live _____ (entertain) from 8 p.m.
9 I was amazed by his _____ (kind).
10 I didn't hear the last _____ (instruct).

pay imitate heavy skate informal direct achieve quote dance fit promote secure

2 Change the words above to the correct noun form and add them to the table.

152

Lesson 6.1 -ING/-ED ADJECTIVES

1 Complete definitions 1—10 with the correct form of the adjectives in the box.

> exciting/excited   terrifying/terrified
> astonishing/astonished
> tiring/tired   fascinating/fascinated
> disappointing/disappointed
> disgusting/disgusted
> frustrating/frustrated
> depressing/depressed
> interesting/interested

1 you want to know more about it, and you give it your attention:
I was _____ in what he had to say.

2 being happy, interested and hopeful because something good has happened, or is going to happen:
The kids are getting really _____ about the trip.

3 very surprising:
It's _____ that you didn't know about this!

4 making you feel that you want to sleep or rest:
It was a long, _____ trip.

5 extremely interesting:
Istanbul is a _____ city.

6 unhappy because something you hoped for did not happen:
I was _____ that I hadn't won.

7 making you feel sad:
It's a very _____ book. I didn't like it at all.

8 extremely unpleasant and making you feel sick:
What's that smell? It's _____!

9 feeling annoyed, upset or impatient because you cannot control/change a situation:
He gets _____ when people don't understand what he's saying.

10 very frightened:
I'm absolutely _____ of spiders!

Lesson 6.1 MULTI-WORD VERBS

1 A Match the phrasal verbs in sentences 1—10 with meanings a)—j).

verb + *off*

1 I called him on the phone, but we got **cut off**.

2 They had to **call off** the football game because of the weather.

3 I have to do this work. I can't **put** it **off** any longer.

verb + *out*

4 I'd like to **check out** some other options.

5 He's wearing a pink jacket so he'll **stand out** from the crowd.

6 I can't **work out** what to do about the problem.

verb + *after*

7 My neighbor is **looking after** my cats when we go away.

8 He **takes after** his father. They are both very good-looking.

verb + *in*

9 Can you print out and then **fill in** the form and send it back to me?

10 Saskia, please **let** me **in**!

a) delay doing something

b) the phone suddenly stopped working.

c) look/behave like an older member of the family

d) get more information about something

e) allow someone to come in

f) decide that a planned event won't happen

g) be easy to see/notice

h) take care of something or someone

i) write the necessary information in an official document

j) decide/plan something to solve a problem

B Label pictures A—F with sentences 1—10.

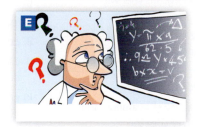

VOCABULARY BANK

Lesson 7.1 SUCCESS

1 A Match expressions 1—8 with definitions a)—h).

1 be on a shortlist   *b*
2 come in first
3 be nominated
4 win an award
5 be on the winning team
6 win a medal
7 be a runner—up
8 get an "A"

a) win
b) be named in a list (chosen from a larger group) to be considered for a prize or job
c) be officially suggested as a possible prize winner (or candidate for an important job)
d) receive a prize/money/title because of an achievement
e) receive a valuable piece of metal because of success in a competition (or bravery, e.g., in war)
f) be part of a group that wins a game/ competition
g) come in second place in a competition, race, etc.
h) get the highest grade for a piece of academic work

B Look at the situations on the right and complete the captions with the words in the box.

> winning   medal   award   got   nominated
> runner—up   shortlist   not come in

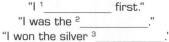

"I ¹_____ first."
"I was the ²_____."
"I won the silver ³_____."

"I won a prize for best student! I ⁴_____ A's on all my exams!"

"I was ⁵_____ for Best Actor, but I didn't win. The Oscar was awarded to Rick Rooney."

"My book was on a ⁶_____ for Book of the Year, but it didn't win. I've never won an ⁷_____."

"I was on the ⁸_____ team!"

Lesson 7.1 VERB PHRASES   with prepositions

1 A In each sentence, the same preposition is missing twice. Complete the sentences with the prepositions in the box.

> to   on   in   for   about   with

1 I couldn't cope _____ my boss any more, so I decided to part _____ the company.
2 The journalist wrote _____ the workers, who were complaining _____ poor working conditions.
3 Always stick _____ what you believe in; this will lead _____ true happiness.
4 She worked _____ a rich family, and her job was to care _____ the sick grandmother.
5 The scientists started working _____ a project, but without any money they couldn't go _____.
6 When she was ten, she took part _____ a play, and this resulted _____ her love of the theater.

B Match the verb phrases in Exercise 1A with definitions a)—k).

a) create a text   *write about*
b) look after
c) refuse to change your mind
d) be involved in
e) be employed by
f) cause something to happen (two phrases)
g) spend time and effort doing something
h) leave
i) continue
j) deal with a difficult problem or situation successfully
k) show publicly that you think something is wrong

Lesson 8.1 GETTING ALONG

1 A Match 1—6 with a)—f) to complete the sentences.

My neighbor:

1 is very helpful. For example,

2 sometimes borrows my tools,

3 drops by most days because

4 lends me sugar or milk

5 is really unfriendly. She

6 is always gossiping

a) but he never gives them back!

b) he fixed my car last year.

c) doesn't even say "good morning."

d) she likes to chat.

e) about people who live on the street.

f) if I need it.

B Underline the words and phrases in 1—6 that match definitions a)—f).

a) comes to my house (informally)

b) not friendly

c) uses my possessions

d) gives me things (that I will later return)

e) helps a lot

f) talking about other people (usually bad things)

C Are any of the sentences in 1A true of your neighbors?

Lesson 8.1 COMPOUND NOUNS

1 A Put the words in the box next to the correct key word to make compound nouns. Which compound nouns are written as one word? Use a dictionary to check.

~~racket~~   office   barrier   screen   mark   shop   machine   lab   tan   court   cup   learner   card   glasses   ball

1 tennis   _racket_
  _____
  _____

2 coffee   _____
  _____
  _____

3 post   _____
  _____
  _____

4 language   _____
  _____
  _____

5 sun   _____
  _____

B Put the key words in the box in the correct places. Which compound nouns are written as one word? Use a dictionary to check.

book   machine   phone   room   shoes

1 running
  sports   _____
  high-heeled

2 check
  picture   _____
  text

3 bed
  dining   _____
  changing

4 sewing
  washing   _____
  vending

5 head
  pay   _____
  cell

check   cheque

Lesson 9.1 HISTORY

1 Use one word from each row in the table to complete sentences 1—12.

	noun	verb	adjective	person
1	~~invasion~~	invade		invader
2	history		historical / historic	historian
3	colonization/ colony	colonize		colonizer
4	democracy	democratize	democratic	democrat
5	liberation	liberate		liberator
6	discovery	discover		discoverer
7	leadership	lead		leader
8	politics		political	politician
9	development	develop	developing	developer
10	invention	invent	inventive	inventor
11	foundation	found	founding	founder
12	independence		independent	

1 1066 is the date of the Norman ____invasion____ of Britain.

2 Edward Gibbon was a great _____. He wrote *The History of the Decline and Fall of the Roman Empire*.

3 India was a _____ of Great Britain until 1947.

4 South Africa's first _____ elections, in which black people could vote, took place in 1994.

5 In the eighteenth and nineteenth centuries, William Wilberforce led a movement to _____ slaves.

6 Alexander Fleming is known for his _____ of penicillin.

7 Fidel Castro was the _____ of the Cuban revolution of 1959.

8 The Kennedys and the Bush family are known for their involvement in American _____.

9 The World Bank lends money to _____ countries, particularly in Asia and Africa.

10 In 1901, Wilhelm Rontgen won the Nobel Prize in Physics for his _____ of the X-ray.

11 Bill Gates is the _____ of Microsoft.

12 Angola gained its _____ from Portugal in 1975.

Lesson 9.2 COLLOCATIONS with *come*, *give*, *have* and *make*

1 Write the words and phrases in italics in the correct places in the word webs below.

1 *across the mountain, with instructions, to dinner, nearer*

come
- *closer* _____ (move toward)
- *a long way* _____ (travel)
- *in blue* _____ (be produced/sold)
- *over* _____ (visit)

3 *a cold, a chance, ideas, 100 calories*

have
- *210 pages* _____ (contain)
- *memories* _____ (thoughts)
- *a disease* _____ (illness)
- *an opportunity* _____ (be able to)

2 *a prize, permission, orders, me a headache*

give
- *advice* _____ (tell someone something)
- *a donation* _____ (present)
- *the go ahead* _____ (allow)
- *me a shock* _____ (cause feelings)

4 *a living, an agreement, a movie, an effort*

make
- *a list* _____ (produce)
- *an attempt* _____ (try)
- *a deal* _____ (collaborate)
- *a fortune* _____ (get money)

 colonize / democratize

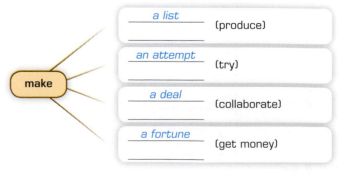 colonise / democratise

Lesson 10.1 THE ENVIRONMENT

1 A Complete the text with the words and phrases from the box with the same meaning as the words and phrases in parentheses.

> global warming   pollution   aerosol sprays   protect
> industrial waste   factory smoke   natural resources
> destroys the environment   harmful   environmentally-friendly
> car exhaust fumes   destruction of the rainforest

Many people are worried about the state of the planet and the effects of ¹_global_____ _warming_____ (an increase in world temperatures caused by an increase in carbon dioxide around Earth). A growing human population is putting pressure on Earth's ²_____ _____, (things that exist in nature and can be used by people, for example oil, trees, etc.) like food and water. Also, a lot of human activity is ³_____ (causes damage), either because it causes ⁴_____ (dirty air, water or land) or because it ⁵_____ _____ _____ (damages the air, water and land so badly that it might not recover). Some of the most common causes of damage are:

- ⁶_____ _____ (chemicals and unwanted materials that factories throw away)
- ⁷_____ _____ and ⁸_____ _____ _____
- ⁹_____ _____ (that contain CFCs—a chemical which damages the ozone layer)
- ¹⁰_____ _____—which increases the amount of carbon dioxide in the atmosphere.

Environmentalists try to ¹¹_____ the environment (keep it safe from harm) by encouraging people to change the way they live (recycling more, using ¹²_____ _____ or "green" products that do not damage the environment, wasting less, etc.) and persuading governments to take environmental issues more seriously.

B Complete the table with words from the text in Exercise 1A.

noun	verb
¹_____	destroy
protection	²_____
³_____	pollute
⁴_____	damage
waste	⁵_____

Lesson 10.1 WORD BUILDING   Prefixes

1 Look at the prefixes in the table and complete sentences 1—12 with a suitable form of the words in parentheses.

in-	invisible
	inappropriate
	inaccurate
	inadequate
	inability
im-	immature
	impossible
	impolite
	immobile
	immoral
ir-	irresponsible
	irregular
	irrelevant
	irrational
ex-	ex-girlfriend
	ex-President
	ex-husband
	ex-boss
	ex-wife

1 The number is not correct. It's _____. (accurate)

2 Let me introduce you to my _____, Amelia. (wife)

3 I can't do it. It's _____! (possible)

4 It's difficult to travel because the buses and trains are very _____. (regular)

5 You can't leave without saying goodbye. It's _____. (polite)

6 She behaves like a child. She's very _____. (mature)

7 You can't come to the office dressed like that. It's _____. (appropriate)

8 He left his laptop on the train. He's very _____. (responsible)

9 I used to work for him. He's my _____. (boss)

10 There is no good reason for it. It's completely _____. (rational)

11 It doesn't do the job. It's _____. (adequate)

12 She refused to move at all. She was _____. (mobile)

Lesson 1.2

3 c Look at your drawing. Does it include these things?

1 wheels   **2** seat   **3** chain   **4** handlebar

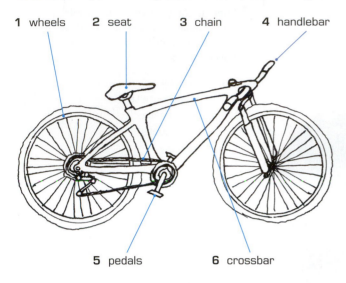

5 pedals   **6** crossbar

Lesson 1.2

7 B Read the text and check your answers.

Stella magazine commissioned YouGov, a research agency, to interview over 1,000 women in the U.K. about everything from their eating habits to their relationships and family values to find out what they really think. Here are some of the results.

Eighty percent of women say that losing their health is their greatest concern, followed by putting on weight (52%) and losing their job (24%). It seems that British women aren't too happy with their bodies: 23 percent of women are on a diet now, and 58 percent have **gone on a diet** in the past. Only four percent of women **exercise** more than seven hours per week, while 21 percent don't exercise at all.

The biggest challenge for modern women is balancing home and work life (82%), followed by bringing up happy children (56%) and finding time for themselves (52%).

As for their love lives, nine percent of women between 45 and 54 met their husbands through the Internet, and 49 percent of women believe that the best age to **get married** is between 25 and 29.

And what about the relationships between men and women? Fifty-nine percent think fathers should **take more responsibility** for their children. These women are also less than content with their husbands' efforts at home: 51 percent say they currently **do** over 75 percent of the **housework**. Despite this, over 70 percent of women would prefer to have a male boss than a female.

And their heroes? The woman they most admire are ex-Prime Minister Margaret Thatcher (7%), followed by the Queen (5%).

Lesson 1.3

8 A Student A: read your instructions below.

You work for a famous business school. Student B wants to enroll in the school. Interview him/her. Use the following prompts and ask about:

- his/her reason for taking classes
- his/her work experience
- his/her expectations from these classes
- his/her plans for the future

Prepare the questions. Remember to ask your partner why he/she is a good candidate for the school and, at the end, if he/she has any questions about the business school.

B Change roles and role-play the interview again.

Lesson 2.1

1 B Read and check your answers.

HOLLYWOOD versus History

Fact or fiction:

1 **Fiction:** the film *The Last Samurai* does tell the story of the samurai rebellion, but the character Nathan Algren did not exist.

2 **Fiction:** in truth, we know very little about William Shakespeare's personal life or what provided his inspiration.

3 **Partly true:** the film *Braveheart* does tell the story of how William Wallace fought to free Scotland, but kilts were not worn in Scotland until 300 years later. And there are many other historical inaccuracies.

4 **Partly true:** the film *Apollo 13* was praised for its accuracy. Much of the dialogue was taken directly from recordings. However, the pilot's exact words were, "OK, Houston, we've had a problem here."

Lesson 2.1

8 A Student B: write *Have you ever ...?* questions using the prompts in the box below.

win a competition/some money
eat something very unusual
break a bone in your body
lock yourself out of the house
ride a horse/motorcycle
climb a mountain/run more than two miles

Lesson 2.4

6 B Student A: Look at the picture story. What happened? Why was the robbery attempt a failure? Prepare to tell your story to your partner using the phrases in Exercise 5C.

Lesson 3.3

6 B Change roles and role-play the situation.

Student B

You are a guest at a hotel. Your room is too small. Ten minutes ago you called reception to ask if there were any suites available. Then room service arrived with a selection of desserts (cakes, ice cream, etc.). Call reception to make your complaint.

Student A

You are a receptionist at a hotel. A guest calls to make a complaint. Start the conversation by saying "Reception. How can I help you?"

"Hello. Yes, I'm afraid I have a problem …" Explain the problem again, and ask if there is a suite available.

Apologize for the misunderstanding. Explain that there are no suites available at the moment, but there will be tomorrow.

Check details and thank the receptionist for his/her help.

Confirm details, apologize again, and end the call.

Lesson 3.2

7 D Check your answers.

1 False. Compare: *This is absolutely correct.* (formal) *This hits the nail on the head.* (informal)

2 True. The order of the words in *hit the nail on the head*, *let's face it*, *close to my heart*, etc. cannot be changed.

3 True. They don't have much time. *They're running out of time.* (present continuous) *We didn't finish. We ran out of time.* (past simple)

4 True. *It's close to my heart* = I feel passionate about it.

Lesson 9.3

5 A Check your answers.

1 Michelangelo 2 Al Gore 3 F. W. de Klerk
4 Gael García Bernal 5 Philips and Sony
6 J. R. R. Tolkien 7 Germany won in 2014.
8 *Jurassic Park*

Lesson 9.3

Student A

7 A Check Student B's answers to your questions.

1 Canberra 2 India 3 Paraguay

)) COMMUNICATION BANK

Lesson 4.1

6 A Work out your score. Add up the number of points (0, 1 or 2) for each answer. Use your total to find out if you work like a millionaire.

Question 1   a) 0   b) 1   c) 2
Question 2   a) 1   b) 2   c) 0
Question 3   a) 0   b) 1   c) 2
Question 4   a) 1   b) 2   c) 0
Question 5   a) 0   b) 1   c) 2

Key:

Score 8–10   You work like a millionaire!
You are very ambitious and enjoy your work. Keep going. Sooner or later, all your hard work will pay off, and you can live like a millionaire, too.

Score 6–7   You have millionaire potential!
You understand hard work, and if you make it your top priority, you could be a millionaire, too. Keep focused on your goal.

Score 0–5   You don't work like a millionaire!
The clearest characteristics of self-made millionaires is that they work hard and they enjoy their work. You seem to prefer a work–life balance, in which work and money are not your top priorities.

Lesson 4.1

8 B Read the vocabulary notes and check your answers.

remember • remind
If you **remember** something, a fact or event from the past or something you earlier decided to do, it comes back into your mind:
He suddenly remembered he had to go to the bank.
If someone **reminds** you to do something, or something reminds you of something, they make you remember it:
Can you remind me?

forget • leave
If you want to talk about something you left behind unintentionally, use the verb **forget**. The verb **leave** can suggest an intentional or unintentional act. Compare:
I forgot my book at home.
I left my keys in the car. I left my keys on the table for you.

listen • hear
If you hear something, you know that sound has been made and can often recognize what it is:
Did you hear that noise?
If you **listen** to something or someone, you pay attention to the words, sounds and music that they are making:
Can you say that again? I'm sorry, I wasn't listening.

fun • funny
Use **fun** to talk about events and activities that are enjoyable, such as games and parties. We can also use it to talk about events that aren't enjoyable.
Being sick on vacation isn't much fun.
Funny is an adjective that describes someone or something that makes you laugh:
Bob's jokes are really funny.

Lesson 2.4

6 B Student B: Look at the picture story. What happened? Why was the burglary attempt a failure? Prepare to tell your story to your partner using the phrases in Exercise 5C.

Lesson 4.2

11 Choose one of the job advertisements below and write your cover letter.

JOB OPPORTUNITIES

FASHION DESIGNER WANTED:

We are looking for a graphic designer with a background in the fashion industry. You should have relevant experience and be up-to-date with fashion trends. Strong hand illustration as well as computer design is essential. Please submit a copy of your résumé with relevant samples of work.

TEACHING ASSISTANT, BAHAMAS

Primary school is looking for a teaching assistant to start ASAP. The school is a short walk from the beach. No formal qualifications are necessary; however, a genuine love for the job is required. Please forward résumés or contact me for further information.

TRAVEL WRITER REQUIRED

Travel writer wanted to join our small team. The successful applicant will travel around the world, stay in luxury hotels, and dine in fine restaurants. He/She will need to send a weekly update, including a short review. No previous experience required, but good communication skills and a love of travel essential.

Lesson 5.2

1 c Check your answers.

1 Nobody has ever done it, but, in theory, yes, it is possible.

2 Because it is made of frozen water. It must be below zero degrees Celsius to freeze.

3 Yes. If you travel, you'll notice that you can see different constellations of stars. This is because the surface of Earth is curved.

4 When we cut an onion, it releases a substance called lachrymatory-factor synthase. When a very small amount goes in your eye, it irritates the eye. We then produce tears (we cry) to wash the substance away.

5 Neither hot nor cold. A rainbow is an optical phenomenon caused by the refraction and reflection of sunlight by water. It is the same temperature as the air around it.

6 Because, the heavier you are, the more difficult it is to push you out of the ring (which is how you win a sumo wrestling match).

Lesson 7.2

4 B Student B: read the text below to see if your ideas are mentioned.

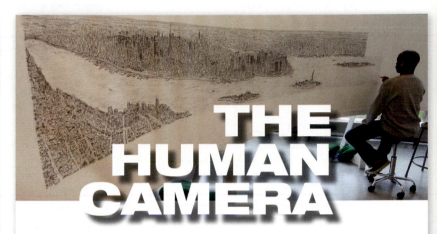

THE HUMAN CAMERA

There is no one quite like Stephen Wiltshire. Born in 1974, Stephen was always different. As a child, he couldn't make friends. In fact, he talked to nobody, showed no interest in school subjects and wasn't able to sit still. Stephen was diagnosed as autistic[1]. He didn't fully learn to talk until he was nine years old, and he didn't manage to pass his exams. But, he found one thing he liked doing: drawing. Art became his way to communicate.

He started by drawing funny pictures of his teachers, but soon began to draw buildings. His eye for detail was perfect. He could see a building just once and remember everything about it. In 1987, at age twelve, he saw a train station in London called St. Pancras. Hours later, in front of TV cameras, he managed to draw this complicated building, with the time on the station clock saying 11:20, the exact time when he was there. The drawing showed every detail perfectly.

Since that television program made him famous in the U.K., many great things have happened to Stephen. He has become a well-known artist, published several books of his drawings, taken helicopter rides above the world's great cities—including London, Rome, Hong Kong and New York—and drawn amazing pictures of them and opened his own art gallery, where he now works, in London.

His drawings are incredibly accurate—he always manages to draw everything in the right place—but also beautiful to look at. In 2006, he was given an MBE[2] by the Queen of England for services to art.

[1]**autistic** /ɔːˈtɪstɪk/ adj – having a mental condition that makes it hard for someone to understand other people and form relationships
[2]**MBE** – Member of the British Empire, an award given by the Queen for outstanding achievements

C Read the text again and answer the questions.

1 How was his behavior different from that of the other children?
2 What special talents does he have?
3 How did the public learn about his special talents?
4 What country/countries has he been to, and what did he do there?
5 What has he published?
6 What is his "job" now?

D Tell your partner about your text. Use questions 1–6 to help.

COMMUNICATION BANK

Lesson 9.1
Student B

2 B Read the texts below and make notes using the prompts below.

- What was the development?
- Where did it take place?
- When did it happen?
- Why was it important?

Learning to Eat Meat

Humans are badly designed animals. We are slow, we have weak teeth, and we don't have tails. That's why we need something extra to match other animals. And that's why eating meat—a development that probably started in Africa around 2.5 million years ago—became so important. Meat gives you fats and proteins that you can't get with other food. But, more importantly, meat-eating led to hunting, and hunting helped to develop our imaginations. When you hunt, you need to see what isn't there, to see what's behind the next tree or over the next hill. We wouldn't have become the most imaginative—and the most intelligent—of the animals if we had continued eating only plants.

Teaching People to Read

Until the end of the twelfth century, Latin was very difficult to learn. Students read and memorized texts for years. Then a Frenchman called Alexander de Villedieu developed a fast method to teach Latin: he used simple rules and wrote them in verse so the students could remember them more easily. Seeing the success of his method, Alexander wrote a grammar book, *Doctrinale*, published in France in 1199. It became a bestseller and spread quickly through Europe, and it started a great literacy movement. This new type of learning became the foundation of modern education. If he hadn't written *Doctrinale*, education would probably have remained the same for hundreds of years.

Lesson 9.1
Student B

7 A Look at the notes and describe a big moment in history. Think about the questions below.

> **The Rise of the Computer**
> - 1981: IBM launched the first personal computer. Microsoft wrote the software.
> - By 1984, IBM was selling three million PCs a year. Apple launched a rival, the Macintosh, which used a mouse and icons.
> - 1985: Microsoft launched Windows and used some of the same tools.

1 Why was this event important?
2 What happened before and after the event?
3 Would the world be different if this event had not happened?

B Describe your big moment to other students.

Lesson 9.3
Student B

7 A You are going to ask Student A the questions below. First, add two more questions of your own. The answers can be found on page 163.

1 Which soccer team won the first World Cup in 1930? Was it Brazil, Argentina or Uruguay?
2 What was discovered in the Alps mountain range in 1991? Was it the body of a 5,000-year-old man, the body of a hairy elephant, or a World War II airplane?
3 When did the European Union introduce the euro? Was it 1979, 1989 or 1999?
4
5

HISTORY

Lesson 1.3

8 A Student B: read your instructions below.

You want to enroll in a famous business school that is well-known for its practical classes. It will give you contacts in the business world. Think about these things:

- the business you want to start
- relevant work experience you have with another company

Student A will interview you for enrollment. He/She will ask about your:

- reason for taking classes
- work experience
- expectations from the classes
- plans for the future

Prepare your answers and think of some questions to ask about the school.

B Change roles and role-play the interview again.

Lesson 10.1

Group B

6 A Look at the photo and read the fact file below. Discuss the questions and make notes about your discussion.

THE CARBON PROBLEM

Did you know ...?

- Transportation is responsible for 25 percent of the U.K.'s carbon footprint, and that doesn't include flying. In the U.K., there are more cars than the number of households. In California, there are more cars than the number of people living there.

- Currently cars are used for 18 percent of trips under a mile and for 62 percent of trips of between one and two miles. 38 percent of car trips are taken by one person alone, and 34 percent are shared by two people.

- Lighting and household appliances, like washing machines, are responsible for around 35 percent of the carbon pollution from your home and most of your electricity bills. If every household in the U.K. put a solar panel on their roof, we would produce more electricity than we need as a nation.

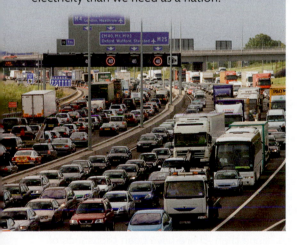

1 Do you think every family needs to have access to a car? Why/Why not?

2 What do you think should be done to reduce the number of miles people drive in cars/fly in airplanes?

3 Do you think people should generate their own electricity using wind/solar power, etc., or should governments choose options like nuclear power?

4 What laws/schemes would you introduce to deal with these problem?

Lesson 10.3

8 A Student B: read the instructions below.

You work in the Tourist Information Center. A customer would like to visit the Australian Outback. Give him/her some advice using the phrases in Exercise 4A and the prompts below:

1 Don't approach dingoes. They can bite. Throw away any leftover food.

2 There are some poisonous snakes. If you see one, move slowly away.

3 Flies can be a problem. You could buy a fly net to attach to your hat.

4 You need to wear a hat and use sunscreen. Take plenty of water/drinks.

5 Don't wear high heels/new, expensive clothes. The land is rough and rocky.

B Change roles and role-play the following situation.
Student B: you are a tourist. You want to go snorkeling on the reef. Ask the dive instructor for advice, e.g., Are there any special clothes you should wear? What equipment do you need?

I'd like some information about going diving. First of all, what clothing do I need to wear?

Lesson 9.1

Student A

7 A Look at the notes and describe a big moment in history. Think about the questions below.

> **Twenty-first-century Natural Disasters**
>
> - Boxing Day Tsunami, 2004, killed 230,000 in eleven countries. Badly affected India, Thailand, Indonesia and Sri Lanka. Underwater earthquake measured approximately 9.2 on the Richter scale (second largest recorded in history).
> - Hurricane Katrina, 2005, killed 1,836, affected mainly poor blacks in New Orleans, U.S.A.
> - Earthquake in L'Aquila, Central Italy, 2009, killed over 300 people.

1 Why was this event important?

2 What happened before and after the event?

3 Would the world be different if this event had not happened?

B Describe your big moment to other students.

Lesson 9.3

Student B

7 A Check Student A's answers to your questions.

1 Uruguay

2 the body of a 5,000-year-old man

3 1999

Unit 1 Recording S1.3

Part One

Is your brain male or female? Well, you might think it's a strange question, but some researchers have found that men's and women's brains are actually wired differently. So, let's do a test to see if your brain is male or female. In a moment, we're going to ask you to draw a picture of a bicycle. So, make sure you have a pen or pencil ready.

Part Two

OK, so I want you to draw a picture of a bicycle. You have exactly one minute, starting now … Make it as beautiful or normal as you like. Include as much detail as you can. You have forty-five seconds left … You have another fifteen seconds … You have five seconds left … four, three, two, one, zero, stop. Right, stop drawing please. Now, write down on your piece of paper, whether you, the artist, are male or female. That's all we need to know for the experiment. Now, turn to page one hundred and fifty-eight to see what a real bike looks like.

Unit 1 Recording S1.4

Part Three

Now, count up the parts on your drawing. Did you include wheels? A handlebar? A seat? A chain? A crossbar? Pedals? Did your bike have at least five parts? And could it work? Now for the difference between the men's drawings of a bicycle and the women's: women's drawings often include a person riding the bike; men's drawings don't usually include a person. This is a clear indication that women think people are important. Men, on the other hand, are more interested in getting the machine right. So, how did you do? Is your brain male or female?

Unit 1 Recording S1.5

Conversation 1

S = student   T = teacher

T: And what about your expectations of the course?
S: Well, as I said, I've studied English for many years and spent time in U.S., but that was a few years ago. So, for me, the most important thing is to just refresh … and try to remember my English and practice speaking and listening.
T: OK. You have a very good level of English, so we'd put you in the advanced class. Is there anything else?
S: Could I ask a question?
T: Of course.
S: I can take the morning class from nine to twelve. Is that right?
T: Yes, that's right.
S: And, in the afternoon, there are options? Optional classes?
T: Yes, these are special classes with a special focus, like English idioms, conversation, pronunciation. We have the full list here.
S: I see. Thank you.
T: No problem. OK, well, thank you very much.

Conversation 2

I = Interviewer   A = Applicant

I: There are a couple of things I'd like to ask about, Jade. Your résumé says you have some experience looking after children?
A: Yes, I was a counselor at a summer camp last year.
I: Can I ask you about that? What types of things did you do?
A: Um, well, I organized games.
I: Games for?
A: The children.

I: OK. And what age were the children?
A: Um … seven to ten.
I: OK. And you enjoyed it?
A: Yes.
I: What aspect, what part did you enjoy, would you say?
A: I suppose I'd have to say I liked the games most.
I: And any problems?
A: Um, no.
I: What about the different ages? We often find that different ages together can be difficult.
A: It depends. In my opinion, you can usually get the older children to help the younger ones.

Conversation 3

I = Interviewer   S = Student

I: I think that's about it. Do you have any questions?
S: Um, yes, actually I do have a question.
I: Yes, go ahead.
S: It's about online classes at the college.
I: Right.
S: If I'm accepted, I saw that there are … urm, that it's possible to take some courses online.
I: That's right.
S: So, I wouldn't need to attend classes?
I: Not for the online courses. But, er… well, one thing I'd like to say is that the online courses are, in many ways, more difficult than face-to-face courses. Certainly in terms of reading and writing, they're really quite demanding.

Unit 1 Recording S1.7

OK, so I'm going to tell you something about myself. My name is Monica Nielson, and I live in a small town near Bologna, in Italy. I think three words that describe me would be happy, talkative and hard-working. One of the things I love about my lifestyle is that I love the house where I live. I live in an apartment with my boyfriend. It's an old apartment in the historical part of town, so it's very beautiful. It's quite small, so I suppose that's one thing I don't like. My favorite smell is the smell of the ocean. We live quite far from the ocean here. But in the summer, I love to drive to the coast and breathe the ocean air. It makes me feel good. And, finally … if I could change one thing about the past, I would bring my grandmother back. She was a nice lady, and I miss her a lot.

Unit 2 Recording S2.3

H1 = Host 1   H2 = Host 2   R = Rosie (a film historian)

H1: Hi, and welcome to *The Movie Show*, where today we're looking at the Hollywood biopic and why it's become so popular. Now, Hollywood has always used true stories in its movies. In fact, it began making successful movies in the 1920s. And, since then, there have been thousands of movies based on true stories.
H2: That's right. But, in recent years, there've been more and more biopics. Directors have turned to the lives of famous people as a source of material. So, why is it that some of the best movies in recent years have been based on real events or inspired by real people?
H1: Today, we're talking to Rosie Truman, an actor and a film historian. Rosie, why do you think Hollywood is doing so many biopics?
R: Well, one reason is that audiences really enjoy movies about people they already know something about, but they want to know more. So, from these movies, we've learned something. We've learned about the difficult lives of some

of the biggest music legends, like Ray Charles and Johnny Cash. And we've learned about the lives of politicians, like George Bush, or sporting heroes, like Muhammad Ali. It's a way in which Hollywood can actually teach us about history in an entertaining way. And it's interesting.

H2: Yes, I think that's right.

H2: But, what about the actors, Rosie? I mean, many of the actors have won Oscars for their roles in these movies. What's it like for them?

R: Well, I think actors just love these roles. It's very exciting to be asked to play a character everyone already knows. Look at Helen Mirren. She won an Oscar for her role playing the Queen, and it's probably one of her greatest successes.

H1: Oh, absolutely! So, how do they do it? How does an actor prepare for a role like this? Do they meet the person they're going to play?

R: Well, yes, obviously, if that person is still alive, then that's a great way for the actor to study the character, to see how they move and how they talk. In fact, I know that Helen Mirren met the Queen for tea, you know, very English. And that really helped her to understand her character. And Will Smith, who played Muhammad Ali … Well, when they met, they got along really well, and … and they became friends.

H2: But what about playing a character everyone knows, like George Bush, for example?

R: Yes, it's funny actually, when you're playing a character people recognize, you have to work really hard at getting the voice right. Josh Brolin played George Bush. And, when he was preparing for the film, he talked to himself all day in a Texas accent. He even phoned hotels in Texas, just so he could listen the accent.

H1: Really? That's funny. What about actors who can't meet the character in person? What do they do?

R: Well, there are other ways to prepare. Audrey Tautou, for example. She played Coco Chanel. So, she couldn't meet her in person, but she watched hours and hours of film footage. She watched her in interviews, and she looked at photographs. Tautou wanted to look like Coco Chanel when she was on screen so that we would recognize her image.

H2: That's right. And it was a beautiful movie.

R: It was, and you know one of the things …

Unit 2 Recording S2.6

H = Host   N1 = 1st news clip   N2 = 2nd news clip
N3 = 3rd news clip   N4 = 4th news clip

H: Hello. I know what I was doing. Do you?

N1: Buckingham Palace has announced the death of Diana, Princess of Wales. The Princess, who was thirty-six, died late last night in a car crash in central Paris.

N2: It's one small step for man, one giant leap for mankind.

N3: Breaking news here at five live. There are reports that a plane has crashed into the World Trade Center in New York. That is, a plane has reportedly crashed into the World Trade Center in New York, setting it on fire …

N4: President Kennedy and Governor John Connally of Texas were shot today from an ambush as President Kennedy's motorcade left the center of Dallas …

Unit 2 Recording S2.8

W = Woman   M = Man

M: OK, so, tell me all about it …

W: Well, in the beginning, I was at home, and … um … this was just one morning before a very important interview …

M: Uh-huh.

W: And … um … I didn't feel well, so my mother had given me some pills, and um … then I didn't think anything more about it. So, anyway, … I then got on to the subway, to go for my interview.

M: Right, and what happened then?

W: Well, clearly I must have fallen asleep because I wasn't feeling great by this time. And um, I'm starting to feel sleepy, so I'm thinking I must have fallen asleep. Anyway, I was getting some funny looks, even before I fell asleep, but anyway. I fell asleep, and then I realized, before long, um … I must have been having a dream, I suppose, about my mother. And all of a sudden, I woke up. But, I didn't just wake up, I woke up shouting the word, "Mom!"

M: No! You're joking!

W: At the top of my voice, in a packed, quiet subway car.

M: Oh, no!

W: Yes, and everybody's staring at me, and that did not help matters. Anyway, I got off the subway, and I then arrived at my interview, put all that behind me, I'm not, I'm still not feeling a hundred percent perfect, but nevertheless arrived at my interview on time. And, I go in, and think, actually "This is going pretty well. They're not saying an awful lot, and, come to think of it, they're looking at me in a really strange way."

M: Then what?

W: Well, the next thing I knew, I'd left the interview, and said, "thank you very much for seeing me," blah-blah-blah … and gone to the ladies' room. And there in the mirror, I could see what everyone was looking at and why they couldn't say anything,

M: What was it?

W: My face had swollen up!

M: Ah! No way!

W: It was bright red, and …

M: No!

W: and covered in blotches, pimples …

M: Oh! You're kidding!

W: No, and the pills that my mother had given me were so out-of-date that they had caused an allergic reaction …

M: Oh! How embarrassing!

W: I know.

Unit 2 Recording S2.9

M = Man   W2 = 2nd woman   W = Woman

M: OK. What do we think? True or false?

W2: Erm … I don't know. I think it might be false because … I don't know …

M: Yeah, she was a little bit slow in telling the story …

W2: I don't know if your mom would give you out-of-date pills …

M: Yeah, would a mother giver her daughter out-of-date pills?

W2: I think false.

M: It sounded like she was trying to think of what to say next, so … you think false? I think false, too.

W: Yes, it was false!

Unit 2 Recording S2.11

OK. This story is about a man called Radu Dogaru, who stole famous paintings from a museum in Rotterdam. In fact, he stole paintings by Picasso, Matisse and Monet. The paintings were worth millions of dollars. What Radu didn't realize was that, because the paintings were so famous, he would have difficulty selling them. So, he tried to hide them at home. Later, the police thought they had caught Radu. However, the problem was that, when they went to search for the paintings, they couldn't find them. It seems that, when Radu's mother, Olga, found out what Radu had done, she destroyed the paintings by burning them in her oven in order to protect her son. In the end, Radu was arrested for the theft.

Unit 3 Recording S3.1

L = Laurie   K = Kenna   J = Javier

L: OK, so what do you think, Kenna? Are you a planner or a procrastinator?

K: Me? Oh, a planner, definitely.

L: Yes, I think so. You generally like to do things ahead of time.

K: Absolutely. Yeah. I like to be organized and know when everything is happening. I have to be like that, actually. It's the only way to get everything done.

J: Really? I hate planning. I like to leave things until the last minute. I mean, you never know what's going to happen. You might need to change your plans, so why bother making plans in the first place? No, I like not knowing what I'm going to be doing.

K: But that's impossible. What about vacations, for example? You must know what you're doing for your next vacation. I mean, you need to decide where you're going, how you're going to travel, reserve the dates, get the tickets … There's so much to organize. Surely you have to plan for vacations. You can't just put that off until later.

J: Not really. I don't mind where I go.

K: No, I don't believe, … you're just saying that. I think you do make plans. You just don't like to admit it.

J: No, really. I much prefer to wait and see what happens. I might get invited somewhere.

L: OK, so maybe for vacations. But what about tonight? Have you made any plans for tonight?

K: Yes. Of course. I can tell you exactly what I'm doing tonight. This evening a friend of mine's coming over. We're eating at my house—I'm going to try out a new pasta recipe. And then we're going to the movies to see that new Argentinian film.

L: Javier?

J: Uhhh … I don't really know. I'll see how I feel. I might go out, or I might just stay at home and relax. I told you. I really don't like to plan.

L: How about at work? Are you more organized at work? Do you multitask? I mean, how do you make sure you get everything done?

J: … Actually, I think I am a procrastinator. I do get jobs done, but I never get started right away. I tend to waste time and get distracted and leave the job for ages. And then, just before the deadline, I work really hard, sometimes all night. And then I don't stop until the job is done. It's quite stressful, but everything gets done in the end.

K: You don't use your time very wisely then? Oh, no. I'd hate that. I don't think I could work with you.

Unit 3 Recording S3.4

Conversation 1

W = Woman   M = Man

W: Hi. Me again. I sent an attachment with all the figures for the last six months. That should be all you need.

M: Sorry—I didn't catch any of that.

W: I sent the figures in an attachment. Is that Tom?

M: You've lost me. Who is this?

W: This is Ana Lucia. Is that Tom?

M: No, this is Willy's Burger Bar. What number are you trying to call?

W: 845-6795.

M: I think you have the wrong number.

W: Oh, I'm sorry.

Conversation 2

W = Woman   M = Man

M: I have a reservation in the name of David Cullinan.

W: Just one moment. Umm, could you repeat the last name?

M: Cullinan. C-u-l-l-i-n-a-n.

W: Cullinan. I can't find the name. Did you make the reservation over the phone?

M: Yes, just yesterday.

W: Sorry, let me see if there are any messages here. I'll only be a moment. I'm sorry. We have no reservations in the name of Cullinan, and we're full tonight.

M: So, you're saying I can't stay here. This is the Sheldon Hotel, yes?

W: No, this is The Felton. With an "F."

M: Really? So, I'm in the wrong hotel.

W: The Sheldon is on Queen's Road, just around the corner.

M: Oh, no. Sorry, can you say that again—where is it?

W: On Queen's Road, just around the corner.

Conversation 3

F = Father   G = Girl

G: You missed the best parts. You're late.

F: What exactly do you mean? The show starts at 7:00, doesn't it?

G: No, it finishes at 7:00!

F: Didn't you say it starts at 7:00?

G: No, it starts at 5:00 and finishes at 7:00!

F: So, what you mean is I've missed the whole show.

G: Yes.

Conversation 4

M = Man   W = Woman

M: We don't have anything for you, I'm afraid.

W: I don't get what you're saying. You're a car rental company, right?

M: Yes, but today's a holiday, and all the cars have been reserved already.

W: Do you mean to tell me that there's nothing at all? No cars available?

M: There's nothing until tomorrow, I'm afraid.

W: But I definitely reserved a car for today, the third of July.

M: It's the fourth of July today. In other words, your reservation was for yesterday.

W: It can't be. Is it?

M: It's the fourth today, ma'am.

W: Oh, no. I have the date wrong.

Unit 3 Recording S3.7

W = Woman   M = Man

W: OK, so we're looking at creating a video channel.

M: Yep. The first thing, I think, is what's our target audience?

W: Yeah, what's our aim?

M: Well, we came up with this idea.

W: Go on.

M: That it would be really cool to do a series of videos about local places but with a special angle.

W: Oh, that sounds good. What's the angle?

M: An hour to kill. So, say you're in Sydney or Istanbul or anywhere really and you have an hour to kill. We have a video of someone describing something to do in that place in an hour or less.

W: Oh, I see. So the target audience is tourists.
M: It could be tourists or local people. Say you find yourself in a part of the city that you don't know very well.
W: OK.
M: And you have a bit of spare time. By going onto our video channel, you get all kinds of suggestions about what to do or where to visit in under an hour. And the clips are filmed on location, so you get to see the places, too.
W: I like it. So who will be the hosts? Will you have any big names?
M: No, we don't have any money! We'd get local people to host each video clip, with just one camera, kind of cheap and cheerful, low production values, but really cool content.
W: Who are our competitors or rivals? It must have been done before.
M: Oh, I'm sure, but I don't know if it's been done with the angle of an hour to kill.
W: OK. Um, what else? How often will we upload videos?
M: Well, we'll try to get coverage of as many cities and towns around the world as possible. So, I don't know, one a day? So in a year, we'll have three-hundred-and-sixty-five. Then we just carry on from there.
W: Wow. Very ambitious. What about a name?
M: We thought of One Hour Wonders.
W: One Hour Wonders. I like it!

Unit 4 Recording S4.2
Luca

Well, I've always loved sports and swimming. As a kid, I used to spend all my free time in the summer on the beach with my friends. We would swim or surf or just play around in the water. And there was always a lifeguard there on the beach, and I used to think, "What a great job!" So, when I left school, I trained to be a lifeguard. I really enjoyed the job for a few years. In the summer, I would work on the beach, and, then, in the winter, I would go skiing. It was my dream job. I loved it. But, after a while, I started to get bored. I was just on this boiling beach all day, watching all the beautiful people, but I couldn't really enjoy myself, you know. I just had to stand there and watch. So, I knew it was time to find something else to do.

Nicola

I used to be an ice cream taster, and, for a while, it was definitely my dream job. I mean, can you imagine anything better than sitting at work eating delicious ice cream all day? I was in heaven. I was working for a big company, with a team of food scientists, and our job was to come up with new ideas for ice cream flavors. So, I suppose that was the problem because, a lot of the time, we had to try new flavors, like curry and lime ice cream or cheese and sausage, and we would have to taste it. Usually it was terrible, really disgusting. Now, most people would just say, "Yuck, I'm not eating that again." But unfortunately, when it's your job, you have to keep tasting it to see if they have made it any better. Sometimes we would taste thirty different ice cream flavors before lunch. So, it wasn't all good.

Amy

I was a professional shopper for a while. It was fun at first. The lady I worked for was a television host, and she needed outfits to wear on television. But, she didn't have time to go shopping. So, I would go out and buy clothes for her. Then, she would try them on at home, and I would take back anything that was no good. It gave me fascinating insight into how some people live. But, as time went on, I realized she was impossible

to please. One time I had to buy her an outfit for a special event she was going to, and I bought her a few different things to try on. But, she didn't like any of them, and she was really **furious** that I hadn't found her something different. It wasn't really my fault, but I lost my job soon after that.

Unit 4 Recording S4.5

W1 = Woman 1   W2 = Woman 2   M1 = Man 1   M2 = Man 2

W1: OK, so we're looking at plans for the new café. First of all, we need to decide on the location. Then we'll look at what kind of food we're going to offer and possible names for the café.
M1: Yes, that sounds good.
W2: OK.
W1: Right. Let's focus on the ideas we had for the location. We looked at some options last time, but we need to make a decision.
M1: I liked the one near the station. It would be really busy during the week when everyone comes in for work. But what does everyone else think?
M2: Yes, I think the station idea is good.
W2: I think we need to decide on the kind of atmosphere we're looking for. The location near the shopping center would be a really nice place to visit on the weekend.
W1: Hmm.
M1: I'm not sure that I agree, actually. The way I see things, we need to choose the location that will give us the most customers. And I think that will be the café near the station.
M2: And it's cheaper.
W2: That's a good point. I suppose so.
W1: So, should we say we'll look at the location near the station?
All: Yes. Good idea. Yes, OK.
W1: Good. So, moving on to the next point, what kind of food are we going to serve? What do you think?
M1: Hmm … How about an Italian café?
W2: Mmm … I'm not sure …We talked about Italian, but there are lots of other Italian cafés around. I really feel that it would be hard to make ours different.
W1: OK—good point. I think we should think about something different then. Any ideas?
M2: Well, I was thinking about a Portuguese café, you know, with delicious cake and pastries. There are quite a lot of Portuguese people in this area, and tourists, too. I think that style of café would be really popular.
W2: Yeah, a Portuguese café. I think that's a great idea. What do you think?
All: That's OK. Yeah. Nice.
M1: That's a nice idea. We could do Portuguese-style lunches, too, for office workers.
W1: Yes, maybe. So, do we all agree? A Portuguese café?
All: Yes. That's fine by me.
W1: OK. Let's recap. A Portuguese café selling and lunches, located near the station. Right. So, what would we call it? Café Express?
M1: I'm not sure about that. I think we need to come back to the type of café we're establishing. So, Café Portugal or something like that …
W2: Why don't we call it Café do Sol? Or Café Lisboa? Café … umm … Café Fado …
W1: I like Café Lisboa. I think it sounds really good, and Lisbon's a beautiful city.
M1: Café Lisboa. I like it.
M2: Yes, that sounds good.

flavor   flavour

W1: OK, we're running out of time. Let's sum up what we decided. It's going to be a Portuguese café. We think the station location might be good. And we like the name Café Lisboa. Is that right?
All: Yes, I think so. That's right.
W1: OK, so we'll need to decide on …

Unit 4 Recording S4.8

I'm a pharmacist, so I work six days a week. The pharmacy opens at 9 a.m., but I need to be at work before then so I can get everything ready. I usually wake up at about 6:30 so I can get the kids up and ready for school and then go for a run before work. I have to leave home by 8:30 at the latest. The morning is the busiest time in the pharmacy. So, the first thing I do when I get to work is start preparing prescriptions so they're ready for customers to collect. It's a community pharmacy, so I know a lot of the patients quite well. Besides giving out medicine, we try to give advice on healthy living. I think people really appreciate being able to talk to someone in the pharmacy and get advice or treatments without having to see a doctor. I usually have lunch at about 1 p.m. Sometimes I bring my own lunch, and, on other days, I like to leave the store and wander around. I might buy something to eat or even try out a new café. The area near where I work is really nice, and I often bump into people I know. In the afternoon, I try to catch up on all the administrative tasks that need to be done. I check my emails and upload information to our website. I often take phone calls from receptionists, nurses and even doctors from the local clinic, checking information about medication.
I leave the store at about 5:30 p.m., but I usually make some deliveries on my way home. Some of our older patients can't travel to the pharmacy themselves, so they rely on this service. I try to get home by about 7 o'clock so that I have time to read to the children and put them to bed. I'm usually too exhausted to do very much in the evening, so I usually just cook dinner and watch some television. And then I like to plan my next day in my head before going to bed. It's a long day, but I love my job.

Unit 5 Recording S5.2

W1 = Woman 1	W2 = Woman 2	M = Man

W1: Why are the windows round on ships?
M: Round windows are stronger, aren't they?
W2: Are they? I have no idea.
W1: That's right. According to the book, they're less likely to break.
W2: Ah.
M: There you go.
W1: What about this second one? How many hairs are there on the human head?
W2: Erm … A million?
M: No, it's not that many, is it?
W2: It depends whose head, doesn't it? On my dad's, there are about three.
W1: The answer is about ten thousand.
M: Oh, really?
W2: I think that's a bit of a stupid question because it depends, doesn't it?
M: Well, it was a four-year-old who asked the question.
W2: Oh, yeah, that's true.
W1: Next question: What happens when your plane flies over a volcano?
W2: Ummm.

M: Nothing happens, does it? Well, it depends on whether the volcano is erupting or whether it's active.
W2: Yeah.
W1: Well, according to the book, Jamieson asked a pilot. And the pilot said that, as he was flying over the volcano, his engines shut down, stopped working completely.
W2: Scary. Did he get hot?
W1: Hmm, it doesn't say. But he obviously survived. So there you go. Anyway, what about this one? Why did the Beatles break up?
W2: Dunno. They got old, didn't they?
M: No. John Lennon went off with Yoko Ono, didn't he?
W1: Well, Jamieson wrote to Yoko Ono, and she replied, "Because they all grew up, wanted to do things their own way, and they did."
W2: Oh, that's interesting.
M: I'm amazed she replied.
W1: Me, too. OK, last one. After watching a violent video game, the little boy asked. "Why is there war?"
W2: Great question.
M: That's a really good question.
W2: Hmm, because men like fighting?
M: Political reasons. One country wants the land or the oil or the gold.
W1: Well, Jamieson asked lots of experts. Most of them didn't or couldn't answer. Then he asked an American army colonel, who said there are four big reasons: different ideologies, a sense of honor, economic reasons, and fear.
M: Uh-huh.
W2: Good question for a four-year-old.
M: And a good answer.

Unit 5 Recording S5.5

Conversation 1

M = Man	W = Woman

M: Arggh. Oh, no.
W: What's the matter?
M: Oh. This ATM's not working. Do you know if there's another machine somewhere? I really need to get some money.
W: Hmm … I'm not sure. There might be one in the shopping mall.
M: Thanks.

Conversation 2

M = Man	W = Woman

W: Argh!
M: What's the matter?
W: My laptop just crashed, again. That's the third time it's happened. Would you mind looking at it for me?
M: Sure.
W: Thanks. It's so annoying. I keep losing my documents. Do you know what the problem is?
M: Let me have a look. There's a lot of stuff on here. Why don't you save the documents onto a memory stick?
W: That's a good idea.
M: And then do you want me to try …

Conversation 3

M = Man	W = Woman

W: Customer service. Good morning.
M: Um, yes. I have a problem with my vacuum cleaner.
W: Could you tell me what the problem is, sir?
M: Yes, I can. It keeps making a funny noise. And it's just not working properly.

clinic surgery

W: You say it keeps making a funny noise …
M: Yes, that's right.
W: OK. Let's see if I can find someone who can help you. Could you hold, please?
M: Yes, of course.

Conversation 4

M = Man   W = Woman

M: Oh. I don't believe it! Excuse me, this machine isn't working. It just took my money. Could you give me a refund?
W: I'm afraid I can't do that.
M: Why not?
W: Well, I'm not allowed to give refunds.
M: But I've just lost my money. And I still need a ticket.
W: I can sell you a ticket, but I can't give you a refund.
M: Well, could you tell me whom I should speak to?
W: Yes, of course. You need to speak to the manager.
M: OK. Would you mind calling him for me?
W: Of course not. I'll just call him.

Unit 5   Recording S5.8

I'm going to tell you about Robo-Chef. Basically, Robo-Chef can prepare and cook all your favorite recipes. It works like this. First of all, it washes and prepares all the vegetables. Then it prepares your dish and cooks it for you on your stove. Robo-Chef comes complete with hundreds of menus already programmed. But, you can also program Robo-Chef with your own recipes. Or, if you want to try something new, you can download new recipes whenever you like. All you have to do is choose the dish you want, decide how many people you want Robo-Chef to cook for, and what time you want the meal to be ready. So, let's say you would like a vegetable lasagne for six people ready by 8 o'clock. Then, just make sure you have all the ingredients in the kitchen, press the button, and that's it. You can go to work, and, when you come home in the evening, your delicious dinner will be ready. What could be easier? Robo-Chef is the chef of the future.

Unit 6   Recording S6.1

R = Radio host   C = Clip   P = Professor   M = Man

R: Welcome to *Start the Day*!
C: Hello—can I help you?
Your call is important to us.
Hello—can I help you?
Sorry, all our operators are busy at the moment. Please hold.
M: They put you on hold for ages, listening to this terrible music. When you finally speak to someone, you're so angry, you just want to shout …
R: Anger. We all know the feeling. A report that came out last year shows that people are getting angrier. One in ten people says that they have trouble controlling their temper. Traffic jams, airports, call centers, computer crashes— they can all leave us feeling angry, and anger is difficult to control. Or is it? Professor Miller from The Metropolitan University is here to tell us about two very different therapies to help deal with stress. First of all, destruction therapy. What's that about?
P: Well, basically, the idea is that a lot of people, when they get angry, they don't know what to do with their anger— they don't deal with it very well. They just keep it inside. But, if you don't deal with your anger, sooner or later it will explode. So, with destruction therapy, you use your anger to destroy something, but in a controlled way. The idea is

that, if you do that, it helps you to feel better.
R: OK, I get angry a lot. Can destruction therapy help me?
P: Perhaps. We can try it. What we do is we take you to a place full of old cars. When we get there, I'll give you a hammer, and you can use it to smash a car to pieces.
R: Really? Is it that simple? If I smash the car to pieces, will I feel better?
P: Yes, a little. But, that's only the beginning. Then, I'll ask you to think about a situation in the past when you felt really angry. And, when you think about that anger situation, you'll hit the car much harder. And the therapy will be much more satisfying. When we finish the session, you'll feel much better.
R: That's amazing. And, businesses are using this kind of therapy in Spain, is that right?
P: Yes, there are some old hotels in Spain. You can pay to go and destroy the hotel. So, some companies who feel that their workers are stressed, or they need to build a team, send their workers to destroy the hotel. And it's a good way for them to get rid of that stress. It works.
R: That's incredible. But there's another idea I wanted to ask you about. People say that laughter is the best medicine. And nowadays, laughter therapy is used in hospitals to help people with pain.
P: That's right.
R: So, how does that work?
P: Well, if people laugh about something, they feel better. On average, children laugh up to 400 times a day, but, when we grow up, we only laugh about seventeen times a day. And it's not enough because, when you laugh, your body produces chemicals—and these chemicals make you feel happier. And they also make you feel less pain. So, in Mexico, for example, they use laughter therapy in hospitals. A group of people goes around the hospital, visiting the patients, and, basically, they make them laugh, by telling them jokes or doing something funny.
R: And does it really work? Do people feel better afterward?
P: Absolutely! They feel better, and they don't need medicine.
R: That's great. So, in Mexico, laughter really is the best medicine?
P: Yes, it looks like it. That's right …

Unit 6   Recording S6.4

Conversation 1

M = Man   W = Woman

M: I have something to tell you.
W: What's that?
M: I've been offered a job.
W: Wow! That's fantastic. Congratulations!
M: There's one thing I have to tell you though.
W: Really? What's that?
M: The job is in Germany. I'm moving at the end of the month.
W: That's awful. What am I going to do?
M: I have to go. I hope you understand.
W: I see.

Conversation 2

M = Man   W = Woman

W: Hello. You came in for a job interview last week.
M: Yes, that's right.
W: First, I'd like to say that we were very impressed with your interview.
M: Oh. Thank you.

stove   cooker

W: However, I'm sorry to have to tell you, but we've offered the job to someone else.

M: Oh. That's a shame. Thank you, anyway.

W: I'm afraid the other candidate had more experience.

M: I understand.

W: But, we'd like to keep your details, in case another job comes up in the future.

M: OK.

Conversation 3

W1 = 1st woman   W2 = 2nd woman

W1: You'll never guess what.

W2: What?

W1: I just won some money in a creative writing competition.

W2: You're joking?

W1: No, really.

W2: That's amazing! How much did you win?

W1: Two thousand dollars.

W2: You lucky dog. How fantastic! How are you going to spend it?

W1: Actually, I have so many bills to pay. I'll spend it on that.

W2: Well, it's good news anyway.

Conversation 4

M1 = 1st man   M2 = 2nd man

M1: I'm afraid I have some bad news.

M2: What is it?

M1: I had an accident. I crashed the car.

M2: Oh, no. That's terrible. Are you OK?

M1: Yes, I'm fine.

M2: That's good.

M1: But, I'm afraid the car isn't.

M2: Oh, that doesn't matter. You can get the car fixed.

M1: Unfortunately, it was your car.

M2: My car? You mean you crashed my car? How did that happen?

M1: Well, you see I …

Conversation 5

M = Man   W = Woman

W: Dad, I have some good news for you.

M: What is it?

W: Well, you know I was waiting to hear from the college?

M: Yes.

W: Well, … I'm really pleased to tell you that … I got in!

M: That's wonderful news, dear! Good for you. I'm so happy for you.

W: There's only one problem though …

M: What's that?

W: It means I'm leaving home.

M: Well, of course we'll miss you, but it's fantastic news.

Conversation 6

M = Man   W = Woman

W: There's something I have to tell you.

M: What's the matter?

W: I split up with Fabio.

M: Oh, no! That's terrible. I'm really sorry to hear that.

W: No, it's OK actually. I'm happy about it, but guess what?

M: What?

W: He already has a new girlfriend.

M: No! That's really annoying.

W: Yeah, and they got engaged.

M: You're joking!

Conversation 7

W1 = 1st woman W2 = 2nd woman

W1: Bad news, I'm afraid.

W2: What is it?

W1: Steve lost his job.

W2: Oh, no. That's awful. I'm really sorry to hear that.

W1: Do you want to hear the good news though?

W2: Yes.

W1: The company is paying him thirty thousand dollars.

W2: Really?

W1: He's going to travel around the world.

W2: That's amazing!

Unit 6 Recording S6.8

One of the most, er, memorable moments, or not moments, rather events, in my life … was a couple of years ago. It all started one day when I was at work, and my brother phoned me out of the blue and said, um, "What are you doing the weekend of Sept. 23rd?" or whatever it was. And I said, "I don't know." He said, "Well, reserve a flight to Norway." My brother lives in Norway, and I live in Boston. So, I said, "Why?" He said, "Oh, I'll let you know when you get here—it's a surprise." So, weeks went on, and I tried to work out what this could be. But, I had absolutely no idea. So the weekend in question came around … I went to the airport, got on my flight, and I was met there by somebody I'd never met before. He just came up and said, "Are you Steve?" I said, "Yes." And he said, "OK. Come with me." So, I went with him to the car. We drove for a little while, and I tried to kind of get it out of him where we were going, but he wouldn't tell me anything. He pulled up outside a hotel, and there was my brother and my half brother, and my two half sisters there waiting for me. I was thinking "What on earth is going on?" And my brother just said, "I realize we don't spend enough time together, so I've gathered you all here and planned a weekend for you." We're like "Oh, cool! So, what are we doing?" "I'm not telling you." "OK, fine." Next thing, we got on a boat and, er, he took us out to a lighthouse. And we spent the first night eating Norwegian shrimp and drinking beer, and we slept in a lighthouse. The next morning, we got up and drove off in his car. We said, "Where are we going?" He said, "I'm not telling you." He took us to a local shopping mall and said, er, "I realize I've done OK in life. I've done better than you guys. Here have a load of money. I want you all to go shopping and buy stuff that you wouldn't normally buy with this money." He said, "The one condition is you're not allowed to buy a gift for me or my family." So off we went in different directions, spent all his money, bought some very nice things., and met back up again. In the evening, he took us out to a blues concert. Then he took us for a five-course meal. And, we spent that night in a very nice hotel. The next morning we had breakfast, and I got back on a plane and went back to Boston. Yeah, that weekend is one of my happiest memories.

Unit 7 Recording S7.1

H = Host   I = Ian

H: Hello, and welcome back to the *Focus* podcast. I'm Jheni Osman, the editor of *Focus*, the monthly science and technology magazine.

He's the hugely influential author of *Blink* and *The Tipping Point*. His work is quoted by academics, presidents and

buddies   mates

your buddies at work. And now Malcolm Gladwell has turned that deft mind of his to a new subject: the science of success. In his new book, *Outliers*, Gladwell argues that, if we want to be successful, we should think less about what successful people are like and more about where they have come from and the opportunities they have had along the way. Now, Ian's read the book, and he joins me. Now … his new book is looking at success …

I: Yes, and what he says is, erm, that, if we think about somebody like Bill Gates, a hugely successful person, and we want to learn from, from his achievements, then what do we look at? We look at what that man is like, you know, what drives him; what does he do on a day-to-day basis; how can we be more like him? But, what Gladwell argues in the new book is, is that we should pay less attention to that side of things and look at where Bill Gates came from. So, how did he get to where he got to, the opportunities he had along the way. And, what he says is that Bill Gates has one thing in common with another group of very successful people, the Beatles.

H: So, what's that?

I: Well, they both practiced what they do, and they practiced a lot.

H: Right, so how much is a lot?

I: A lot is 10,000 hours. That's like the magic number if you're going to become world-class at anything in the world. You need to put 10,000 hours' practice in.

H: Oh, OK.

I: So, the Beatles, they, they were doing gigs, you know, like all-night gigs in Hamburg, in these little clubs, and just the number of hours that they put in on the stage allowed them to master their craft …

H: I think the 10,000 hours magic number is really interesting because, as you know, I used to play tennis professionally, and I hit a load of tennis balls when I was younger. And I'm sure, I must have done 10,000 hours' worth, you know. I must have done four hours a day and stuff. And I remember speaking to Martina Hingis' mom about why she thought her kid was so good, such a prodigy. She basically said, "My daughter has been hitting tennis balls since the age of three, and she has hit X number of tennis balls for X number of hours, and it's, you know, I'm sure she's …" So once you're over that magic number of 10,000 … yeah.

I: The same goes for people like Beethoven … It's incredible how …

H: But, at the end of the day, you have to have talent.

I: You have to have raw talent; you have to have belief in what you can do; and you have to have the will to put those hours in … but you also need the opportunity.

H: Uh huh.

Unit 7 Recording S7.4

T = Tim   J = John   P = Peggy

T: So, what about your memory, Peggy? How good is it?
P: It's OK, which is lucky 'cause I need to remember lots of things.
J: Like what?
P: Well, I'm a sales rep for a publishing company, so I'm usually out visiting schools, trying to sell books.
J: So you need to remember … what exactly?
P: Oh, lots of things. The worst thing when I started was just trying to remember how to get to these schools in my car. I used to get lost all the time. I'm not very good at directions. Then, once you're there, you have to remember the names

and faces of the people you're talking to. I once spent a whole hour calling this woman Sally when her name was Samantha.
T: And she didn't tell you?
P: For some reason she didn't tell me. And then there's all the product information.
J: Product information? What, the books?
P: Yes. We sell about five hundred different books, and I have to know about all of them. I mean, it gets easier, thank goodness, but I still make mistakes occasionally. What about you, John? You're an actor, right?
J: Yeah. The main thing I have to remember is my lines. Fortunately, I have a good memory for words, and I don't find it that hard to memorize them. So, I mean, yeah. The other thing you have to remember when you're in the theater is the blocking.
T: What's that?
J: Blocking? It's where you stand or move to, you know? Like, when you say your words you might have to walk quickly across the stage or move in front of someone. It's all planned, and you have to remember it.
T: Oh, I see.
J: But it's funny: for, for other things I have a terrible memory. I'm totally useless. I always forget birthdays and dates. I'm always late for things. It's just … luckily, I'm OK with my lines.
P: What about you, Tim?
T: I'm probably the same as all other students, at least all other history students. I have to memorize dates and also names. But it's not that difficult because you read about them so much you can't really forget them. But, for other things, I have a really bad memory. I can never remember jokes or movies. Sometimes I'm watching a movie, and, after an hour, I realize I've seen it already. I'm completely hopeless like that.
J: Oh, me, too …

Unit 7 Recording S7.5

M = Man   W = Woman

M: It's interesting. One of the most intelligent people I know is a ten-year-old boy from Egypt. He doesn't go to school, and he works in a touristy area in Cairo. And he sells things to tourists, little souvenirs. Now, the reason I say he's intelligent is that he can sell you something in about fifteen languages. I once spent an afternoon watching him, and it was incredible. Most of the time he uses English, but he guesses where you're from, and then he starts speaking your language. For example, he can speak a little bit of French, Spanish, Japanese, Italian, etc. It's amazing. He knows enough in all these languages to say "hello" and sell you something.
W: How did he learn the languages?
M: I asked him that, and he said he learned them by talking to tourists.
W: That's amazing. Just talking to people, you can learn so much.
M: So, like I said, he doesn't go to school, but, for me, he's super-intelligent. Let me give you another example. I have a friend who built his own house. He just taught himself how to do it: bought some land, bought the materials and the equipment and just did it. No qualifications—no certificates, no college degree.
W: In my view, that's impressive. I couldn't do that.
M: This is someone who left school at fifteen to do an apprenticeship.
W: Degrees and certificates aren't everything, but, you know, having said that, I do think they are useful in some

ways. For one thing, they show that you're able to complete a course of study—that you're motivated enough.

M: Yeah, I think that's true.

W: But, I must say, real life experience, traveling and meeting people … these give you an amazing education, too.

M: Exactly. That's what I was saying. Like the boy from Egypt.

Unit 7 Recording S7.8

A couple of years ago, I learned how to scuba dive, which was really exciting, really good experience. And, when you're learning, half of the, the training is in the classroom, and half is, er, practice in a swimming pool. So the classroom stuff was fine. I found it really quite easy. I was learning with my mom, and she was really worried about doing the kind of more academic stuff and passing the test. But, I found that part OK. It was the practical stuff that I had trouble with, and she was really lucky, she was really good. But you go and you learn all the technical stuff, you know, how to go underwater, how to clear your mask if you get water in it, and so on. And then you have to do two dives outside in a, in a kind of reservoir or a quarry or, you know, something like that. But obviously, because I'm in Canada, it was really, really cold. And we woke up on the morning of our dive, and there was ice on the water. So, when we got there, we were very nervous and didn't want to get into the water. But, once I was in, it was so freezing that I tried to go under the water. But, the more I tried, the harder it got. And then I got very frustrated and started to cry, and then all my ears got blocked up, and I couldn't get under. But eventually I managed to do it and went down, passed my test, did all of the skills that you need to do. Despite the fact that I was so terrible at it, I managed to pass. And now, erm, now that I passed, I can go anywhere I want. So I'll make sure it will be somewhere very hot. So, erm, to sum up, although it was a really difficult, really difficult challenge, I'm so glad I managed to do it. For me, it was quite an achievement, and, and I'm proud of myself for having done it.

Unit 8 Recording S8.2
Speaker 1

I'm in a band, so I use the Internet all the time just to promote it. So, for example, we have to have a website. I didn't really know anything about the Internet, but I absolutely have to. So, we have a website, and, from there, it links to things like Twitter and Facebook and other social media. And then, every time we have a gig coming up, we use it as a promotional tool: we can send out newsletters by email to people who sign up to the website and let them know what we're doing. Then, when we're actually in the process of a gig, we'll, you know, put photos online and post quotes talking about what we're doing so people can see it. Then, it usually leads, you know, from one person to the next person to the next person. They share it on their wall, for example, or they'll post the photo. It just means you can reach a ton of people rather than, you know, the old-fashioned way of just showing somebody a photo after the event—that's no good. So, the Internet's amazing for that. You can just reach thousands really quickly, which is exactly our goal.

Speaker 2

So, I have a food blog where I review restaurants and post my reviews onto this blog, just as a hobby. It's something I really enjoy doing, but it means I take a lot of photos of food. You know, anything I eat I take a photo of it. So, for me, using Instagram, which is social media for uploading photos, is the perfect sort of tool for advertising my blog because it's free and people love looking through pictures of all the different dishes. So I find that, you know, I have about two … over two thousand followers just from people wanting to look at photos of a steak or a piece of chicken, which sounds crazy, but it's very popular. So, I use Instagram a lot to link up with my blog.

Speaker 3

Um, well I use Facebook, mainly because I work from home and I don't really chat to people much during the day. So, it's a good way of … of staying in touch with people. You know, it's an online community, isn't it, and I like to keep in touch with people that way—and, you know, old friends. Probably one of the best uses, though, is organizing parties and things because you can just do one blanket invitation to everyone. Most people usually get a notification in their email inbox to say they've been invited to something, don't they? So I think … I think it's really handy. Rather than calling a lot of people, you can do it all through social media rather than making lots of phone calls. But, probably what I like most about it is just seeing people's family photographs. People are always posting their … their … the pictures of their children or … or you know … parties or friends, and it's just … it's nice to see those and keep in touch with people.

Unit 8 Recording S8.5
Conversation 1

A: I'm really hungry. Can I have some of this?

B: Help yourself.

Conversation 2

A: Come on in.

B: Thanks.

C: Have a seat.

Conversation 3

A: Hi.

B: What a day! I'm so tired!

A: I'll make you some coffee. Put your feet up.

Conversation 4

A: Can I just quickly use your phone?

B: Be my guest.

Conversation 5

A: Welcome!

B: Thank you. What a nice room.

A: Make yourself at home.

Unit 8 Recording S8.6
Conversation 1

W = Woman   M = Man

W: Hi, Dave. Sorry. Do you mind?

M: What?

W: We don't smoke in the house.

M: Oh, sorry about that. I didn't know.

W: That's all right. It's no problem.

Conversation 2

M1 = 1st man   M2 = 2nd man

M1: So they've invited me to dinner at their house.

M2: Great. And they're also from Morocco?

M1: The same as you. From Morocco.

M2: That'll be fun.

M1: So, do I need to take a dish? Like, take some food?

M2: No, it's not necessary. You can take a small gift if you want, but you don't need to take food.

Conversation 3

M = Man   W = Woman

M: Hello?

W: Hello?

M: Hi, I'm Richard Davies. From Brooklyn? I'm here to visit your offices.

W: Ah, hello.

M: I'm a bit early. Is this a bad time?

W: Umm.

M: I can come back later.

W: I wasn't expecting you so early. Can you come back in ten minutes? I just need to finish some work here, and then I'll be able to show you around.

M: Of course. Sorry about that.

W: Not at all. It's fine.

Conversation 4

W1 = 1st woman   W2 = 2nd woman

W1: So, I walked into your parents' house, but I forgot to take my shoes off. Did I do something wrong?

W2: Oh, I see.

W1: My shoes weren't dirty or anything, but I still felt really bad.

W2: It's OK—I'll tell my parents you forgot. Don't worry about it.

W1: I don't know. Should I call them up to apologize?

W2: No, it's nothing. You really don't have to apologize.

Conversation 5

W = Waiter   C = Customer

W: Excuse me, sir. Would you mind putting this on?

C: What?

W: Put on your jacket. In this restaurant, you have to wear a jacket.

C: My apologies. I didn't know.

Conversation 6

W = Woman   M = Man

W: So, we're staying with an American family for Thanksgiving.

M: For what?

W: Thanksgiving. You know, people from the United States celebrate it.

M: So, what's the problem?

W: Americans always eat turkey on Thanksgiving, don't they? But we're vegetarians—we never eat meat. So, well, what should we do?

M: Um … If I were you, I'd tell them the problem, and maybe they can cook a turkey while you and your family just eat something else.

Unit 8   Recording S8.8

B = Ben Jacques   S = Sharon Hills

B: So, Sharon, imagine you had to start a brand new community.

S: Yes?

B: I know it's a difficult question, but ideally where would it be?

S: Erm, I'd probably choose somewhere quite warm, so you didn't have any issues of flooding or, you know, too much snow to deal with—something like that. And then I'd choose another place most people would probably choose, not an island …

B: Where … where exactly?

S: But, I think, hmmmm … somewhere in France, I don't know why.

B: Oh, somewhere in France? OK and who would be there: the French only or a mixture of people?

S: No, I … well, it would need to be a mix of people, and they'd need to be able to help one another.

B: In what way?

S: Well, … I'd like to take one person who's an expert in one field, another person who's an expert in another field, so you have—you know—arty people, manually skilled people, good speakers, good writers …

B: Ah, so a whole range of skills …

S: Exactly!

B: … all going into the melting pot.

S: Yes, but, I wouldn't have too many people to start with, although, if it's too small a group, then I suppose you risk, erm, not getting along with each other. But I think if you keep that group fairly small to begin with, then you can draw up your own special laws, you know, to govern yourselves.

B: Would it need laws do you think … this, this utopian society?

S: Mmmm … well, ideally there'd be no laws, but, because people are human, I think you would probably have to come up with some ground rules, yes.

B: What would be the most important one?

S: Oh! Erm, I think, … not to physically hurt somebody else, I suppose.

B: Right, so pretty much like we have now …

S: Yes, I guess so …

Unit 9   Recording S9.4

Speaker 1

Yeah, I grew up in the nineties. For me, film and music are two important aspects of my life, and it was a fantastic decade for both of those. In terms of movies, there were some excellent ones that came out, erm, my favorites being *Forrest Gump*, *Pulp Fiction* and *The Shawshank Redemption*. In terms of the music, … probably the most famous bands of the time were Oasis and Blur. Ah, one of the most memorable moments of the nineties was Euro '96 … obviously the soccer tournament. I was lucky enough to go to the opening ceremony myself. Obviously, as we were entering the end of the millennium, the celebrations toward the end of the nineties were huge, and so were the celebrations on the actual night. Also, Mother Teresa died, sort of Mother Teresa was, erm, the famous charitable missionary.

Speaker 2

Ah, the seventies. Well, they were wonderful I think. If somebody asked if it was a good decade or a bad decade, personally I have to say it was a good decade to grow up in. I think of it as a very lucky experience when generally the world that I lived in, which was London and England, which was the post-war period and therefore an era of a certain amount of, erm, restriction was all ending, and things were freeing up. And that happened just at the time that I was leaving home and finding my own independence. It all seemed as though it happened at the same time. Erm, technology was changing and improving. Um, everything seemed to be developing and getting better in many ways. The fashion was getting rid of short hair and regimented kinds of looks. Erm, individuality was very much the order of the day. Great people were emerging in the arts. John Lennon, for example, was an icon for me, I think, as a creative artist with a message as well in his work.

Great artists in film, Scorsese: *Taxi Driver*, Spielberg: *Duel*, these were emerging artists of tremendous skill and artistry, but they were just starting out then when I was.

Speaker 3

I was a teenager in the eighties, and I remember thinking that I didn't like a lot of the fashion and the music from back then. But, now it's obvious in retrospect that I did like it. I love looking back on like a nostalgia trip at the way we used to dress and how much hair gel I used and how much hair spray the girls used, and er, now in the 2000s there's sort of a trip back into that time, you know? Girls are wearing big earrings again and geometric patterns on their clothes. Erm, the music in the eighties became quite computerized sounding, quite electronic, and disco faded away, although we did still have soul. People like Luther Vandross and Billy Ocean were making soul music. New Romantic was another style that came out in the early eighties, where the men started wearing lots of make-up and had big shoulders and small waists. And, Madonna was a big trendsetter for girls, and, at one point, she cut her hair really short in the mid eighties and almost like a boy's, and then all the girls started cutting their hair short, too. I wasn't very fashionable myself. I used to spend most of my money on records, not clothes. There were some good movies around in the eighties too, things like *Back to the Future* with Michael J. Fox, *Desperately Seeking Susan* with Madonna, *ET*, *Police Academy* … Um, I'm gonna be forty this year, and I imagine my birthday party is going to be a big nostalgia trip back to the eighties.

Unit 9 Recording S9.5

M = Man   W = Woman

M: So, yeah … so question one.
W: Yes, about the religious leader, any ideas?.
M: Yeah. Spoke out against racism in South Africa, worked as an English teacher? Um … no idea.
W: Well, it could be a few different people couldn't it?
M: I have no idea. I … I don't know. I don't know.
W: Want to guess?
M: If I were to guess … oh, no I don't have a clue on this one. I'm sorry.
W: OK. I'm gonna tell you it was B—Desmond Tutu.
M: Oh, really?
W: Yes.
M: Oh, no. I didn't know that.
W: Fair enough.
M: I didn't know that.
W: All right. So the second one is about the politician being killed by her own bodyguards.
M: Well, it's definitely not A.
W: Oh … OK, yes.
M: Definitely not A, so … it's B or C. Um …
W: Can you remember?
M: I can't remember. I've forgotten.
W: So you're just gonna have to guess.
M: Yes, um …
W: Come on! I'm gonna press you now. If you used to know it, you can take a shot—it's in there somewhere.
M: I'm gonna go for B.
W: Oh, no. It was the other one. It was C—Indira Gandhi.
M: Oh.
W: Never mind.
M: Oh, well. I didn't know that …
W: Well, there you go. Um … so—number three, any ideas, uh, about the anthropologist feeding bananas to wild chimpanzees?

M: Jane Goodall, Louis …?
W: Louis Leakey, Margaret Mead.
M: Well. Well, I'm sure it isn't Margaret Mead.
W: How about B?
M: Um, I'm … I'm sure it isn't … I'm sure it isn't B.
W: OK.
M: So that leaves A.
W: It leaves you with A. Very good. It was Jane Goodall.
M: Yes, that's right!
W: OK, and now the scientist …
M: Which inspirational scientist spent his free time playing the violin?
W: Free time …
M: … When he wasn't changing the world? Um, I … I think I know this one.
W: OK.
M: I'm … I'm … yeah …
W: Uh, be careful 'cause all of those … changed the world.
M: I'm not a hundred per cent certain, but it might be Albert Einstein.
W: Right, are you saying B?
M: B.
W: Yes, you're right.
M: Excellent.
W: And we're almost there, with number five, uh, the activist who refused to give up the bus seat. You must remember this.
M: Oh, no. I can't remember.
W: You must!
M: Uh, its one of those things I used to know.
W: Start of the Civil Rights Movement.
M: I used to know, but I … I've forgotten.
W: All right.
M: Che Guevara?
W: Sure?
M: No.
W: No.
M: But …
W: OK, it was C—Rosa Parks.
M: Oh!
W: You're right. You didn't remember.
M: Oh.
W: So the last one.
M: It's interesting. Oh, dear.
W: The last one then.
M: Right.
W: Um, which amazingly original and creative writer was banned from the U.S. for years?
W: Have you heard of them?
M: I, … I, well, … I know it wasn't Charles Dickens.
W: Right.
M: So it's one of the other two. Oh.
W: Go on. Take a guess.
M: I'm gonna go for C.
W: Good choice.
M: Ah! That's right, that's right!
W: It was C!
M: Excellent! Excellent!
W: Well done. You did very well.
M: Yes, yeah, not too bad.

Unit 9 Recording S9.7

OK, well, someone whose work really influenced me is Gabriel García Márquez. I like his short stories, but I fell in love with his novels, particularly *One Hundred Years of Solitude*. That book really made its mark on me. Anyway, Márquez was a Colombian writer. I think he was born in 1928. He's a Nobel Prize winner—he won the Nobel Prize in Literature—and his books have been translated into dozens of languages. He was one of the best-known writers in the style that's called magical realism. This means he wrote kind of realistically, but there's magic. I mean, magical things happen in his books, like ghosts appear and all kinds of crazy things happen. I'm a big fan of that type of writing. Anyway, his novels are kind of funny, but it's black humor or satire. He invented all these amazing, unforgettable characters, like, corrupt officials and devoted lovers, vicious policemen and stupid revolutionaries. And, through it all, you're laughing at the characters, but you also see their world is falling apart. I haven't read his work in Spanish, only English, but the style is amazing. His dialogue is fast and funny, and he wrote amazing descriptions of places and people. And, well, it was finding Márquez's work as a teenager that really made me become a reader.

Unit 10 Recording S10.2

Speaker 1

My favorite food city is, ah, Hiroshima, in Japan … They have all sorts of food. They of course have the really famous sushi that everyone thinks about when they think of Japanese food. But, they have so much else to offer. Hiroshima's really famous for its *okonomiyaki*, which is like a cross between a pancake and a pizza … It's a kind of egg and flour mixture with cabbage and noodles and meat and sometimes cheese. It's really good. One of my favorite restaurants is a place called, ah, Daikichi, which specializes in grilled chicken. You can get grilled chicken with cheese, grilled chicken with plum sauce, and a really good soup with rice and ginger in it. I'd love to take you to Daikichi, you'd love it. They have good beer, too. But also you can get *tempura* in Hiroshima, which is like shrimp and vegetables deep fried in a really light, fluffy batter … It's really good. And then, you also have the informal restaurants that are called *izakaya* where you go with a group of friends. You order lots of dishes, and everyone shares and eats from the middle of the table. So, it's a great way to try lots of different kinds of food. Actually I know a really good *izakaya* restaurant that I should take you to.

Speaker 2

Well, my favorite food city would be Madrid. I lived in Madrid, in Spain, for around ten years on and off, and the quality of the food is, is wonderful—it's sensational. Spanish people always say that Spanish food is the best in the world, and I always argued while I lived there, that I felt there was a lot more variety of food in the U.S. But, when I moved back to the U.S., I really started to miss the richness, the quality of the food in Spain. I think my favorite restaurant in Spain was a tiny, little Galician place—Galicia is a part in the northwest of Spain. It's a seafood restaurant in a small little bar. It was a very, it wasn't posh or expensive; it was cheap and basic, but just served the most wonderful seafood followed by lots of white wine and a great *tarta de Santiago*, a great pastry dessert, afterward. Another great thing, obviously, about Spanish food, which you'll have heard of is *"tapas"* where everyone gets together on Sunday afternoon to have a few bites to eat and a few beers together. It's a lovely social atmosphere, and it's nice to go out and try a variety of different food. I once tried pig's ear, which I have to say was possibly the worst thing I've ever tasted, but generally the quality was sensational.

Unit 10 Recording S10.5

Conversation 1

W = Woman   M = Man

W: Is there anything I should know for when I arrive at the airport?
M: Yes, watch out for the taxi drivers who tend to hang around outside the airport. Most of them aren't licensed, so you really shouldn't use them.
W: OK.
M: If you do use one, make sure you find out how much the ride is supposed to cost. Don't get in until you've agreed on the price with the driver, or else you could find that you have to pay three or four times the amount you should pay for the trip.
W: Oh, right. That's good to know.

Conversation 2

M = Man   W = Woman

M: Hi. I'm going to J.F.K. airport tomorrow, and my plane leaves at 3 p.m. Latest check in time is 1:40. What time do you think I should leave downtown Manhattan?
W: For J.F.K.? Well, you'd better leave plenty of time because often there are delays on the subway. Are you going on the subway or the train?
M: The subway, I think.
W: The subway? If I were you, I'd allow about an hour and a half. So, if you want to be at the airport at 1:30, … then you'd better leave at about 12 o'clock.
M: OK. That's great. Thanks.

Conversation 3

M1 = 1st man   M2 = 2nd man

M1: Be careful when you take trips into the jungle in the north. Generally, there are a lot of mosquitoes there, so remember to take mosquito nets and insect repellent. It's a good idea to wear long pants and shirts with sleeves in the evening. And don't forget to take your malaria pills.
M2: Oh, yes. I must remember those.
M1: And, whatever you do, don't drink the water, or you'll have stomach problems.
M2: Oh, I didn't know that.
M1: Yes, always be sure to boil the water first or drink bottled water. You have to be careful when you eat raw food, too, like fruit if it's been washed in water.
M2: OK.

Conversation 4

W1 = 1st woman   W2 = 2nd woman

W1: We're going there on vacation, and I've heard that there's a lot of street crime. Is that true?
W2: Not really, no. I mean, it's like any big city. You need to watch out for groups of young children on the streets. They try to distract you and then sometimes take your bag.
W1: Oh. OK.
W2: It's not very common, but don't walk around the city obviously carrying money in a big money belt or anything.
W1: Of course.
W2: The most important thing is to remember to hold on to your purse, and things like that, but no, there isn't really much crime. On the whole, it's a pretty safe city.
W1: That's useful. Thanks.

Unit 10 Recording S10.8

One place that I think everyone should have the chance to see is Venice. But, the problem is that this beautiful and charming city is slowly sinking. Ever since the fourteenth century. engineers have tried to work out a way to stop the floods in Venice, but so far nobody has managed. Sometimes there are as many as forty floods per year between March and September, and Venice is actually sinking at a rate of two and a half inches every decade. It's very possible that your grandchildren and their grandchildren will never have the chance to see this fragile city. Everyone should have the chance to enjoy the city, to walk across its famous bridges, through its ancient squares. There are no cars in Venice, and many people think it helps this to be one of the most romantic cities in the world. So, can it be saved? Well, they are trying. Barriers are being put up to try to stop the water from getting too high. This is viewed as a temporary measure, although it should work for a hundred years. So the problem is finding a permanent solution. If you want my advice, go there while you still can, and then together we can put pressure on the government to spend the money it needs to find a permanent way to keep this beautiful and historic city for future generations. We have an opportunity now to save this city, and we must, before it's too late.

Catalogue Publication Data

Authors: Antonia Clare, JJ Wilson

American Speakout Intermediate Student Book with DVD-ROM and MP3 Audio CD

First published

Pearson Educación de México, S.A. de C.V., 2017

ISBN: 978-607-32-4062-8

American Speakout Intermediate Student Book with DVD-ROM and MP3 Audio CD & MEL Access Code

ISBN MEL: 978-607-32-4054-3

Area: ELT

Format: 21 x 29.7 cm   Page count: 184

Managing Director: Sergio Fonseca ■ **Innovation & Learning Delivery Director:** Alan David Palau ■ **Regional Content Manager - English:** Andrew Starling ■ **Publisher:** A. Leticia Alvarez ■ **Content Support:** Erin Ferris ■ **Editorial Services Manager:** Asbel Ramírez ■ **Art and Design Coordinator:** Juan Manuel Santamaria ■ **Design Process Supervisor:** Aristeo Redondo ■ **Layout:** Lourdes Madrigal ■ **Cover Design:** Ana Elena García ■ **Photo Research:** Beatriz Monsiváis ■ **Photo Credits:** Pearson Asset Library (PAL)

Contact: soporte@pearson.com

This adaptation is published by arrangement with Pearson Education Limited

Pearson Education Limited

Edinburgh Gate
Harlow
Essex CM20 2JE
England
and Associated Companies throughout the world.

© Pearson Education Limited 2015

Used by permission and adapted from
Speakout 2ND EDITION Intermediate Students' Book
ISBN: 978-1-2921-1594-8
First published, 2015
All Rights Reserved.

First published, 2017

Esta obra se terminó de imprimir en marzo de 2018, en Editorial Impresora Apolo, S.A. de C.V., Centeno 150-6, Col. Granjas Esmeralda, C.P. 09810, México, Ciudad de México.

ISBN PRINT BOOK: 978-607-32-4062-8

ISBN PRINT BOOK MEL: 978-607-32-4054-3

D.R. © 2017 por Pearson Educación de México, S.A. de C.V.
Avenida Antonio Dovalí Jaime #70
Torre B, Piso 6, Colonia Zedec Ed. Plaza Santa Fe
Delegación Álvaro Obregón, México, Ciudad de México, C. P. 01210

Impreso en México. *Printed in Mexico.*

1 2 3 4 5 6 7 8 9 0 - 20 19 18 17

www.PearsonELT.com

Pearson Hispanoamérica

Argentina ■ Belice ■ Bolivia ■ Chile ■ Colombia ■ Costa Rica ■ Cuba ■ República Dominicana ■ Ecuador ■ El Salvador ■ Guatemala ■ Honduras ■ México ■ Nicaragua ■ Panamá ■ Paraguay ■ Perú ■ Uruguay ■ Venezuela

Acknowledgements

The Publisher and authors would like to thank the following people and institutions for their feedback and comments during the development of the material: **Australia:** Erica Lederman; **Hungary:** Eszter Timár; **Mexico:** Hortensia Camacho Barco; **Poland:** Konrad Dejko; **Spain:** Sam Lanchbury, Victoria O'Dea; **UK:** Lilian Del Gaudio Maciel, Joelle Finck, Niva Gunasegaran.

Text acknowledgements

We are grateful to the following for permission to reproduce copyright material: Extract on page 25 from "Fraud Fugitive in Facebook Trap", 14/10/2009, http://news.bbc.co.uk/1/hi/world/americas/8306032. stm, copyright © BBC Worldwide Limited; Extracts on pages 37, 70, 161 from Longman Active Study Dictionary, 5th edition, Pearson Education Ltd, copyright © Pearson Education Limited, 2010; Extract on page 44 from "Millionaires prefer Gap to Gucci" 05/10/2003,http://www.bbc.co.uk/print/pressoffice/pressreleases/stories/2003/10_october/05/mind_millionaire.shtml, copyright © BBC Worldwide Limited; Extract on pages 44-45 from "Have you Got What it Takes to be Millionaire ?", The Telegraph, 05/06/2014 (Shirley Conran), copyright © Telegraph Media Group Limited; Extract on page 80 adapted from 'The secret of success' interview with Malcolm Gladwell, BBC Focus, Issue 197, 01/12/2008, p.23. Presenters Jenny Osman & Ian, copyright © Immediate Media Company Bristol Ltd; Extract on page 105 from "12 Giant leaps for mankind" by Rob Attar, BBC History Magazine, Vol.10, no.7, pp.42-47, copyright ©Immediate Media Company Bristol Ltd; Extract on pages 116-117 adapted from "I am the Ethical Man" by 22/02/2006 and "We are all ethical men and women now" 13/04/2007 by Justin Rowlatt,http://news.bbc.co.uk/1/hi/programmes/newsnight/4736228.stm,http://www.bbc.co.uk/blogs/newsnight/2007/04/we_are_all_ethical_men_and_women_now.html, copyright © BBC Worldwide Limited; and Extract on page 121 adapted from "Top Ten New Restaurants in East London", Traveller, 09/05/2013, source:http://www.cntraveller.com/recommended/food/top-10-new-restaurants-east-london/viewall. Reproduced with permission from Conde Nast.

Illustration acknowledgements

Fred Blunt: 29, 66, 90, 159, 160; Lyndon Hayes: 26, 27, 74, 75; Eric Smith: 129, 133, 135, 137, 140, 149, 150, 151, 152, 153, 154, 157.

Photo acknowledgements

The Publisher would like to thank the following for their kind permission to reproduce their photographs:

(Key: b-bottom; c-center; l-left; r-right; t-top)

123RF.com: Andrei Shumskiy 7b (icon), Wavebreak Media Ltd 7l, Photoroad 8-9 (background), Wavebreak Stock Media Ltd 8c, Mikhail Vorobiev 12b, Andrei Shumskiy 19b (icon), Andrei Shumskiy 31b (icon), Lightwave Stock Media 32l, Eunika Sopotnicka 33, 123vector 37 (car), Diego Alies 37 (Book), AnnSunnyDay 37, jehsomwang 37 (wind), Roman Malyshev 37 (microscope), nazlisart 37 (Flag), Andrei Shumskiy 43b (icon), David Smith 43r, Andrey Bayda 44tl, tetyanka 45 (car), Ihor Obraztsov 46r, David Smith 52-53 (balloon), Andrei Shumskiy 55 (icon), Andrei Shumskiy 67b (icon), Andrei Shumskiy 79b (icon), agencyby 84/8, Sean Nel 84/9, serezniy 84/1, veralub 84/3 (a), 123vector 86br, Andrei Shumskiy 91b (icon), sjenner13 96, Andrei Shumskiy 103b (icon), Andrei Shumskiy 115b (icon), kritchanut 116-117 (background), lightwise 117t, Gabriel Gonzalez 121, andersonrise 148 (young girl with brown hair), Jacek Chabraszewski 148 (young girl), Brian Eichhorn 148r (grandma), Elena Elisseeva 148 (son), Warren Goldswain 148 (mature man), goodluz 148 (father), Paul Michael Hughes 148 (Young boy), Kurhan 148 (aunty), Kurhan 148 (uncle), lammeyer 148 (mother), Nyul 148 (brother), 148 (cousin), 148 (husband), Aigars Reinholds 148 (grandpa), rido 148 (man), robinsphoto 148 (young woman), Dmitriy Shironosov 148 (daughter), Eric Simard148 (ME), stylephotographs148 (mother-in-law), Cameron Whitman 148 (sister), 148 (young man), Lisa Young 148r (grandpa); **Alamy Images:** Gregg Vignal 10; Garry Gay 43l, Davide Piras 43cl, Davide Piras 47/C, ableimages 48t, Cultura Creative (RF) 48b, Ian Goodrick 55cr, Blend Images 59 (F), Cultura RM 60, Deborah Ernest 61, Anatolii Babii 62/C, Ian Goodrick 62/B, Isowork Images 62/E, M. Timothy O'Keefe 62/D, culture-images GmbH 65b, StreetStock 7cl, StreetStock 71, Vincent Abbey 87b, Thierry Grun 87c, Catchlight Visual Services 91cr, David J. Green-lifestyle 291cl, Agencja Fotograficzna

Caro 94br, Pixellover RM 8 97, Catchlight Visual Services 98tr, PeterBarritt 103r, Everett Collection Historical 103l, Heritage Image Partnership Ltd 104c, LondonPhotos /Homer Sykes 108tr, Tim Graham 110bl, David Pearson 110tr, The Illustrated London News Picture Library. Ingram Publishing. Alamy 110br, Creation of Adam fresco on the ceiling of the Sistine Chapel by Buonarroti Michelangelo Vatican Museum Rome Italy Europe 112-113b, Images-USA 117 (bus), Eddie Linssen 151t, Arterra Picture Library 157/1; **BBC Photo Library:** Hladik, Martin 36; **BBC Worldwide Ltd:** 16 (inset), 28 (inset), 40 (inset), 52l (inset), 55r, 64 (inset), 76 (inset), 100 (inset), 124r (inset); **Comstock Images:** 99 **Corbis:** LWA / Larry Williams 16-17, Bettmann 23b, Jon Hrusa /Epa 24, 68/Ocean 25 (background), 25cl, Amelie-Benoist /Bsip 31t, Edgar Su /Reuters 35l, Ingo Bartussek / Westend61 50r, Andersen Ross /Cultura 52-53, Photo Media 67l, Lan 80t, Bettmann 81tr, Hemant Mehta / India Picture 87t, Bettmann 103cr, Arnie Sachs / CNP /AdMedia 104l; Photo Media /Classicstock 108l; **Fotolia.com:** cunico 38tr, Kaesler Media 38l, Monkey Business 38r, Raven 38 (food icon), arphoto 44 (notes), Banana Republic 44-45 (background), Željko Radojko 44 (watch), Maksim Striganov 44(ring), photorealistic 51,Eyematrix 56 (background), nacroba 67cr, Taiga 67r; Dp3010 76 (cake), Robsonphoto 76-77 (heart background), surasaki 76-77 (flower background),Esolla 77 (flowers), sumnersgraphicsinc 77(cork), Andrey Burmakin 79cr, Cifotart 80-81 (background), Fontanis 84/6, Joe Gough 84/11,karandaev 84/10, Login 110(background), 118 dominiquelavoie 151c; **Getty Images:** George Hoyningen-Huene / RDA / Contributor 21 (F), Bilderlounge 31cr, Jeff Giniewicz 31r, Hero Images 34b, iStock / Getty Images Plus 35c, Bilderlounge 38tc, Jeff Giniewicz 40-41, Tom C. Robison 43t, Hero Images 47/A, Judith Haeusler 56b, Fotog 59/C, FPG 67t, 68/C, Massive 68/A, Westend61 68/B; Tatiana Morozova 69/E, Stan Honda /Staff 79r, Al Bello /Staff 88-89 (background), Stan Honda /Staff 88-89 (foreground), Buda Mendes 91t, Philip Game / Lonely Planet Images 91r, Philip Game /Lonely Planet Images 100-101, Frank Barratt 103cl, Terry Fincher 107,Photo 12 110tl, 112-113t, Vincenzo Lombardo 115cl, Photonica World 115cl, BBC News & Current Affairs /Jeff Overs 116l, Zhang Peng 119r, Photonica World 119l, Tim Graham 163; **NASA:** NASA / JPL / ASU 95; **Nicola Krebill:** 56t; **Pearson Asset Library:** Ryan Rodrick Beller 25(t), elen_studio 45(t), RAGMA IMAGES 49(t), baranq 57(t), Boris Djuranovic 61(t), zeljkodan 72(t), Andy Dean Photography 73(tr), John Panella 76(t), Jason Nemeth 81(t), angstrup 82(t), Andrey Burmakin 97(t), Andrey Burmakin 105(tr), Norman Chan 106(t); **Pearson Education Ltd:** Sophie Bluy 63; **Photolibrary.com:** Sugar Gold Images. Denkou Images 68/D; **Plainpicture Ltd:** Julian Love / Cultura 43cr; **Press Association Images:** Fiona Hanson 65cr; **Reuters:** Dylan Martinez 79t; Chip East 161; **Rex Features:** Design Pics Inc 7r, 16b, Rex Features19cl, 21(B), 21(G), 23t 52r(inset), Everett Collection 21(D), Franck Leguet 21 (A), Scott Myers 21 (C), Niviere /Villard 21 (E), Ron Sachs/ Pool via CNP 21 (H), Cultura / REX 32r, Solent News 47/B, Steve Meddle /ITV 72, PictureGroup 79l, 80cr, 80bl, Ron C Angle 80br, KeystoneUSA-ZUMA 81tl, Universal History Archive /Universal Images Group 81bl, 81br, Geraint Lewis 83b, Cultura 84/3 (b), WestEnd61 98tl; 104r, Brian Rasic 108br, Agencia EFE 110cl, Stuart Clarke 110cr, ITV 111, I Love Images 115l; **Robert Harding World Imagery:** P. Schickert 91l, 92; Nick Bonetti 93, Fernanda Preto 94cl; **Science Photo Library Ltd:** David A. Hardy 31cl; Amelie-Benoist / Bsip 35r; **Shutterstock.com:** Dizain 8(t), Rob Marmion 9(t), Justanotherphotographer 10(t), wavebreakmedia 11(t), Minerva studio 12(t), Peter Bernick 12 (tc),Valentin Agapov 12(c), Lexa _1112 12(c), Samuel Borges Photography 13(tl), Creativa images 13(tc), Pressmaster 13(tc), Photographee.eu 13(tr), racorn 14(t), Kzenon 15(t), Chamille White 16(t), AnjelikaGr 17(t), Zeynep Demir 19(t), InesBazdar 19(tr), Bannosuke 20(t), Helga Esteb 21(tl), Tinseltown 21(tr), Spass 22(tl), Tsuguliev 22(tc), marilook 22(tc), Ruslan Guzov 22(tr), Litwin Photography 23(t), Prazis 24(t), creatista 26(t), file404 27(t), speedkingz 28(t), Kzenon 29(t), Wavebreakmedia 31l, Rawpixel.com 32(t), Stocklite 33(t), Antonov Roman 34(t), Alexander Tolstykh 36(t), stockshoppe 37(t), slog21 38(t), Kzenon 39(t), Bloomua 40(t), Quinky 41(t), bikeriderlondon 44(tl), Africa Studio 44(rc), CandyBox Images 46(t), Piotr Marcinski 47(t), Andrey Armyagov 48(t), 06photo 48c (butterfly), Pakhnyushcha 49, Zurijeta 50l; Maridav 51(t),RG-vc 55cl, Chamille White 55t, Minerva Studio 56(t), ImageFlow 58(t), EpicStockMedia 59/E, Graham Prentice 59/D, Sailorr 59/A, Sozaijiten 59/B, Gelpi 60(t), nito 62(t),

Robcocquyt 62/A, sylv1rob163(t), Shaun Jeffers 64-65, Vladimir Mucibabic 69/F, stockyimages 70(t), Monkey Business Images 73, Antonio Guillem 74(t), Jaroslaw Grudzinski 76 (rings/rose), Dragon Images 77(t), pixeldreams.eu 79cl, Your Design 80(t), Monkey Business Images 82(tl), spass 82(tc), Ivica Drusany 83(t), pixeldreams.eu 83 (background), taa22 84(t), Franck Boston 84/12, damato 84/7, Greg Epperson 84/5, mhatzapa 84/4 (b), Rido 84/4 (a), Kiselev Andrey Valerevich 84/2, auremar 86tr, leedsn 85(t), bikeriderlondon 86tl, WitR 87(t), Jimmie48 Photography 88(t), Iakov Filimonov 92(tl), Iakov Filimonov 93(tl), Rrrainbow 94(t), Tupungato 94bl, Toria 95(t), PiXXart 96(t), Talent Release 98(tr), Alta Oosthuizen 99(tr), vesna cvorovic 99(tr), docstockmedia 99(tr), Andrey Burmakin 103t, nobeastsofierce 104-105, Olivier Le Queinec 105r, is am are 107(t), Africa Studio 108(t), Anteromite 109(t) elwynn 110(tl), Sergey Nivens 111(t), FloridaStock 115r, Roman Vanur 115t, Artens 116(tl), J. Lekavicius 117(tr),Dan Thornberg 117 (flag), Rich Carey118(t), holbox 120(t) Zhukov Oleg 121(t), 06photo 122, Africa Studio 123(t), Sam Dcruz 124(t),FloridaStock 124-125, guentermanaus 125(t), Inga Ivanova 151b, Christopher Kolaczan 157/5, M. Shcherbyna 157/2, Ssuaphotos 157/3, Three one five 157/4; **SuperStock:** Cultura Limited 7t, RubberBall 7cr, Science Photo Library 7cl, Science Photo Library 11l, Science Photo Library 11r; Cultura Ltd 14b, F1 Online 14t, Cusp / Cusp 19r, Cusp/Cusp 28-29, Blend Images 98tc; **The Kobal Collection:** Warner Bros. / James, David 19l; **TopFoto:** Ronald Grant Archive / ArenaPAL 23c; 2005 155; **www.playpumps.co.za:** 55l, 56c.

All other images © Pearson Education

Every effort has been made to trace the copyright holders and we apologize in advance for any unintentional omissions. We would be pleased to insert the appropriate acknowledgement in any subsequent edition of this publication.